Creating Meaning

Reading and Writing for the Canadian Classroom

Second Edition

Kathy Block and Hannah Hofer Friesen

OXFORD

UNIVERSITY PRESS

OXFORD
UNIVERSITY PRESS

Oxford University Press is a department of the University of Oxford.
It furthers the University's objective of excellence in research, scholarship, and education by publishing worldwide.
Oxford is a registered trade mark of Oxford University Press in the UK and in certain other countries.

Published in Canada by
Oxford University Press
8 Sampson Mews, Suite 204,
Don Mills, Ontario M3C 0H5 Canada

www.oupcanada.com

Copyright © Oxford University Press Canada 2012

The moral rights of the author have been asserted

Database right Oxford University Press (maker)

First Edition published in 2000

Library and Archives Canada Cataloguing in Publication

Friesen, Hannah
Creating meaning : advanced reading and writing for the Canadian classroom / Hannah Hofer Friesen, Kathy Block. – 2nd ed.

ISBN 978-0-19-544572-5

1. English language--Textbooks for second language learners. 2. English language—Rhetoric.
3. College readers. I. Block, Kathy II. Title.

PE1128.F75 2012   808'.0427   C2011-901411-4

Cover image: The Indian in Transition, 1978, Daphne Odjig
Canadian Museum of Civilization, III-M-15, IMG2008-0624-0001-Dm

Oxford University Press is committed to our environment.
This book is printed on Forest Stewardship Council® certified paper
and comes from responsible sources.

Printed and bound in Canada.
1 2 3 4 — 15 14 13 12

Introduction

Creating Meaning: Advanced Reading and Writing, Second edition, has been written for advanced learners who are preparing for academic studies. At college and university, students are expected to work with large amounts of information presented in written form. More specifically, they must be able to comprehend information and ideas, select and synthesize relevant information, and communicate information accurately and analytically in their own writing. To be successful in the academic milieu, then, students must be actively involved in the construction of meaning in both reading and writing.

Students must also be able to integrate what they read with what they write. Research in academic writing clearly demonstrates that, for the vast majority of university assignments, students are expected to base their written work on source texts in their fields. University-bound students must learn to paraphrase as well as quote and document what they read. More importantly, they must be able to compare points of view or data or both and integrate these into their own creative frameworks. One of the central purposes of this text is to help learners for whom English is an additional language make the transition into academic writing in a Canadian context by practising these skills. To this end, students are guided through a process of reading, discussing, and writing.

This text contains a variety of authentic readings grouped around specific themes, an approach that allows learners to read widely on specific topics and to reflect on them from a variety of angles. It provides learners with enough material to practise selecting and synthesizing relevant information in writing. It also exposes learners to words in meaningful contexts, thus allowing them to develop stronger vocabularies and the ability to express their ideas in depth.

Most of the readings in *Creating Meaning* are Canadian in their content and are related to academic fields, including sociology, psychology, management, law, medicine, and geography. We have selected readings that we believe will engage students deeply in their new social and academic milieu and that will serve as springboards for discussion in the classroom.

In addition, the book has been organized so that learners will practise strategies for academic reading and vocabulary development. Before starting to read, the students discuss or write or both in order to draw out what they already know. They also skim the text, examine illustrations, and make predictions. They develop flexibility in the way they read; that is, in most cases they are encouraged to read for depth of understanding, but occasionally they are encouraged to scan a passage for specific information. Through the book, learners also read texts in all four rhetorical modes (description, narration, exposition, and argumentation). They analyze a variety of specific organizational structures (e.g., cause and effect, comparison, and definition) as a means of increasing their comprehension, their ability to remember information, and their ability to organize information in writing.

For purposes of vocabulary development, the book has been organized so that the students build up their vocabulary by focusing on words in context. Vocabulary exercises are created around words that are listed on the Academic Word List. However, as the book progresses, the vocabulary exercises become more open-ended. For example, the students select key words and devise means of understanding these words in context.

Finally, the book has been organized so that the writing tasks become progressively more complex. For example, Chapter 1 briefly reviews the four types of sentences and the components of a well-organized paragraph and Chapter 2 reviews basic essay structure. This foundation in academic writing is developed throughout the text. As students work through the book, they practise a variety of increasingly complex writing tasks, such as answering short-answer examination questions, and writing summaries and a formal critique, until, in Chapter 10, they write a research paper.

Each reading passage is accompanied by the following types of exercises:

- pre-reading exercise (oral or written discussion, skimming and predicting exercises)
- comprehension check
- vocabulary-in-context exercise
- critical analysis discussion questions
- writing task
- revising task

Each chapter contains an academic writing task that pulls together the skills practised and the content of the readings.

For those who have used *Creating Meaning: Advanced Reading and Writing*, First edition, the basic structure of the chapters and the skills that are practised are the same in this second edition. However, in the second edition, the themes and readings have been updated. For example, Chapter 10, while maintaining the focus on the academic skills of citing and referencing, provides readings and opportunities for discussion and writing around the theme of global citizenship.

Dedication

This book is dedicated to my soul mate and life partner, Ralph Friesen, himself a lover of the written word. As well, to Nathan and Zea Friesen, my much-loved son and daughter who appreciate the intrinsic worth of the written page.

—Hannah Hofer Friesen

For Anthony and Noah, my beautiful children, and for Steve, my beautiful partner in life.

—Kathy Block

Acknowledgements

The authors wish to thank the many people who have contributed to this book, including Cindy Angelini and all the folks at Oxford University Press Canada. Acknowledged also are the teachers who provided feedback on the first edition of *Creating Meaning: Advanced Reading and Writing* and therefore, assisted in creating a well-rounded textbook for *Creating Meaning*, Second edition.

Creating Meaning
Big Picture

Creating Meaning
Big Picture (continued)

CHAPTER 1

Our Families, Ourselves

Introduction to the Chapter

In this chapter you will read about families from three points of view. The first reading gives a definition of family, the second is a personal account by a foster mother, and the third is an essay about the importance of both fathers and mothers in the family. It describes what each parent contributes to the children. Each reading focuses on different aspects of family.

For each reading you will do a comprehension check and study new vocabulary. You will also be asked to analyze and discuss the topic. Finally you will complete academic writing assignments that begin with the four sentence types and progress to well-written paragraphs.

Reading 1—*Changing the Definition of Family*

Pre-reading Exercises

Pre-reading exercises help you get a quick overview of the content and organization of the reading and can remind you of what you already know about the topic. As a result, you will be able to follow what the author is trying to say more easily and you may be able to read faster. Think of it as getting the big picture—the map for where you are going.

Thinking about the Topic

One pre-reading technique is to think about the topic and discover what you already know about the subject matter.

EXERCISE 1. PRE-READING DISCUSSION

To prepare for the first reading, discuss the following questions before you read.

1. Is your family the same size as your parents' or your grandparents' families? If not, what are the reasons for the change in size?

2. In what ways is your family important to you? Give an example.

3. How are the families you know changing?

Other Pre-reading Techniques

Before you read "Changing the Definition of Family," follow the pre-reading techniques below. They will help you predict what is in the reading.

- Read the title.

- Read the introduction.

- Read any headings.

- Read the first sentence under each heading.

- Study any graphs, pictures, and typographical aids.

- Read the last paragraph or summary.

Changing the Definition of Family

[1] The family is under stress. The number of divorces has increased dramatically around the world. In many countries more people prefer to live in common-law relationships and there are fewer people getting married. There is also a significant increase of single-parent families. Nevertheless, optimists say the family is merely changing as it has done for thousands of years.

[2] Information from Canada's Vanier Institute of the Family in Ottawa tells us that it is important to realize that families have always changed in response to circumstances. For instance, families have altered in size, structure, and patterns of functioning. Over the centuries families have been in a constant state of adaptation to the natural environment as well as to current political, religious, and social conditions. However, there have been few periods in history during which families have changed as much as they have in the second half of the twentieth century.

[3] There are a number of reasons for the changes in the family:

i) The extended family that was once common is now relatively rare. Older people now have greater financial security and tend not to live with their grown children.

ii) Nineteen out of twenty Canadians move at some point in their adult lives, and half of all Canadians move at least once every five years. Nuclear families move from one community to another in search of economic opportunity. Grown children leave their community.

iii) Contraception gives women a choice in the number and spacing of their children. Great numbers of women choose to work outside the home rather than stay at home to raise their children as has been the custom.

iv) Liberalized divorce laws affect the family in that men and women can choose to leave less than satisfactory relationships. This has resulted in increased numbers of single-parent families. (Definition is the Problem, 1997, pp. 9–10)

[4] According to the Vanier Institute, Canadians say in surveys that family is important to them. However, what we value now in families is not what we valued in the past. For instance, many people believe that it is not the marriage certificate we value as much as the way in which we try to care for one another.

[5] With so much change taking place at such a rapid pace, how do we re-define family? According to a 1997 report, psychologists who studied textbooks for definitions of the family could not find a true or specific definition. They noticed families were defined through pictures and stories referring to family life. They were largely defined by who was in them. As well, families are shown in a great many different ways; for example, families with both parents, families with single parents of only a father or mother, and also couples without children.

[6]   The Vanier Institute of the Family believes that families should be defined by their function rather than who is in them. In other words, "We can no longer define families by who belongs to them because they are all so different. However, we can define families by what they do, because most of them still must handle the same tasks they have handled for many, many generations." Furthermore, they say that the family is "the primary unit of learning, education, and socialization, a source of emotional sustenance and support, a significant unit of both economic production and consumption." (Transition Not Crisis, 1997, p. 3)

[7]   An inclusive definition of families and their functions must admit diversity and be culturally neutral. Furthermore, it must be societally neutral and not rely on any one national, historical, religious, or ethical set of assumptions. This is a matter of great importance in a free and pluralistic society.

[8]   The Vanier Institute's functional definition of family:

> **Family**
> Any combination of two or more persons who are bound together over time by ties of mutual consent, birth and/or adoption or placement, and who, together assume responsibilities for various combinations of some of the following:
>
> - Physical maintenance and care of group members
> - Addition of new members through procreation or adoption
> - Socialization of children
> - Social control of members
> - Production, consumption, distribution of goods and services
> - Affective nurturance—love
>
> (Vanier Institute of the Family)

[9]   Just as individual human beings are both actors within society and act upon it, so families can be thought of as simultaneously active and receptive agents within society. Families, the many forces at work on them, and their contribution to society are best understood as systems, the sum of many interacting parts. Moreover, families are open systems. Families are open to all kinds of

social, political, economic, and natural influences. At the same time, families greatly influence their environment. For example, families in advanced industrial societies appear to have fewer children. In turn, smaller families result in many other changes in society such as empty schools, lower demand for big cars and houses, and a smaller workforce. Those changes, in turn, may influence families. (Vanier Institute of the Family)

Source: Adapted from Anonymous. (1997). Definition is the Problem. *Canada and the World Backgrounder, 62*(5), 3.
Anonymous. (1997). Transition Not Crisis. *Canada and the World Backgrounder, 62*(5), 8–11.
Vanier Institute of the Family, http://www.vifamily.ca/

EXERCISE 2. COMPREHENSION CHECK

1. List the ways in which Canadian families have changed in the last few decades.

   _____

   _____

2. State four reasons for these changes.

   _____

   _____

3. Canadians say that what they value in families now is the same as what they valued years ago. True or False? Explain your answer.

   _____

   _____

4. Why is it necessary to come up with a new definition of family? How was family defined in the past?

   _____

   _____

5. In your own words, state what is meant by "open systems."

   _____

6. The Vanier Institute of the Family has defined family in a new way. Who makes up a family?

   _____

7. According to the definition, what are the functions of a family? The first answer is supplied for you.
   a) Physical maintenance and care of group members
   b) _____
   c) _____
   d) _____
   e) _____
   f) _____

8. Using the information from questions 6 and 7, write the Vanier definition of family in your own words. This definition will be a summary of the information in the reading. When you summarize, you need to use your own words in expressing what the author has said and to use your own sentence structures as well. These need to be different from the author's words or sentences. In this way, you avoid plagiarism.

_____

_____

_____

Critical Analysis

In each chapter you will have two opportunities to participate in critical analysis of the topic. In these analyses you will be expected to reflect more deeply on what you have read; that is, to go beyond a factual, literal level of a reading topic. This kind of exercise conforms to your instructor's expectation that you use your knowledge and understanding to apply, analyze, synthesize, and evaluate ideas and information. Critical analysis, then, is an opportunity to go deeper, to discuss or write at a more intensive level.

EXERCISE 3. ANALYZING QUOTATIONS

The following quotations are taken from the reading. After reading each quotation, discuss the following questions with your classmates.

1. "According to the Vanier Institute, Canadians say in surveys that family is important to them. However, what we value now in families is not what we valued in the past. For instance, many people believe that it is not the marriage certificate we value as much as the way in which we try to care for one another." (paragraph 4) Do you agree that society's values have changed? Drawing on your own experience, discuss what is valued in families today.

2. "An inclusive definition of families and their functions must admit diversity and be culturally neutral. Furthermore, it must be societally neutral and not rely on any one national, historical, religious, or ethical set of assumptions. This is a matter of great importance in a free and pluralistic society." (paragraph 7) Do you agree that the Vanier Institute has defined family to be truly inclusive and societally neutral? Is it possible to be societally neutral? How can this be achieved? Give reasons for your answer.

Vocabulary Study: Signal Words

The reading "Changing the Definition of Family" contains numerous signal words, such as _however_, _for example_, and _furthermore_. These words function as transitions, that is, they link one idea to another or one paragraph to another.

In addition, these signal words can provide a suggestion or cue for the reader to speed up, to maintain the present speed, or to slow down. (Your speed may vary when you read a textbook or research material, depending on the importance of the material.)

An understanding of the function of the words in the chart below gives you information that can help you understand the text.

SIGNAL WORDS AS AIDS TO COMPREHENSION

Signal Words (map, GPS)	Purpose
again *in other words, that is, to illustrate, for example, suppose,* *for instance, such as*	1. Indicate it is possible to speed up • repetitious information • examples
likewise, similarly, also, furthermore, and added to, *in addition* *first, second, . . . next, then, (1), (2), . . .*	2. Indicate need to maintain speed • continuation • enumeration (listing)
however, nevertheless, instead of, despite *in summary, for these reasons, to sum up, in brief* *in conclusion, thus, therefore* *above all, indeed, most important, it is essential*	3. Indicate need to slow down • change in information • summary • conclusion • emphasis

Source: Adapted from McWorter, K. (1996) *Efficient and Flexible Reading* (4th ed.). New York, NY: HarperCollins.

EXERCISE 4. SIGNAL WORDS

1. Scan "Changing the Definition of Family" for signal words. Make a chart similar to the one above, in which you list the signal words from the reading and indicate their function as an aid to comprehension. Are you meant to maintain speed, slow down, or speed up?

2. Then, in pairs, discuss the author's possible reasons for using these signal words at this particular point in the reading.

EXERCISE 5. VOCABULARY IN CONTEXT

The sentences below are taken from the reading. For each underlined word choose the closest meaning: a, b, or c.

1. "Nevertheless, optimists say the family is merely changing as it has done for thousands of years." (paragraph 1)

   a) people who take a hopeful view
   b) people who agree
   c) people who disagree

2. "For instance, families have altered in size, structure, and patterns of functioning." (paragraph 2)

   a) refused to change
   b) changed
   c) improved

3. "The extended family that was once common is now relatively rare." (paragraph 3)

   a) abnormal
   b) uncommon
   c) crowded

4. "Great numbers of women choose to work outside the home rather than stay at home to raise their children as has been the custom." (paragraph 3)

   a) difference
   b) tradition
   c) law

5. "Liberalized divorce laws affect the family in that men and women can choose to leave less than satisfactory relationships." (paragraph 3)

   a) narrow-minded
   b) open-minded
   c) foolish

6. "The Vanier Institute of the Family believes that families should be defined by their function rather than who is in them." (paragraph 6)

   a) lifestyles
   b) what they do
   c) number of individuals

   We know that the word *function* is a noun. How does the addition of the suffixes "-ing"—*functioning* (paragraph 2)—and "-al"—*functional* (paragraph 8)—change the part of speech?

7. "Furthermore, they say that the family is the primary unit of learning, education, and socialization, a source of emotional sustenance and support, a significant unit of both economic production and consumption." (paragraph 6)

   a) nourishment
   b) forgetfulness
   c) abandon

8. "An inclusive definition of families and their functions must admit diversity and be culturally neutral." (paragraph 7)

   a) confusion
   b) variety
   c) disagreement

9. "This is a matter of great importance in a free and pluralistic society." (paragraph 7)

   a) made up of many cultures that have equal status
   b) made up of one culture that is dominant
   c) made up of urban culture that is pervasive

Reading 2—*James*

EXERCISE 6. PRE-READING DISCUSSION

Discuss the following questions before you read.

1. Have you ever wished you could choose your parents or family?

2. Describe a time when you and your mother did something on your own.

3. In your country of birth, how are single parents regarded? Are they accepted?

To help your comprehension of this next reading, follow the pre-reading techniques below. You should follow these techniques for each of the readings.

- Read the title.

- Read the introduction.

- Read any headings.

- Read the first sentence under each heading.

- Study any graphs, charts, pictures, and typographical aids.

- Read the last paragraph or summary.

In the following article, a single mother writes about her experience in raising a son.

James

[1] My son, James, is 11 years old now. I am his foster mother. He has lived with me for seven years, so we seldom think of it as a foster-care relationship. I am his "real" mom and he is my "real" son. It is a permanent relationship and a permanent placement by Child and Family Services. We do not and have not for many years used the word "foster." Somehow I think that might make him (and me) feel that we both do not quite have the relationship that other moms and sons have. He and I both feel secure in our relationship. We have the same needs that biological families have.

[2] I am a single parent. This adds some extra pressure, but it also makes things less complicated in some ways. There is no negotiating with a partner about what is best for James, but on the other hand James has only one parental role model and influence. It also means that when I am tired there is no other adult to take over for me. This means that at times James has to deal with me when what I really need is some space.

[3] James is Aboriginal. Maintaining his cultural awareness is important and I believe that it should not be ignored or replaced just because it is not the same as mine. My approach has been to let him take the lead here. At certain ages he has been more interested in his culture than at other times. This preteen age is a time when kids focus more on what they have that is the same as other kids rather than what sets them apart. I expect that as he gets older, he will start asking more about it again.

no more than 13 yrs

[4]   I worry sometimes about how people view him and how, as he grows older, this will affect him. At this point, he seems oblivious to any prejudice because of his culture. I have seen how some storekeepers, for example, watch him a little more than other children. Though it does not happen often, it does happen, and as he grows older, he may start to notice this.

[5]   When he was younger, I took him to some powwows and read him books written and illustrated by Aboriginal writers and artists. At a certain age, he seemed to become uninterested. At this time, I make sure that he has books written by people of his culture and some more informational books about legends and traditions of "his people" as he calls them. He loves reading and is an excellent reader so he takes in lots of information. What I could have and should probably still do is learn more myself about his culture instead of just providing him with the information. Parenting is a constant learning experience.

[6]   James has some special needs. By the time he was four years old, he had moved from home to home at least 16 times. My focus has been on giving him a predictable and stable home atmosphere. More than anything I believe he needs to know that he is safe and that I am present—physically as much as emotionally. He has some difficulty establishing his own limits and usually feels better about himself when they are set out clearly. To succeed, he needs to know what the rules, boundaries, and limits are. We keep quite a regular schedule—as I have often heard social workers say about children like James, "routine, routine, routine."

[7]   As a single parent working full-time, I know I often miss the small things and this is something that has become clear to me, especially recently. I miss day-to-day things like stopping to listen to him tell a story about something that happened at school, or tell me about a book he is reading or a dream he had. I do well with the big decisions—about what I think will be in his best interest, where we should live, what school would be best for him, and so on.

[8]   I believe that all parents set their priorities according to what they believe to be crucial. I know that more than in any other area of my life I struggle with parenting. It seems to me that it is the most important role I have at this time. I often wonder about how I am doing, what I might be missing, what I need to change or let go of as my boy grows older. I learn as I go.

Source: Yvonne Block.

Exercise 7. Comprehension Check

1. How do we know this mother–son relationship is positive?

_____

2. How does the author feel about being a single parent?

    Pro: make things less complicated in some ways; only one parental role model and influence

    Con: extra pressure; no negotiating with partner; no one can take over for me.

3. What does the author mean when she says, "My approach has been to let him take the lead here." (paragraph 3)

_____

_____

4. Who are "his people"? (paragraph 5)

Aboriginal people

5. What does this mother do to ensure James knows his culture?

_____

Why is this necessary?

_____

6. What is James especially good at?

reading

7. How is this mother like other mothers?

_____

_____

8. How do James and his mother fit the Vanier Institute's definition of the family? Respond to each of the points in the definition. The first one has been done for you.

a) She cares for him
b) *foster relationship* _____
c) _____
d) _____
e) _____
f) _____

EXERCISE 8. VOCABULARY IN CONTEXT

From the list, choose the word that fits best in each of the following sentences.

seldom (paragraph 1) rarely

negotiating (paragraph 2) bargaining

maintaining (paragraph 3) continuing

oblivious (paragraph 4) unaware

stable (paragraph 6) unwavering

routine (paragraph 6) regularity

priorities (paragraph 8) preferential ratings

crucial (paragraph 8) essential

1. Although the summer storm brought down trees outside the house, the baby was _oblivous_ to it as she slept in her crib.

2. If watching hockey on television were not one of his _priorities/routine_, we would have been able to finish the project by now.

3. It is _crucial_ for the patient to follow the doctor's orders regarding the medication.

4. _Maintaining_ a good relationship with the parents of your spouse is essential.

5. Since both my partner and I have jobs now, our finances have become _stable_.

6. I _seldom_ eat chocolate cake because it is too fattening for me.

7. When people come back from holidays, it is sometimes difficult for them to re-establish a _routine_.

8. It is helpful to have good _negotiating_ skills when you go to a garage sale.

EXERCISE 9. WRITING: UNDERSTANDING THE READING

Write a paragraph describing in your own words what particularly struck you about this reading passage. In other words, what did you think was interesting or unusual?

Reading 3—Two-Parent Families: The Special Role Each Parent Plays

EXERCISE 10. PRE-READING DISCUSSION

Discuss the following questions before you read.

1. When you think of your father or mother, what memory stands out?

2. Describe a time when you did something special with either your mother or father. How did it make you feel?

3. What do you know about your father or mother when he or she was the age that you are now?

The author of "Two-Parent Families: The Special Role Each Parent Plays" presents information about families and the contributions that fathers and mothers make. As you read, try to identify what each parent contributes to the children's lives. Notice how that information helps create a fuller picture of the importance of both a man and a woman in the life of a child.

Two-Parent Families: The Special Role Each Parent Plays

Parents Together

[1] A strong relationship with one's spouse is the bedrock of a child's family life and influences how the child will eventually relate to his own partner. But the rush of daily life, especially during the busy years of soccer teams, and dance lessons, may push the adult relationship into second place. Nevertheless, it is important for a couple to love and support one another. In order to keep the couple's relationship strong, those Saturday night dates are as important as any of the children's events.

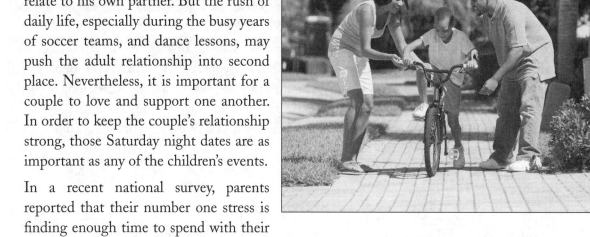

[2] In a recent national survey, parents reported that their number one stress is finding enough time to spend with their children. One way to increase the time spent with children is to involve them in the daily activities of running the home such as preparing meals, tidying up, looking after the pets, and doing the laundry. This way, the whole family becomes a team in maintaining the home.

[3] In building a family team, it is important that the adults be co-captains. Children need to know their parents are in charge. Slowly though, children need to be given more and more independence and opportunities to make their own decisions. It is a parent's job to eventually do themselves out of a job.

[4] Parenting is best handled as a team effort because men and women bring different influences to the family and affect their children's development in different ways. Research reveals that children tend to do better when they are exposed to different parenting styles.

The Role of Fathers

[5] Evidence is mounting that the involvement of a father has a greater influence on his children than previously acknowledged. It appears that a father's interest increases children's social development, their sense of self-worth and their chances of academic success. The reason seems to be that a man's involvement in child-rearing is different from a woman's. Fathers influence their children's social confidence because they are the first "stranger" or "other" in their child's life unlike mothers whom infants appear to regard as an extension of themselves. Fathers set the groundwork for dealing with strangers later. Fathers play a significant role in a child's emotional health and development of their self-worth. As the children grow older, fathers tend to push them to take chances in situations in which mothers have a tendency to urge more caution. Both approaches are important to the child's development.

[6]   Dads, of course, provide boys with something that women can't: a model of what it's like to be a man. Children learn more from what you do than from what you say, although both actions and communication are important. Fathers can show boys how a man conducts himself with dignity, integrity, and respect for others.

[7]   Girls also seem to rely on their fathers in developing a sense of their own femininity. A girl's relationship with the opposite sex seems to be based on the relationship she had with the first male in her life—her dad. If a father has a loving relationship with his daughter, she'll have a better chance of creating a good relationship with a male partner in later life.

[8]   Some studies suggest that the average father spends only 15 to 20 minutes a week in one-on-one discussions with his children. One of the most effective ways of becoming an involved father is to spend more one-on-one time with your children in real two-way conversations. When you're a father who is genuinely engaged in raising his children, you're doing something good for your children as well as for yourself. Kids are sponges who soak up love, and when they get enough, they aren't shy about giving it back to you.

The Role of Mothers

[9]   Researchers have made some important observations about maternal influence. It appears that mothers have a stronger role than fathers in teaching children the skills of social interaction. Women tend to put more emphasis on building and maintaining relationships, both inside and outside the family. They also tend to have a more flexible style of discipline than fathers and are more open to negotiation as a means of reconciling conflicts. Children learn from them how to handle the give-and-take that's part of any strong relationship. Moms also tend to have an important influence on the academic performance of their children because, possibly, they spend more time with them, even if they have a job outside the home. Moms also more often take on the role of guardian of the family's health.

Encouraging Daughters

[10]   A mother can play a major role in her daughter's developing self-esteem. Girls look for role models as they try to figure out how they fit into society, especially how they relate to men. They look to their own mothers to provide a strong model of confidence and equality with the men in their lives. As well, mothers can provide a healthy model for girls who worry about their body image. Talking to a daughter about the idealized images on TV and in magazines encourages her to be aware and reassures her that there is no one "acceptable" body type. Encouraging a daughter to care about her grooming is essential, but it is not beneficial to be judgmental about any perceived physical shortcomings.

[11]   A daughter relies on her mother to be the model of how to be a mother herself. She learns to maintain strong family relationships, to care for other family members, and to continue family traditions, whether it's a family picnic on Canada Day or hosting a gathering of the extended family during the holidays. However, this teaching does not mean that a mother's role is to sacrifice for the family. That's the message she might get if her mother automatically calls on

her first for help around the house or when she sees that her mother takes on most of the responsibilities for the family's everyday care. Both mothers and fathers are involved in running the household and both sons and daughters share household responsibilities.

Encouraging Sons

[12]   Throughout his childhood, a son is happy to spend time with his mother. As he gets older and begins to focus more on friends, he starts to spend less time with mother. By the time he's about 9 or 10, a boy may pretend he doesn't need his mother, partly because of society's messages about how boys should behave and partly to avoid teasing. He may fuss if his mother continues to kiss him goodbye in public, but he actually needs the closeness. It is best not to show this closeness in front of his friends!

[13]   Many mothers play a major role in demonstrating important qualities such as sensitivity, compassion, and caring. These help their sons develop into complete human beings. Boys also learn from their mothers about the nature of relationships with the opposite sex. If a boy has a good relationship with his mother, the first woman in his life, it can lead to positive relationships with women later on. Boys who grow up with mothers who aren't emotionally available to them tend to be less secure and more emotionally fragile. Boys rely on maternal sensitivity to respond to them as they develop. Teaching a son how to relate to the world emotionally will also prepare him to be a better, more involved father one day.

Source: Adapted from Christine Langlois (Ed.), "Two-Parent Families." *Raising Great Kids* (Ballantine Books, 1999).

EXERCISE 11. COMPREHENSION CHECK

Answer true or false to the following questions according to the reading.

1. The author believes that a nurturing relationship between a father and a mother is the foundation of the family. _____

2. The author believes having one parent in the home is better than having two. _____

3. In part, girls learn that they are worthy of love from the love they receive from their fathers. _____

4. The presence of fathers in the home does not necessarily benefit boys. _____

5. Fathers and mothers provide the model for their children's future positive relationships. _____

6. Mothers are generally the guardians of family health. _____

7. The main idea of this reading is that both fathers and mothers make specific contributions to a family. _____

Exercise 12. Critical Analysis

1. You have now read different views relating to family. Compare the author's views in "James" with the author's views in "Two-Parent Families: The Special Role Each Parent Plays." On a separate sheet of paper, make a chart in which you list the similarities in the views of the two authors, the differences, and finally your own views. Discuss your chart with your class.

2. The author of "Two-Parent Families: The Special Role Each Parent Plays" presents strong views and recommendations. In your opinion, are her views inclusive of diversity as recommended by the Vanier Institute? Explain your answer.

| Vocabulary Study |

The author of "Two-Parent Families: The Special Role Each Parent Plays" has used a wide range of vocabulary, much of which can be understood from the context. Complete the exercises below, and try to find the meaning of the words from the context. When this is not possible, you may need to use a dictionary.

Exercise 13. Definitions (A)

Match each word in column A with its meaning in column B. The first answer is given for you.

A	B
1. *eventually* (paragraph 1)	a) study, examination
2. *bedrock* (paragraph 1)	b) self-respect
3. *stress* (paragraph 2)	c) in time
4. *survey* (paragraph 2)	d) preserving
5. *co-captains* (paragraph 3)	e) shared leadership
6. *maintaining* (paragraph 2)	f) honesty
7. *significant* (paragraph 5)	g) anxiety, strain
8. *approaches* (paragraph 5)	h) foundation
9. *dignity* (paragraph 6)	i) important
10. *integrity* (paragraph 6)	j) particular ways of doing

EXERCISE 14. DEFINITIONS (B)

The following sentences are taken from the reading selection. Choose the best meaning for the underlined word or words.

1. "Research reveals that children tend to do better when they are <u>exposed to</u> different parenting styles." (paragraph 4)

   a) pictured
   b) shown, experiencing
   c) disposed to

2. "<u>Evidence</u> is <u>mounting</u> that the involvement of a father has a greater influence on his children than previously acknowledged." (paragraph 5)

   evidence   *mounting*
   a) proof   a) elevation
   b) mystery   b) truth
   c) science   c) growing, increasing

3. "Girls also seem to <u>rely on</u> their fathers in developing a sense of their own femininity." (paragraph 7)

   a) ignore
   b) depend on
   c) commit to

4. "One of the most effective ways of becoming an <u>involved</u> father is to spend more one-on-one time. . . ." (paragraph 8)

   a) present and engaged
   b) absent and distant
   c) busy and working

5. "It appears that mothers have a stronger role than fathers in teaching children the skills of <u>social interaction</u>." (paragraph 9)

   a) aggressive behaviour in society
   b) appropriate behaviour in society
   c) inappropriate behaviour in society

6. "They also tend to have a more <u>flexible</u> style of discipline than fathers and are more open to <u>negotiation</u> as a means of <u>reconciling</u> conflicts." (paragraph 9)

   flexible   *negotiation*   *reconciling*
   a) changeable   a) confrontational   a) segregating of
   b) dig in   b) compromise   b) bringing solutions to
   c) severe   c) disagreement   c) insisting upon

7. "Talking to a daughter about the <u>idealized</u> images on TV and in magazines. . . ." (paragraph 10)
   a) unobtainable or presented as better than they really are
   b) scant and frightening
   c) useless and unlawful

8. "As he gets older and begins to <u>focus</u> more on friends. . . ." (paragraph 12)
   a) avoid contact
   b) become absentminded
   c) centre attention

A Word about Summaries

- How are summaries useful?

  When a condensed overview is needed, summaries are very helpful. They are useful when preparing for examinations, obtaining key points from readings or research for a seminar, summarizing lab reports, or summarizing historical or literary documents or readings.

- What does a summary contain?

  A summary is a condensed restatement of the main ideas of a passage. Unlike a paraphrase, a summary does not contain all the information presented in the original. Only the gist of the text and a few details are included. Most of the background information and explanations are also omitted. In length, summaries are often one-quarter or less of the original.

- What steps do I follow as I summarize?
  1. Carefully read the whole text; look up any difficult words not clear from the context. It is essential to understand the passage before you summarize.
  2. Underline or highlight the sentences or phrases that contain the main idea or thesis of the passage. Write the thesis in your own words; then find the supporting details. The thesis and supporting details provide a rough outline.
  3. Write the summary in your own words, expressing the information in the outline. A good way to ensure you are using your own words is to give an oral summary before you write. Be sure to change words to synonyms and to vary the word order in your sentences.
  4. Decide what to omit. Abridge and combine the information where possible. Present the ideas in the same order that they appeared in the reading. Leave out repetitions, examples, anecdotes, digressions, dialogue, quotations, parenthetical statements, figures of speech, jokes, minor descriptive details, and most statistics.
  5. Reread your summary and ensure that no essential information has been left out and that all the information comes from the reading.

Exercise 15. Summarizing

Choose the best summarization of each statement below.

1. "A strong relationship with one's spouse is the bedrock of a child's family life and influences how the child will eventually relate to his own partner." (paragraph 1)
   a) Maintaining a close connection with a partner is the only model for the child to learn how to have a strong relationship.
   b) How a child relates to a partner in the future is strongly influenced by the parents' earlier relationship.

2. "Kids are sponges who soak up love, and when they get enough, they aren't shy about giving it back to you." (paragraph 8)
   a) When children receive sufficient love, they do not hesitate to return this love.
   b) Children never receive sufficient love and so become dependent on it.

3. "Encouraging a daughter to care about her grooming is essential, but it is not beneficial to be judgmental about any perceived physical shortcomings." (paragraph 10)
   a) It is not important to criticize a girl or to remind her about cleanliness.
   b) It is unhelpful to criticize a daughter about her looks, although teaching her about being clean and tidy is important.

Exercise 16. Understanding the Organization of the Reading

"Two-Parent Families: The Special Role Each Parent Plays" is an essay that shows good organizational technique. The writer begins by providing a title that informs the reader about what can be expected. There follows a "hook," a statement that introduces the essay and catches the reader's attention. It describes, generally, the importance of parents maintaining a close relationship. The thesis statement is found in the final paragraph of the introduction, paragraph 4. Therefore, the reader knows that the unique functions of what fathers and mothers contribute in raising their children will be discussed next. This information is conveyed through paragraphs that explain, describe, or support according to the author's own knowledge, experience, and research. Throughout the body of the essay, there are recommendations for how to improve relationships in the family.

This exercise will help you understand the organization of "Two-Parent Families: The Special Role Each Parent Plays." Make notes in each category with information from the reading.

Then write a summary that includes that information, beginning with the thesis statement and ending with the recommendations.

Two-Parent Families: The Special Role Each Parent Plays

The thesis statement is found in paragraph 4: "Parenting is best handled as a team effort because men and women bring different influences to the family and affect their children's development in different ways."

In the supporting paragraphs we find the following information:

1. What fathers contribute: Name the three ways that a father's interest contributes to his children's lives.

   _____

   _____

   _____

2. Unique qualities: What unique qualities do fathers bring?

   For sons: _____

   _____

   For daughters: _____

   _____

3. Role of mothers: Identify four qualities that mothers bring to a child's life.

   _____

   _____

   _____

   _____

4. Unique qualities: What unique qualities do mothers bring?

   For daughters: _____

   _____

   For sons: _____

   _____

5. Recommendations: List recommendations the author makes throughout the reading regarding parental and family relationships.

   _____

   _____

Writing

Four Types of Sentences for Academic Writing

To write accurately and to revise your own work, it is essential to know what constitutes a complete sentence. To the second-language student, it often seems that the varieties of sentences in English are endless and to learn them all would be an overwhelming task. In fact, sentences can be classified into four basic types: simple, compound, complex, and compound-complex. Every sentence fits one of these four sentence types.

In this chapter, the four types of sentences—simple, compound, complex, and compound-complex—will be reviewed and practised.

A. Simple Sentences

A simple sentence is an independent clause (complete sentence).

1. It must have a subject and a verb, but it can be very short.

Example: The dog barked.
                     subject   verb

or

2. A simple sentence can be longer with a subject, a verb, and phrases.

Example: Yoko flew (to Jasper) (during the holidays).
               subject verb prepositional phrase   prepositional phrase

or

3. A simple sentence can have a compound subject and a compound verb.

Example: Yoko and Claudia flew to Jasper during the holidays and skied all week long.
             compound subject   compound verb

B. Compound Sentences

A compound sentence consists of two independent clauses (simple sentences) that have been joined by a coordinating conjunction or a semicolon (;).

1. Two independent clauses may be joined by a coordinating conjunction (*and, but, or, for, nor, so*).

The following three examples from the readings use some commonly found coordinating conjunctions: *and, but, so*.
   - "Both mothers and fathers are involved in running the household and both sons and daughters share household responsibilities."
   - "This adds some extra pressure, but it also makes things less complicated in some ways."
   - "He has lived with me for seven years, so we seldom think of it as a foster-care relationship."

Relationship of Clauses Joined by Coordinating Conjunctions	
Additional information	*and*
Contrasting information	*but*
An effect after a cause	*so*

2. The two independent clauses may also be joined by a semicolon. This kind of compound sentence is possible only when the two independent clauses are closely related in meaning. If they are not closely related, they should be written as two simple sentences, each ending with a period.

   Example: They should have seen his death coming; grandfather had been growing increasingly weak, deaf, and unable to care for himself.

   Example: I washed the dishes today; tomorrow someone else should do it.

3. A compound sentence can consist of two independent clauses joined by a semicolon and a conjunctive adverb. Some common conjunctive adverbs are as follows: *however*, *nevertheless*, *consequently*, *therefore*, *thus*, *furthermore*, *moreover*, *also*. They should usually be followed by a comma.

   Example: The student residence is located on campus; therefore, it takes very little time for Mario to get to his classes.

   Example: Koji was happy with his score on the TOEFL exam; however, he soon realized his academic standing was not acceptable to the University of Calgary.

EXERCISE 17. SENTENCE-COMBINING

Combine each pair of sentences (or independent clauses) to form compound sentences. Use semicolons and conjunctive adverbs.

1. Air fares have increased dramatically. Most people still prefer to travel by air.

   _____

2. The flood of the century in Manitoba was destructive. Many people had to leave their homes.

   _____

3. The price of the house has been reduced. It seems nobody wants to buy it.

   _____

4. We like to cross-country ski in the winter. On weekends we just pack up the car and go.

   _____

5. The museum in Spain has been hailed as a monument to the imagination. It is being studied by architects everywhere.

   _____

6. The sky was dark and threatening. It did not rain.

_____

7. My brother is an engineer. He intends to apply for the job advertised in the *Calgary Herald*.

_____

On a separate sheet of paper, write four compound sentences using the following conjunctive adverbs: *nevertheless*, *consequently*, *moreover*, and *furthermore*.

C. Complex Sentences

A complex sentence is made up of an independent clause (complete sentence) and one or more dependent (subordinate) clauses. A subordinate clause is introduced by a subordinate conjunction and modifies the main clause or some element in it.

Example: (*main, principle, or independent clause*) On the playground

fathers often get the child to swing ever higher, (*dependent clause*)
‾‾‾‾‾‾‾   ‾‾‾
subject   verb

while mothers are cautious, worrying about an accident.
   ‾‾‾‾‾‾ ‾‾‾
   subject   verb

Example: It would be difficult for a newspaper to eliminate weekend
   ‾‾ ‾‾‾‾‾‾‾
   subject   verb

colour comics (*dependent clause*) because many people consider them
                                       ‾‾‾‾‾‾‾‾‾ ‾‾‾‾‾‾‾
                                           subject   verb

an integral part of the enjoyment in reading the newspaper.

Note: An independent clause can stand alone as a complete sentence; however, a dependent clause by itself is a sentence fragment.

Example: The legislature passed a sales tax.   (complete sentence)

When the legislature passed a sales tax.   (fragment)

He had already failed twice.   (complete sentence)

Because he had already failed twice.   (fragment)

The following words can change a complete sentence (an independent clause) into an incomplete sentence (a dependent clause).

although	which	before	until
since	because	if	unless
when	after	whether	whereas

Relationship of Clauses Joined by Subordinating Conjunctions	
Time	*while, before, until*
Cause and effect	*because, since, as*
Contrasting information	*although, even though*

Note: Punctuation of complex sentences

If the dependent clause comes before the independent clause, a comma is necessary.

Examples:

- Although he did not score, he made the best play of the game.
- He made the best play of the game although he did not score.

EXERCISE 18. COMPLETING COMPLEX SENTENCES

Using some of the subordinating conjunctions in the chart, complete the following complex sentences.

1. _____ I do not like pizza, I ordered fillet of sole.

2. The librarian called to ask _____ you could return the books you borrowed a month ago.

3. I would not bother to read that comic strip _____ I did not find it amusing.

4. _____ we had been at my sister's wedding, my friends and I went to an all-night party at the beach.

5. Most Canadians drink milk _____ most Vietnamese do not.

6. _____ I have mostly perennials in my garden, there is still too much work.

7. I will have to buy you a new violin case _____ I can repair the damaged one.

8. _____ the doctor can diagnose the disease, a sample will have to be sent to the lab.

D. Compound-Complex Sentences

A compound-complex sentence consists of two or more independent clauses and one or more dependent clauses.

Examples:

- When the legislature passed a sales tax of 14 percent, many people complained, but the prime minister refused to remove it.
- Jack worked for his brother, and this was a good arrangement although they sometimes disagreed.

EXERCISE 19. WRITING SENTENCES

After reading "Two-Parent Families: The Special Role Each Parent Plays," you made notes under each of the headings in the organizational exercise, Exercise 16. Now, write complete sentences under each of the headings, using simple, compound, and complex sentences. In some categories you may be able to include all the information in one sentence, whereas in other categories you will need to write two or three sentences.

EXERCISE 20. WRITING COMPLETE SENTENCES

We know that each family has good times and bad times; each family has its positives and negatives. Make a chart showing how your family members, or those of another family you know, "pull together," that is, try to be united, or how they draw apart, that is, move away from one another. Then write complete sentences for your points. Try to vary your sentence structures according to the four sentence types discussed earlier.

Paragraph Development

A well-written paragraph contains a series of sentences that develop a main idea. Usually, a paragraph begins with a topic sentence—a sentence that introduces a topic and contains the main idea in the paragraph. But the topic sentence can also be found in the middle or at the end. Some paragraphs may lack a topic sentence altogether; the main idea is implied or suggested through the details.

A well-written paragraph should

1. be unified: All the sentences should be related to the main idea of the paragraph

2. be coherent: Every sentence should be logically connected to the preceding and following sentence. Transition words, such as *however, nevertheless,* and *in addition,* can assist writers in achieving coherence.

3. contain supporting information: The main idea in a paragraph should be supported by facts, examples, reasons, explanations, quotations, or personal experience.

4. be well organized. Paragraphs should have logical patterns of organization, such as chronological order, illustration, comparison and contrast, or cause and effect. Additional rhetorical devices that can be used to organize paragraphs are description, narration, classification, process analysis, and definition. These devices will be practised in subsequent chapters.

> **Example of a well-written paragraph:**
>
> **(Topic and main idea)** Children's lives are enriched in several ways when fathers are engaged in their lives. **(Supporting information)** From research we know that children's social development is enhanced, their sense of self-worth increases, and their academic performance improves. The reason for this seems to be that a man brings something unique to a child's life. Fathers tend to be willing to push a child to achieve and to persist in the face of discouragement. **(Conclusion)** A supportive father's contribution to his children is invaluable on many levels.

EXERCISE 21. TOPIC SENTENCES (A)

With a partner, read paragraphs 5, 9, 10, 11, and 13 in "Two-Parent Families: The Special Role Each Parent Plays." Underline the topic sentences, and then identify what kind of supporting information the author is using. Are any of the topic sentences implied?

EXERCISE 22. TOPIC SENTENCES (B)

Return to the paragraphs that you wrote previously. Underline your topic sentences and identify what type of support you used.

EXERCISE 23. WRITING: DESCRIBING YOUR FAMILY

Now write a paragraph or paragraphs describing your family or the most influential member of your family. In supporting your topic sentence, consider using examples, comparison, or description. It may be helpful to study the following three examples before you write.

1. Exemplification

"Information from Canada's Vanier Institute of the Family in Ottawa tells us that it is important to realize that families have always changed in response to circumstances. For instance, families have altered in size, structure, and patterns of functioning. Over the centuries families have been in a constant state of adaptation to the natural environment as well as to current political, religious, and social conditions. However, there have been few periods in history during which families have changed as much as they have in the second half of the twentieth century." From "Changing the Definition of Family."

2. Comparison

"I am a single parent. This adds some extra pressure, but it also makes things less complicated in some ways. There is no negotiating with a partner about what is best for James, but on the other hand James has only one parental role model and influence. It also means that when I am tired there is no other adult to take over for me. This means that at times James has to deal with me when what I really need is some space." From "James."

3. Description

This example is taken from *Red China Blues* by Jan Wong. Here the author describes a person.

"Like me, Scarlet was nineteen. She was a head taller than I and serious-faced, with a tendency to furrow her thick brows whenever she was perplexed. She was also voluptuous, and slouched self-consciously most of the time—the Cultural Revolution was not the best time in Chinese history to look sexy 'Welcome you!' used up one-third of her English vocabulary. She knew four other words: 'Long live Chairman Mao!' Scarlet was a world history major, chosen to match my major at McGill. In fact, the entire female section of her class had been moved into Building Twenty-five to keep me company. . . ." p. 44.

| Questions to Aid in Revising |—————————————

1. Does your paragraph contain a topic sentence introducing the main idea?

2. Are all the ideas within the paragraph related to the main idea?

3. Is the main idea adequately supported with facts, examples, a comparison, or a description?

Ask another student in the class to read your paragraph and summarize your main idea in a few words. Does her or his summary express your main idea?

CHAPTER 2

Innovators: People Who Make a Difference

Introduction to the Chapter

An innovator is someone who introduces something new; it could be a new idea, a new way of doing something or creating a new device that has not been a part of our lives before. The readings in this chapter concern people who have done things differently and their unique creations. The first reading is about David Suzuki, a man of many talents especially in raising awareness regarding the environment. The second reading is about a woman from India, Vandana Shiva, who is passionate about saving seeds and ensuring that these are available to farmers. The final reading is about architect Frank Gehry, his extraordinary creativity and gifts, and how he uses these in creating unusual and special buildings around the world. The focus of the writing exercise in this chapter is on essay writing. The final exercise asks you to write an essay on innovation.

Reading 1—*David Suzuki: Educator, Broadcaster, and Activist*

EXERCISE 1. PRE-READING DISCUSSION

Discuss the following questions before you read.

1. When you think of environmental protection, who, in general, comes to mind? Identify what this person has accomplished.

2. If you had the power to make changes to the environment, what would you choose to do? Explain your answer.

3. In what way has the thinking about the environment changed? Is it different than it was in your parents' generation, for instance?

4. Why do you think there is so much discussion and controversy around the environment?

Vocabulary Specific to the Environment

The term *environment* covers all the elements of the natural world, from the earth, the oceans, the air, and the climate to the plants and the animals that live there. It also relates to where we live, how we live, and the people that surround us.

In "David Suzuki: Educator, Broadcaster, and Activist," the author uses specific vocabulary and phrases normally used in discussions about the environment. The following chart identifies some words and phrases from the reading that are associated with the environment. It provides meanings and parts of speech where possible.

Vocabulary Related to the Environment	Meanings (N = noun, Adj = adjective, Adv = adverb)
environment (paragraph 1)	(N) The physical conditions something exists in. The conditions that affect the behaviours and development of something.
environmental (paragraph 1)	(Adj) Connected with the natural conditions in which people, animals, and plants live.
environmental threats (paragraph 10)	Possible dangers to the environment. Words frequently used together include *environmental damage*, *environmental harm*, *environmental clean-up*, *environmental assessment*, and so on.
interaction with the environment (paragraph 8)	Act of relating with the environment. To interrelate with the physical environment.
sustainable (paragraph 4)	(Adj) Involving the use of natural products and energy in a way that does not harm the environment. Words frequently used together include *sustainable within a generation*, *sustainable living*, *sustainable future*, *sustainable forestry*, and *sustainable fishing*.
sustainability (paragraph 12)	(N) Ability to be maintained or to continue without destroying the balance of nature.
unsustainable (paragraph 10)	(Adj) Unsound; not defensible or acceptable.
impact on the earth (paragraph 8)	The effect that something or someone has on the world.
functions well within its natural limits (paragraph 12)	Works well within its usual or normal restrictions or confines.
clean energy (paragraph 11)	Energy that is not harmful to the earth.

EXERCISE 2. USING ENVIRONMENTAL VOCABULARY

Complete the paragraph by inserting one of the words or phrases from the chart above.

David Suzuki believes that our ___environment___ is quite imbalanced and often irresponsible. It is, therefore, ___unsustainable___ and leads to global warming. According to Suzuki, the ___impact on the earth___ is not separate from us; it is us. All of us are responsible for creating a positive ___sustainability___. To make our actions ___sustainable___, we need to focus on using ___clean energy___. This energy, which ___fuctions well with its natural limits___, can continue to be used without doing irreparable harm. The _interaction with the environment_ of our actions serves to decrease the _environmental threats_ to our world. Finally, our environmental activity, that is, our footprint, suggests responsible behaviour for humans on the earth.

David Suzuki: Educator, Broadcaster, and Activist

If we take the position that humans are part of a much greater whole,
we recognize that whatever we do to our surroundings, we do to ourselves,
because there is no separation from it. —*David Suzuki*

[1]   David Suzuki, a Canadian of Japanese descent, has had a significant impact on Canada and the world. He is considered a person who can inspire audiences on issues that concern everyone, from environmental and civil rights to the future of science and technology. He is a clear thinker, a person who has had a life-long passion for science and the environment. His career has been extraordinarily wide-ranging and influential, particularly in the field of education, in radio and television and as an activist for the environment.

[2]   Suzuki refers to his upbringing as the basis of his training, where it all began for him. In 1949, the Suzuki family, comprising David, his three sisters, and his parents, chose the farming community of Leamington, Ontario, as their new home. However, this choice was made after the family was released from a detention facility in Slocan City, BC, at the end of World War II. They had been deprived of their possessions, their rights and privileges, and were exiled east of the Rocky Mountains. Despite this painful period in the family's life, David Suzuki became known as a person with a positive outlook on life who cares deeply about the world at large.

Storyteller

[3]   A highlight of the academic year at Leamington District Secondary School in the 1940s was the yearly, oratorical contest. In this contest, Suzuki drew the topic "If I Were Three Inches Tall." The subject might have worried others, but as a child, he had spent hours in the BC wilderness camping, hiking, and fishing and had a highly developed general knowledge of the world. Suzuki spoke of an imaginary journey, in which he tumbles out of a fishing boat and is immediately eaten by a bass. After a slippery ride down its digestive tract, the boy frees his penknife and slices into the fish's air bladder. There, he safely hides until his father hooks the fish and frees his son in the course of cleaning it for dinner. Not surprisingly, the story was a crowd-pleaser, and Suzuki won first prize. His father, Suzuki tells us, was always a great believer in the importance of being able to speak well.

Honours

[4]   Currently, David Suzuki continues to be a progressive thinker and a persuasive grassroots activist: Suzuki is Canada's leading spokesperson for sustainable development. He possesses a long list of credentials that include award-winning scientist, author of more than 30 books, celebrated broadcaster and host of the country's longest-running science and nature television series, radio personality, recipient of 16 honorary doctorates, several First Nations honours, Officer of the Order of Canada, and founder of the David Suzuki Foundation.

[5] The common threads that connect the prize-winning speaker of 1949 with the environmental champion of today are an unwavering pursuit of excellence and the ability to tell a story that people want to hear. "My father expected that I would always do my best," he says. "When some high school friends wanted me to run for school president, he was angry when I said I wouldn't because I knew I would lose. He told me there would always be someone better than me, but that is no reason not to try." In the end, Suzuki ran and won.

Education

[6] After graduating from high school in London, Ontario, in 1954, Suzuki left for Amherst College in Massachusetts on a scholarship. By 1961, he had completed a Ph.D. in zoology at the University of Chicago. Suzuki was a research geneticist who spent his early career searching for a genetic mutation in *Drosophila*, fruit flies. By 1963, he was on his way home to his birthplace, Vancouver, and the University of British Columbia (UBC), where he remained a faculty member for 38 years.

Broadcaster

[7] In 1971, Suzuki launched *Suzuki on Science* on CBC Television in Vancouver. Five years later, the program was reborn as *The Nature of Things with David Suzuki*. From the beginning, he distinguished himself as the thinking person's television host. Through skilled storytelling, he made information accessible and entertaining and challenged his audience. Suzuki explains, "I've always thought of myself as a simplifier. When I was young, my father used to make me practise my lessons and speeches." He would always tell me, "If you can't make me understand it, how will you explain it to others?"

[8] His encounter with John Livingston, executive producer of *The Nature of Things*, signalled a turning point in Suzuki's thinking about science. Livingston, a professor of environmental studies, helped Suzuki see the imbalance of human impact on the earth. This resulted in the eight-part series *A Planet for the Taking* in 1985. Suzuki explains, "Till then, I had always taken the position that humans were at the centre of everything and that we had to limit our interaction with the environment. *A Planet for the Taking* made me realize that we are deeply rooted in a far more complex world than we understand. If we take the position that humans are part of a much greater whole, then we recognize that whatever we do to our surroundings, we do to ourselves, because there is no separation from it."

[9] The almost two million loyal viewers of *A Planet for the Taking* believed Suzuki's message. Under his guidance, CBC's science and nature programming on television and radio since the late 1970s has been very successful. *The Nature of Things* has a devoted weekly following and is broadcast in more than 50 countries.

Activist

[10] Suzuki had always imagined that popularizing science would empower individual Canadians. But he discovered early on that it offered him a platform, and that ignited his activism. Beyond the walls of the studio, Suzuki was a relentless advocate for old-growth forests and First Nations land claims, and a fearless critic of many environmental threats, including James Bay hydroelectric

projects, offshore oil drilling, unsustainable forestry, BC aquaculture, genetically modified foods, and the country's official policy on climate change. "As a young man, I was taught that I had no choice but to stand up for what I thought was right," says Suzuki. He has been run off the road on South Moresby and had his living-room window shattered by gunshots.

The David Suzuki Foundation

[11]   Suzuki's determination to mobilize Canadians eventually led to the establishment of the David Suzuki Foundation. "My wife, Tara, helped me understand that people are frightened. You can't just give them half the story and not offer help or an option for something they can do," Suzuki says. "The foundation grew out of a need to give people a sense of power." The Vancouver-based not-for-profit organization was launched in 1990 as a science-based, action-oriented centre. It focuses on four key areas: oceans and sustainable fishing; forests and wild lands; climate change and clean energy; and sustainable living.

[12]   While the foundation offers practical advice for the Canadian public, it has also provided Suzuki with a vehicle for social change. Last year, he and his team created a forceful blueprint for the future. "We got together and asked ourselves, Where do we want to be in 25 years?" Suzuki explains. "There was a long list of things about which we all agreed. We want clean air, clean water, wildlife, wilderness; we want to be able to eat the fish that come out of our lakes and rivers." The result, *Sustainability within a Generation: A New Vision for Canada* (*SWAG*), is a how-to guide for a thriving and competitive country that functions well within its natural limits.

[13]   Suzuki says that after they identified their goals, they asked themselves, "How do we get there and what do we need to do?" The answer was to send the document to all senior officials in Ottawa, who were amazed by the contents. *SWAG* is comprehensive and the conclusion of Suzuki's lifelong commitment to careful thinking and critical analysis inspired by his belief that it is always possible to do better. Possibly for the first time, it gives grassroots activists, government, and industry a common goal for the environment. And, as always, it is David Suzuki who raises the bar for all.

Source: Adapted from "David Suzuki: Citation of Lifetime Achievement, 2005." *Canadian Geographic*, http://www. canadiangeographic.ca/cea/archives/archives_lifetime.asp?id=81, retrieved 6 June 2011.

EXERCISE 3. COMPREHENSION CHECK

1. Name three issues that concern David Suzuki. (E BA)

   His long passion for science and environment at the end of world war II

2. Describe what is meant by "this painful period." (paragraph 2)

   After _His family was released from a detention facility in sloan City. Be-_
   They had been deprived of their possessions, their rights and privileges. and were
   exiled east of the Rock Mountains.

3. What three personal characteristics can be identified from Suzuki's performance in the oratorical contest at Leamington District Secondary School? These characteristics also remain true in his later life.

   imaginative; knowledgable; and bravely .

4. In what way was John Livingston particularly influential?

   helps Suzuki see the imbalance of human impact on the earth.

5. How did *A Planet for the Taking* change Suzuki's entire way of thinking?

   made him realize that we are deeply rooted in a far more
   complex world than we understand.

6. What was the purpose of establishing the David Suzuki Foundation and what is its central focus? (N)

   The foundation grew out of a need to give people a sense of power.
   focus on four key areas: _Moblizer Canadians_

7. What is meant by, "And, as always, it is David Suzuki who raises the bar for all"?

   David Suzuki is a pioneer of environmental protection.
   in the fields of

| Vocabulary Study: Synonyms |

Synonyms are words or phrases that have the same (or nearly the same) meaning.

> **Example:** The mother and daughter, who had not seen each other for a long time, *embraced* (*hugged*) when they met at the airport.

However, because synonyms do not always have the same meaning in all senses, they cannot always be used in the same context. For instance, the word embrace has two meanings, "to hug" or "to accept." One could say that the scientist embraced the ideas presented by respected colleagues, but one could not say that the scientist hugged the ideas.

Finding synonyms helps you understand new vocabulary and expand your vocabulary. When you need to find a word that expresses a specific idea or thought, an especially useful tool is a thesaurus, which is a dictionary of synonyms. Thesauruses are written for the specific purpose of grouping words with similar meanings.

EXERCISE 4. SYNONYMS

In this exercise, the synonym and paragraph number of the original word have been provided. From the reading, find the original word that matches the synonym in meaning.

1. *topics* (paragraph 1)   *issues*
2. *deported* (paragraph 2)   *exiled*
3. *spoken* (paragraph 3)   *oratorical*
4. *receiver* (paragraph 4)   *recipient*
5. *owns* (paragraph 4)   *possesses*
6. *familiar links* (paragraph 5)   *common threads*
7. *inequality* (paragraph 8)   *in balance*
8. *stage* (paragraph 10)   *platform*
9. *choice* (paragraph 11)   *option*

EXERCISE 5. VOCABULARY IN USE

To further extend and consolidate your knowledge of language relating to the environment, research and produce a poster about different endangered species. You can find out more about endangered animals on the World Wildlife Fund website. More research could then be carried out about earth or air, or other environmental issues, such as acid rain, aerosols, drought, famine, fossil fuels, the greenhouse effect, the hole in the ozone layer, natural disasters, oil spillages, overpopulation, or traffic in our cities.

| Main Idea |

The main idea of a paragraph or other written piece is the controlling or central idea. One of the most important skills you can develop as a good reader is the ability to recognize the main idea in a piece of writing. The sentence that states the main idea of a paragraph is called the topic sentence. To understand a reading, it is necessary to be able to pick out the main idea. Each paragraph in the reading draws the reader's attention to a main idea, which is supported with description, explanation, facts, and so on. Although main ideas are most frequently placed at the beginning of a paragraph, they can be found in various places in the paragraph: at the beginning, in the middle, or at the end. Furthermore, the main idea can simply be implied. To understand or to identify the main ideas as you read, you should ask yourself the following questions.

1. What is the main point that the writer is trying to make?

2. What does the writer want me to understand or to remember about this topic?

3. How does the writer develop or advance her or his main point?

The following examples show the main idea at different positions in a paragraph.

Example 1:

Reading 1, paragraph 11 shows the topic sentence at the beginning of the paragraph with supporting details following. This is the most common way to organize information.

"Suzuki's determination to mobilize Canadians eventually led to the establishment of the David Suzuki Foundation. 'My wife, Tara, helped me understand that people are frightened. You can't just give them half the story and not offer help or an option for something they can do,' Suzuki says. 'The foundation grew out of a need to give people a sense of power.' The Vancouver-based not-for-profit organization was launched in 1990 as a science-based, action-oriented centre. It focuses on four key areas: oceans and sustainable fishing; forests and wild lands; climate change and clean energy; and sustainable living."

Example 2:

In paragraph 10 of the reading, the topic sentence follows the introductory sentence.

"Suzuki had always imagined that popularizing science would empower individual Canadians. But he discovered early on that it offered him a platform, and that ignited his activism. Beyond the walls of the studio, Suzuki was a relentless advocate for old-growth forests and First Nations land claims, and a fearless critic of many environmental threats, including James Bay hydroelectric projects, offshore oil drilling, unsustainable forestry, BC aquaculture, genetically modified foods, and the country's official policy on climate change. 'As a young man, I was taught that I had no choice but to stand up for what I thought was right,' says Suzuki. He has been run off the road on South Moresby and had his living-room window shattered by gunshots."

Example 3:

In this paragraph, which is based on a reading that introduces Canada's first influential painters, the Group of Seven, the topic sentence is at the end of the paragraph.

"In painting the true landscape of Canada, the Group of Seven dared to think innovatively, that is, in a different way than the norm of the time. They chose to celebrate through their paintings the beauty of nature in this country even though it was wild and untamed. As a result, people did not buy their work and art critics in newspapers severely criticized them. However, they formed a group which gave them the power they needed to eventually be accepted and change the way painting was done in Canada."

Example 4:

In this paragraph, which is taken from an editorial, the topic sentence is implied.

"Among the great geniuses of the Renaissance, many were artists, like Michelangelo, Vandyke, and Rembrandt. Others were poets, such as Shakespeare and Jonson. Still others were pioneers in science: Galileo and Kepler in astronomy, for instance, and Harvey and Vesalius in medicine."

The implied topic sentence here is "The Renaissance produced many creative geniuses."

EXERCISE 6. WRITING MAIN IDEAS

The following sentences have been taken from various places in the reading. Write the main idea in your own words.

1. "Not surprisingly, the story was a crowd-pleaser, and Suzuki won first prize." (paragraph 3)

   _____

2. "From the beginning, [Suzuki] distinguished himself as the thinking person's television host." (paragraph 7)

   _____

3. "Livingston, a professor of environmental studies, helped Suzuki see the imbalance of human impact on the earth." (paragraph 8)

   _____

4. "Last year, he and his team created a forceful blueprint for the future." (paragraph 12)

   _____

EXERCISE 7. TOPIC SENTENCES

1. After completing the exercise in identifying main ideas in sentences, read "David Suzuki: Educator, Broadcaster, and Activist" again, and with a partner underline the topic sentence in each paragraph. At what point in the paragraphs do the topic sentences appear? Do any of the paragraphs have an implied topic sentence? Explain your answer.

   _____

   _____

2. Supporting details: Each topic sentence you underlined contains details that support it. Writers use details, such as examples, facts, reasons, descriptions, explanations, or opinions, to clarify the point for the reader. For each topic sentence, highlight the supporting details and identify their function.

EXERCISE 8. WRITING

1. As you read the topic sentences from paragraph to paragraph, you will be aware that they provide a kind of summary of the reading. Now, in your own words, write a summary paragraph of the reading.

   _____

   _____

   _____

   _____

   _____

   _____

2. Imagine you are a tour guide in a museum of science and the environment. It is your job to describe and explain the work of scientists and environmentalists. Choose one who interests you particularly and research what he or she has contributed to the sustainability of the earth. Then write a speech explaining his or her major work and how it helps the environment. Finally, give your speech to the class and answer any questions they may have.

—| Reading 2 — *Saving Seeds Is a Political Act* |—

EXERCISE 9. PRE-READING DISCUSSION

Discuss the following questions before you read.

1. What food is most commonly eaten in your home? Where is this food grown and by whom?
2. Name some foods that you know are imported from another country. Why is this necessary?
3. How is the food you eat protected? Who protects it?
4. What is your response to the following quotation from Vandana Shiva? What is she teaching?

"In India we have a wonderful ancient legend that tells us that this amazing world of abundance has been given to us to share. We are to use its gift within limits, to not become greedy, because in greed we are stealing someone else's share of the resources." (Vandana Shiva, in her speech to the United Nations Conference on Sustainable Development, 2010)

—| Saving Seeds Is a Political Act |—

[1] "Seeds are our mother," declares Vandana Shiva, a physicist and activist from India. Shiva has a passion for seeds and what they represent. She is the founder of the revolutionary Indian seed-saving organization Navdanya. The organization's name translates as "nine crops." Its mission is to support local farmers as well as rescue and conserve crops that are being pushed into extinction. Shiva believes that seed is the first link in the food chain. Furthermore, she believes that saving seed is our duty and that sharing seed is a cultural value.

[2] Farmers everywhere have been saving seeds for centuries, preserving the most durable ones for replanting. Female farmers in India were no different; that is, until 1995. That year India signed an international trade agreement giving multinational corporations permission to patent, own, and sell seeds. As a result, seeds are becoming the private property of a handful of corporations, transforming the tradition of saving seeds into a subversive political act. Tiny seeds are stirring up controversy.

Women Say "Enough!"

[3] Female farmers are the poorest and most underprivileged group in India, and they have become activists. Led by Vandana Shiva, and inspired by Mahatma Gandhi's concept of non-violence, the women of Navdanya refuse to obey international trade laws or heed the rules of market economy.

[4]   With the new laws in effect, multinational corporations patent seeds and sell them at high prices to small farmers. For these farmers, cost of production soars and profit margins decrease, often leading to hunger and bankruptcy. Recently Shiva and women of Navdanya declared that they strongly believe Indian farmers are finding themselves on the brink of a crisis of extinction because the patent laws discriminate against them and benefit corporations. The paradox, Shiva says, lies in the fact that female farmers, also the consumers of patented seeds, are really the ones responsible for developing them in the first place. She believes "Women have been seed experts, the seed breeders, seed selectors, the biodiversity conservers of the world. And if today we have seeds that we can save, if today we have communities that can tell us the unique properties of different crops and different seeds, it's because we've had generations of women not recognized as agronomists, not recognized as breeders, not recognized in any way as having knowledge. The 10,000 years of human expertise in feeding us is women's expertise."

[5]   According to Shiva, corporations take from farmers. "Most patents today are based on straight forward biopiracy, the pilfering of women's innovation of centuries." She explains that farmers lose control over their means of survival because they become dependent on the patented, genetically modified (GMO) seed. Finally, she believes that where the freedom of seed disappears, the freedom for farmers disappears also.

Revolution in the Rice Fields

[6]   Women of Navdanya are waging a multi-faceted revolution. They are taking a stand for the environment by mobilizing farmers across India to refuse buying GMO seeds that they believe are damaging Indian biodiversity. They are campaigning against the use of pesticides and herbicides. They are educating farmers on the benefits of native seeds. Admirably, they have established 34 community seed banks across the country that preserve native Indian seeds and distribute them at no cost to all interested farmers.

[7]   Furthermore, they have started an economic revolution. They have mobilized some 10,000 farmers to disobey international trade agreements India has signed and create their own independent markets. Small farmers organized by Navdanya have shut corporations out of their fields, are using their own native seeds, and grow food for survival and continuation instead of planting a single crop that is to be sold.

[8]   Moreover, Navdanya's ecological and economic revolution is political in nature. The women have organized some 35,000 Indian villages into declaring themselves "biodiversity republics." These republics are organized around the principle of "living democracy," meaning democracy that is participatory, values sharing, community minded, and environmentally responsible. Whereas the Indian economy is governed by free trade, these republics are pockets of fair trade and economic independence.

[9]   Shiva has been accused of being naive and unrealistic. Some argue that it is not possible to sidestep the world market system. They say traditional systems of farming and trade belong to the past and are not plausible in today's globalized world. Primarily, they argue that ancient systems of farming cannot successfully feed today's poor and hungry people.

[10]   Shiva, however, refuses to budge. She points out that the reason so many people are going hungry is because of unjust trade relations and not organic farming based on diversity. She calls for a revision of the World Trade Organization agreements so that the interests of farmers are taken into consideration.

[11]   Finally, Shiva calls for a return to an economic and political system grounded in sharing and not one based on profits and private property only. This system should be based on women's knowledge, women's traditions, and women's legacy. Shiva states, "The women of India have evolved two hundred thousand rice varieties, work done over millennia by hundreds of thousands of unknown grandmothers." And, she declares that sharing seeds continues to be vital. There really was no point at which any of those women told her sisters that she has bred this new rice and it is her property; furthermore, others must pay her royalties. That system, Shiva argues, is not part of Indian culture but sharing is.

Source: Adapted from "Seeds of Resistance." International Museum of Women, http://www.imow.org/wpp/stories/viewStory?storyid=1236, retrieved 31 May 2011.

EXERCISE 10. COMPREHENSION CHECK

1. In paragraph 1, we learn that Vandana Shiva believes, "that seed is the first link in the food chain." What does this mean?

    _____

2. What occurred in India in 1995 that changed things for female farmers?

    _____

    _____

3. What is surprising about women refusing to obey international trade laws?

    _____

4. What is the "paradox" that Vandana Shiva talks about in paragraph 4?

    _____

    _____

5. Indicate five changes that the women of Navdanya have been able to achieve.

_____

_____

_____

_____

_____

6. Explain the multifaceted revolution referred to in paragraphs 6 to 8.

_____

_____

7. This question has two parts.

   a) In what way do Shiva's critics believe she is naive?

   _____

   _____

   b) How does Shiva answer her critics?

   _____

   _____

8. What is the main point of paragraph 11?

   _____

EXERCISE 11. CRITICAL ANALYSIS

Discuss the following questions with your classmates.

1. Compare the beliefs of the innovators David Suzuki and Vandana Shiva. What do they have in common? List their similarities and their differences. What significance does their work have on the environment in particular?

2. Describe an innovation of the country you are from and explain the effect it has had on people.

3. To what extent should government put money toward innovative ideas? Alternatively, how can people who have innovative ideas be encouraged to develop them?

EXERCISE 12. VOCABULARY IN CONTEXT

All quotations in this exercise are taken from "Saving Seeds Is a Political Act." Choose the best meaning for each underlined word.

1. "She is the <u>founder</u> of the <u>revolutionary</u> Indian seed-saving organization Navdanya." (paragraph 1)

   founder
   a) failure
   b) creator
   c) writer

   revolutionary
   a) successful
   b) powerful
   c) groundbreaking

2. "As a result, seeds are becoming the private property of a handful of <u>corporations</u>. . . ." (paragraph 2)

   a) large companies
   b) small conglomerates
   c) large contracts

3. "Led by Vandana Shiva, and inspired by Mahatma Gandhi's <u>concept</u> of non-violence. . . ." (paragraph 3)

   a) action
   b) idea
   c) aversion

4. "The 10,000 years of human <u>expertise</u> in feeding us is women's <u>expertise</u>." (paragraph 4)

   a) resistance
   b) failure
   c) skill

5. The word *economic* is used several times in paragraph 8 and then again in paragraph 11. It is an adjective describing the noun with which it is connected: <u>economic revolution</u>, <u>economic independence</u>, and <u>economic system</u>. Write the meaning of each term below.

   economic: _____

   _____

   economic revolution: _____

   _____

   economic independence: _____

   _____

   economic system: _____

   _____

6. The word *diversity* in paragraph 10 comes from the word *diverse*. Give the meaning of the word *diversity*.

   _____

7. "She calls for a <u>revision</u> of the World Trade Organization agreements. . . ." (paragraph 10)

   a) change
   b) acceptance
   c) approval

EXERCISE 13. USING SPECIFIC VOCABULARY

The words and phrases below are from the reading. The words in the left column can be paired with the words in right column to create terms with different meanings; for example, *economic revolution* or *seed expert*. Make a sentence with each of your combinations.

Example: The strong economic system of Canada is what allows it to remain stable during upheavals in other parts of the world.

economic	*revolution, independence, system*
corporations	*multinational, benefit, take from, discriminate against*
expert *expertise*	*seed, human, women's*
cultural (adj)	*value*

Writing

Organizing Ideas

Before you write, it is a good idea to organize your thoughts and ideas. One way to do this is to use a technique called clustering, a kind of concept map. This method allows you to see how ideas are related to one another. It shows clearly how the main idea is related to the supporting information. Below is an example of clustering. The graphic is based on Reading 2, "Saving Seeds Is a Political Act."

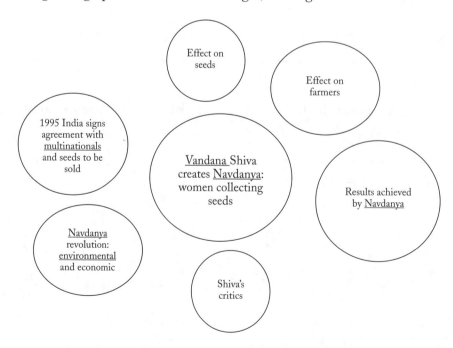

In this example you can see that the topic is "Vandana Shiva creates Navdanya: women collecting seeds." The rest of the clusters provide information connected to the main idea of collecting seeds: the historical agreement India made, its effects on farmers and the seeds, how Navdanya is fighting back environmentally and economically, Shiva's critics, and finally Navdanya's success.

EXERCISE 14. SUMMARY WRITING

1. Using the information from the clusters to guide you, write a summary of "Saving Seeds Is a Political Act."

   or

2. Make notes regarding what you have learned about Vandana Shiva, the innovator. What makes her an innovator? Write a description of her.

Main Idea and Outlining

Reading 1, "David Suzuki: Educator, Broadcaster, and Activist," discussed the importance of main ideas in readings and showed examples where main ideas may be found. Each paragraph in Reading 2, "Saving Seeds Is a Political Act," supports a clear main idea.

Example of an Outline Showing Main Idea and Support

Paragraph 6. "Women of Navdanya are waging a multifaceted revolution. They are taking a stand for the environment by mobilizing farmers across India to refuse buying GMO seeds that they believe are damaging Indian biodiversity. They are campaigning against the use of pesticides and herbicides. They are educating farmers on the benefits of native seeds. Admirably, they have established 34 community seed banks across the country that preserve native Indian seeds and distribute them at no cost to all interested farmers."

Outline of Paragraph 6

Main Idea
The women of Navdanya are trying to change the way seed collection and distribution are done.
 	
Support (facts: list actions)
1. environment
   – mobilize farmers to refuse GMO seeds believed to damage biodiversity
   – campaign against the use of pesticides and herbicides
2. educate
   – instruct farmers on the benefits of using native Indian seeds

Conclude Express success of Navdanya – 34 community seed banks established to safeguard native Indian seeds – seeds are distributed free to farmers

EXERCISE 15. GROUP EXERCISE AND WRITING

A. Group Exercise

First the class is divided into small groups. Then each group is assigned several paragraphs to outline from Reading 2, "Saving Seeds Is a Political Act." All the paragraphs are assigned since the object is to outline every paragraph. Each group must state the main idea of each paragraph and list the supporting details, as illustrated in the example outline. Also include what type of support was used, that is, facts, opinion, description, examples, or research. Finally, when all have finished, each group shares its outline with the class.

B. Writing

From the group outlines, compose a piece of writing in which you use the main ideas and supporting details identified for each paragraph.

Reading 3—*Frank Gehry, Architect Extraordinaire*

EXERCISE 16. PRE-READING DISCUSSION

Discuss the following questions before you read.

1. Consider the architecture in the country you are from. Describe its characteristics.
2. Is your favourite style of architecture modern or traditional? Explain.
3. To become an architect, what skills do you think would be required?
4. How is architecture unique to a country?

EXERCISE 17. SCANNING THE READING FOR INFORMATION

1. Which activity first influenced Frank Gehry?
2. Name some of the buildings Gehry has designed.
3. What kind of reaction is Gehry looking for from people who see his buildings?
4. What do Gehry's unusual forms reveal?
5. Who is especially inspired to take risks by Gehry's designs?

Frank Gehry, Architect Extraordinaire

Hanging on, being relentless, just never giving up, I guess that's patience, and having a vision. You've got to know where you want to go with it, and how to explain it.　　　—*Frank Gehry*

[1]　　According to Frank Gehry, it all started when he was a little boy growing up on Beverley Street in Toronto. His grandmother would go to a nearby wood shop to get wood for her stove. The pieces that she brought home had been cut into a variety of strange shapes. Before his grandmother

burned these pieces in her fire, she would sit on the floor with him and build cities (Enright & Gehry, 1998). Now Gehry is considered by many to be one of the greatest architects of our time. The unusual way in which he manipulates shapes and common materials characterizes much of his work; it is a reflection of his approach to architecture and his underlying philosophy. His architectural signature, which reflects his approach and philosophy, can be seen in the unique designs of many of his buildings, including the Art Gallery of Ontario, in Toronto; the Guggenheim Museum in Bilbao, Spain; the Dancing Building in Prague, Czech Republic; and the Lou Ruvo Center for Brain Health in Las Vegas, Nevada, to name a few.

Dancing Building in Prague

[2]   At first glance, the Guggenheim museum in Bilbao, Spain, appears to be a collage of shapes which move and even clash in unexpected ways. Although the blocks somehow fit together, the effect can be overwhelming. Gehry's work has been described as utterly confusing and disorganized. Nevertheless, Gehry explains his building style in this way, "Basically, I am trying to make buildings and spaces that will inspire people, that will move people, that will get a reaction. Not just to get a reaction, but to get a positive reaction, hopefully, a place that they like to be in" (Academy of Achievement & Gehry, 2010).

[3]   Gehry's collection of unusual forms is typical of much of his work. It reflects both the process in which he engages as an architect and his philosophy of the modern city and democracy. Gehry's way of working is to begin by listening closely to his clients. He genuinely cares about them and the people he works with. He says, "My greatest thrill is to still be friends with the clients and people that helped me make the buildings" (Academy of Achievement & Gehry, 2010). Gehry not only takes note of their explicit requests, but also their body language and facial expressions to give him cues as to their desires and wishes (Tomkins, 1997). He then works as a sculptor, using his intuition to guide him in the creation of shapes and forms that will appeal to his client. According to Tomkins, when he has created a model that is similar to what his clients had wished for, Gehry's own design process really begins. He experiments with the model, modifying forms and the relationships between the forms, pushing his model further and further. When describing his process, Gehry explains as follows:

> You develop a base of information. You look at what's around you, you take things in, you absorb. I think the most important thing is the people, finally, it's a human thing. It's how you interact with people and how you interpret their wishes and yearnings. It's intuitive.

It's very difficult to explain why you do things, why you curve something. It becomes an evolution of thought and ideas. I feel like the picture of the cat pushing the ball of string. You just keep pushing it and it moves around. Then it falls off the table and creates this beautiful line in space." (Academy of Achievement & Gehry, 2010)

From what he says, we can see that Frank Gehry lets his imagination and creativity guide his designs.

[4] The unusual forms in Gehry's work also embody his philosophy of the modern city and democracy. According to Gehry, the unity and uniformity of the nineteenth-century city no longer exist; because our modern society is democratic, our cities are more chaotic. They reflect the pluralism within our societies, and the forms within them are "collisive" (Enright & Gehry, 1998). This new reality is expressed in the unusual and "collisive" shapes of Gehry's buildings and is evident in his building designs; they are an expression of his view of contemporary life. Gehry himself says, "And yet, somehow we muddle forward and make things. So out of that comes inspiration, believe it or not, and leads to ideas. For instance, I've been interested in the sense of movement in architecture. Well, who cares whether a building looks like it's moving or not? . . . That's something that interested me. Maybe it comes from the fast society, the fast world around me, that I'm trying to make some kind of connection to. So I think you've just got to keep your eyes open, keep your ears open and understand what's going on. And then play with it, and move with it, and make your expression grow from that" (Academy of Achievement & Gehry, 2010).

[5] In addition to the striking shapes which characterize Gehry's Guggenheim museum, Gehry incorporated unusual materials into his design. He used titanium, a material more frequently used in aircraft landing gear, for the roof. He chose titanium because "it has a wonderful characteristic of changing in the light. When it rains, it goes golden, so just when the grey skies come, which is a lot of the times in Bilbao, the building radiates . . ." (Enright & Gehry, 1998). In designs of different buildings, Gehry has woven other unusual materials, such as chain link, right into his designs. Again, the use of these materials reveals his thinking about life and architecture. According to Gehry himself, he wants to understand the materials that are commonly used in our culture. And he wants to use these in a different way than has been done previously. He is fascinated by a whole array of materials which he continually experiments with. Different from others perhaps, Gehry is interested in using what is around, what is sometimes easily accessible.

[6] While Gehry's designs may at first seem strange and even jarring, they express his understanding of modern contemporary life. These designs are now inspiring a younger generation of architects, who, he hopes, will be encouraged to take risks and express their own understanding through their work (Enright & Gehry, 1998). In the meantime, we are left to enjoy and find our own meaning in Gehry's work, the art which is architecture.

References:

Academy of Achievement (interviewer) & Gehry, F. (interviewee). (2010, September). Building the Inspiring Space. Retrieved from http://www.achievement.org/autodoc/page/geh0int-1

Enright, M. (Interviewer) & Gehry, Frank. (1998, February 25). This Morning. Toronto, ON: CBC.

McGuigan, C. (1997, January 13). Basque-ing in Glory. Newsweek, 129, 68–70.

Tomkins, C. (1997, July 7). The Maverick. The New Yorker, 73, 38–45.

Exercise 18. Comprehension Check

1. Which of the following is the main idea of this article?

   a) Frank Gehry is considered to be one of the greatest architects of our time.

   b) Frank Gehry learned his skills from his grandmother when he was a small boy.

   c) The Guggenheim museum is his most important building because it reflects his approach and philosophy to architecture.

2. List five words or expressions that have been used to describe Gehry's buildings.

   _____

   _____

3. Describe Frank Gehry's process as he works, including both what others say about it and what he explains about the process.

   _____

   _____

   _____

4. What reason does Gehry give for our modern cities being more chaotic?

   First, define chaotic:

   _____

   Give Gehry's reason:

   _____

5. What do the materials Gehry uses reveal about his thinking?

   _____

6. What influence does Gehry hope to have on young architects?

   _____

7. Both David Suzuki and Vandana Shiva consider themselves activists. In what way is Frank Gehry an activist for change?

   _____

   _____

Exercise 19. Critical Analysis

Discuss the following questions with your classmates.

1. Frank Gehry says, "And yet, somehow we muddle forward and make things. So out of that comes inspiration, believe it or not, and leads to ideas." (paragraph 4)

   We do not normally imagine that concrete ideas to make complex buildings take shape and flow from a confused state of mind. From the quotation, what do we learn about how Gehry works? To what extent does this quotation characterize and apply to other professionals, such as engineers, scientists, surgeons, teachers, or artists?

_____

_____

_____

2. Inventors, designers, artists, and scientists often seek to make the world a better place or to create something that will elevate human beings. In this regard what do Frank Gehry, Vandana Shiva, and David Suzuki have in common?

_____

_____

_____

3. Vandana Shiva considers herself a revolutionary. Name some people whom you would characterize as revolutionary. List pros and cons regarding revolutionaries.

_____

_____

_____

EXERCISE 20. VOCABULARY IN CONTEXT

Provide a synonym or a definition for the underlined word in the following sentences. Try to get the meaning from the context before you consult a dictionary.

1. "The unusual way in which he <u>manipulates</u> shapes and common materials characterizes much of his work; . . ." (paragraph 1)

_____

2. The following words come from paragraph 2, where the building is described and where the descriptive words make the building seem real and extraordinary.

a) "<u>collage</u> of shapes"

_____

b) "which move and even <u>clash</u> in unexpected ways"

_____

c) "Although the blocks somehow fit together, the effect can be <u>overwhelming</u>."

_____

d) "Gehry's work has been described as <u>utterly</u> confusing and <u>disorganized</u>."

_____

3. "He then works as a sculptor, using his intuition to guide him in the creation of shapes and forms that will appeal to his client." (paragraph 3)

    intuition: _____

    appeal: _____

4. "Gehry not only takes note of their explicit requests. . . ." (paragraph 3)

    _____

5. "He experiments with the model, modifying forms and the relationships between the forms, pushing his model further and further." (paragraph 3)

    modifying
    a) erasing
    b) changing
    c) notifying

    "pushing his model further and further"

    _____

6. "In addition to the striking shapes which characterize Gehry's Guggenheim museum, Gehry incorporated unusual materials into his design." (paragraph 5)

    _____

7. "While Gehry's designs may at first seem strange and even jarring, they express his understanding of modern contemporary life." (paragraph 6)

    jarring: _____

    contemporary
    a) old-fashioned
    b) up to date
    c) out of date

Writing

Writing an Essay

What is an essay? An essay is composed of a series of paragraphs about a particular topic or subject. It has an introduction, several developmental paragraphs, and a conclusion.

Usually an essay begins with an introduction in which the information presented moves from general to specific. It begins with background information, which is general, and proceeds to the thesis statement, which is specific. The thesis statement states the main idea and reveals the author's purpose in writing and his or her point of view.

The paragraphs that follow the introduction to the essay make up the body of the essay. This is where the writer develops the argument or point of view presented in the thesis statement. This development is in the form of supporting details, such as examples, facts, reasons, descriptions, explanations, or opinions.

The conclusion may restate the topic, summarize the main points, or add a question or two for further reflection on the topic.

The essay is shaped like the diagram below, which shows the introduction, body, and conclusion.

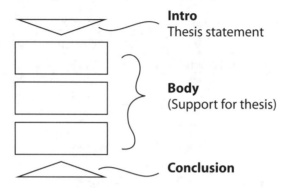

EXERCISE 21. OUTLINING THE ESSAY

"Frank Gehry, Architect Extraordinaire" is an essay that shows good organization. It is a model that shows how to develop the introduction, the body, and the conclusion of an essay. In this exercise, please reread the essay and create an outline by answering a series of questions.

The Introduction

1. What is the "hook" that the writer uses to interest the reader?

    _____

2. What is the thesis statement?

    _____

3. What ideas or questions does the thesis statement prompt? That is, what do you expect will be answered in the body of the essay?

    _____

    _____

The Body

4. There are four body paragraphs in this essay: paragraphs 2, 3, 4, and 5. Underline the topic sentences, write what each paragraph is about, and provide the supporting details.

    For paragraphs 2 to 5, answer the following:

    a) What is the topic sentence?

    _____

    _____

_____

_____

b) What is the paragraph about?

_____

_____

_____

_____

c) Provide the supporting details.

_____

_____

_____

_____

The Conclusion

5. What information does the conclusion include? How does this serve to round out the essay?

_____

_____

EXERCISE 22. ESSAY WRITING ASSIGNMENT

You have read about innovators and discussed innovations. Now write an essay of at least two pages on one of the following topics:

1. An innovative person who helped change someone's life
2. An innovation that changed the world
3. An innovation you would work on if money were no object
4. A topic of your choice related to innovation

Preparing to Write

The following suggestions can help you plan and organize your paper.

1. Brainstorm for information. List all your ideas about the topic.
2. Choose the most relevant ideas and connect them to your topic. To help you organize, you could use various techniques, including, listing, clustering, creating a flow chart, or outlining as previously completed. See the examples under "Organizing and Generating Strategies."
3. Write down the main idea or thesis statement.
4. Prepare a plan.
5. Develop your ideas with examples, explanations, facts, or personal experience.
6. Write your first draft.

Organizing and Generating Strategies

1. Listing (Example from the Frank Gehry reading)

    Topic: Frank Gehry's unique and unusual style in creating buildings

    Body: {
      Description of buildings and Gehry's comments
      How Gehry works: his process
      Gehry's philosophy
      Unusual materials used
    }

    Conclusion: Further influence of Gehry's work

2. Clustering (Example from "Saving Seeds Is a Political Act")

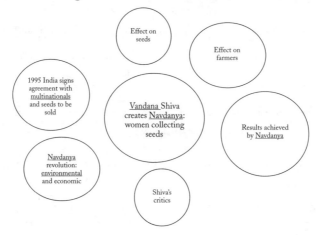

3. Flow chart

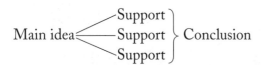

    The Frank Gehry reading is organized in this way.

After You Write

After you have completed the first draft of your essay, you need to revise it. The following questions will help you.

1. Does your thesis statement express the main idea of your essay?

2. Does each paragraph further develop an idea that relates to the thesis statement?

3. Is each supporting idea thoroughly developed?

4. Does the conclusion make a logical and clear summary statement?

CHAPTER 3

Natural Hazards across Canada

dangerous thing

Introduction to the Chapter

Each year, natural disasters cause great suffering and damage in many parts of the world, including Canada. The readings in this chapter concern some of the natural disasters that have affected Canadians and the causes of these disasters. The first reading provides an overview of natural hazards and disasters in Canada. Readings 2, 3, and 4 focus on two types of natural hazards that occur in Canada: tornadoes and avalanches. Reading 2 describes tornadoes while Readings 3 and 4 focus on avalanches.

At the end of this chapter you will be asked to complete one of the following essay-writing assignments:

1. Describe a natural disaster that affected you or someone you know. Describe your reactions to the disaster or the reactions of others.

2. Choose one type of natural hazard (e.g., hurricanes or earthquakes) that occurs or has occurred in Canada or another country. Describe the steps in the process that lead to the formation of this natural hazard with reference to such factors as landforms and weather conditions. (You may have to do some research.)

Reading 1—*Natural Hazards*

EXERCISE 1. PRE-READING DISCUSSION

Discuss the following questions before you read.

1. Have you or someone else you are close to ever experienced a natural disaster? What was the disaster and what were its effects?

2. Examine the map of Canada on the next page. What types of natural disasters have affected the province, territory, or region in which you are living?

3. Which areas of Canada seem particularly affected by natural disasters?

4. In your view, are natural disasters inevitable? Why or why not?

Natural Hazards

[1]   It is hard to think of a natural hazard that hasn't occurred in Canada—earthquakes, floods and land-slides—we've seen them all. A natural hazard is a potentially damaging process or phenomenon that occurs, or has the potential to occur, in nature. A natural hazard, such as the earthquake (seismic) hazard on Vancouver Island, exists even when no earthquake has actually occurred. When an earthquake happens, it is termed an event. How fast the event happens is an important consideration. Some natural hazards are slow to evolve (for example, drought and permafrost melting), whereas others strike quickly (for example, earthquakes, landslides, volcanic eruptions, certain floods, and snowstorms).

[2]   Natural hazards become natural disasters when people are injured and when buildings, transportation corridors or power and communication systems are destroyed and the local community is unable to cope. In disaster scenarios, one hazard can trigger another; for example, by destroying the vegetation on the flanks of mountains, forest fires make the land more susceptible to erosion,

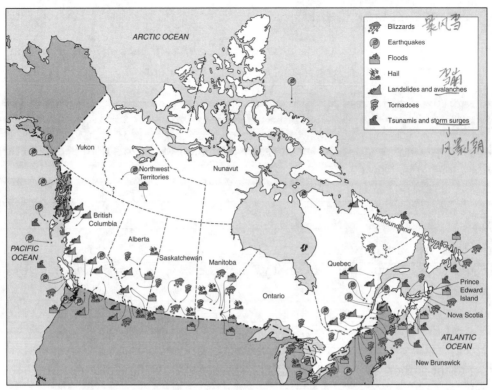

Source: Public Safety Canada. "Natural Hazards of Canada: A Historical Mapping of Significant Natural Disasters." Government of Canada, http://www.publicsafety.gc.ca/res/em/nh/hazardsmap.pdf, retrieved 5 October 2011.

which can lead to landslides. Hurricanes can result in flooding. This multiplication of events, or cascading failure, further complicates the emergency response required.

[3]   Natural hazards will directly or indirectly affect most of the population at least once in their lifetime. Canada is vulnerable to catastrophes similar in scale to those that have occurred elsewhere in the world, such as the 2004 earthquake and tsunami in Indonesia. Earthquakes on Haida Gwaii; tornadoes that have torn through Edmonton, Alberta, and Barrie, Ontario; catastrophic landslides in Frank, Alberta and Saint-Jean-Vianney, Quebec; extensive flooding in Manitoba; and devastating ice storms in eastern Ontario and southern Quebec have all contributed to Canadians' awareness of the potential for damage from natural disasters. These are examples of catastrophic events, but the cumulative effects of smaller but more frequent disasters, such as a river flooding, can sometimes cause more damage and have as much impact on the population as one major event.

[4]   Natural hazards can rarely be stopped, but robust building codes, construction of new physical infrastructure such as debris dams and retaining walls in landslide-prone areas, careful land-use planning, and any measures that increase personal and community resilience will all contribute to reducing how severely individuals and communities are damaged. These are all examples of mitigative actions; however, the first step in mitigation is education. By increasing your knowledge about natural hazards you are one step closer to being prepared.

Source: Adapted from Natural Resources Canada. "Natural Hazards." Government of Canada, http://atlas.nrcan.gc.ca/site/english/maps/environment/naturalhazards/1/, retrieved 5 October 2011.

EXERCISE 2. COMPREHENSION CHECK

1. In this article, the author uses the terms *natural hazard*, *event*, and *natural disaster*. In your own words, explain the meaning of each of these terms, as used by the author.

   _____

   _____

2. Does the author believe that Canadians are safer from natural hazards than people in other parts of the world? How do you know?

   _____

   _____

3. In paragraph 2, the author discusses the "multiplication of events." In this paragraph, find (a) two examples that show what the author means by the phrase *multiplication of events*, and (b) a paraphrase of this phrase.

   _____

   _____

4. According to the author, can natural hazards be stopped? Can natural disasters be stopped? Explain your response.

   _____

   _____

| Main Ideas: Marginal Notes |

When you are reading magazine articles, journal articles, or textbooks, one strategy to help increase your comprehension is to make marginal notes. That is, you may summarize the main idea of each paragraph in a few words in the margin. These notes will later give you a general overview of the information covered in the text.

Example of a Paragraph Annotation

It is hard to think of a natural hazard that hasn't occurred in Canada—earthquakes, floods, and land-slides—we've seen them all. A natural hazard is a potentially damaging process or phenomenon that occurs, or has the potential to occur, in nature. A natural hazard, such as the earthquake (seismic) hazard on Vancouver Island, exists even when no earthquake has actually occurred. When an earthquake happens, it is termed an event. How fast the event happens is an important consideration. Some natural hazards are slow to evolve (for example, drought and permafrost melting), whereas others strike quickly (for example, earthquakes, landslides, volcanic eruptions, certain floods, and snowstorms).

explanation of natural hazards and events

Exercise 3. Main Ideas

For Reading 1, "Natural Hazards," note the main idea of each paragraph in a few words in the margin. Compare your notes to those of your classmates.

Exercise 4. Critical Analysis

The author of "Natural Hazards" states that "robust building codes, construction of new physical infrastructure such as debris dams and retaining walls in landslide-prone areas, careful land-use planning, and any measures that increase personal and community resilience will all contribute to reducing how severely individuals and communities are damaged." (paragraph 4)

Discuss the following questions with your classmates.

1. What does the author mean? What examples can you think of in which damage to people and property from a natural disaster could have been reduced if there had been better planning?

2. Can you think of other examples in which damage was minimized because of good planning?

3. If development takes place in an area that has the potential for a serious natural disaster, who should be responsible for paying for reconstruction? Be prepared to support your opinion.

Exercise 5. Group Exercise

Reading 1 provides general information about natural hazards in Canada. In the mind map below, fill in the blanks with words that you associate with some of the natural hazards that occur in Canada.

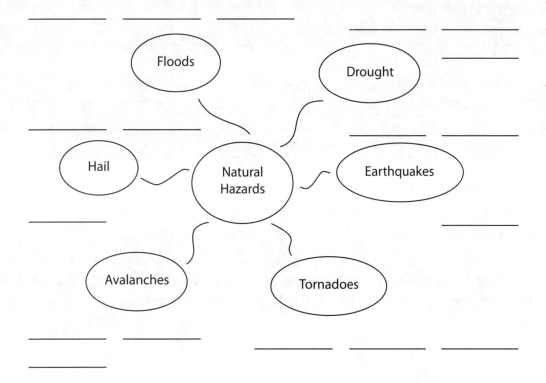

Vocabulary Study: Suffixes

Many words in English are made up of root words combined with suffixes. The addition of a suffix to a root word changes the part of speech of the root word. For example, in Reading 1 of this chapter, the phrase *catastrophic events* is used. In this phrase, the word *catastrophic* is used as an adjective to describe *events*. The noun form of the word *catastrophic* is *catastrophe*. These words have related meanings but are written in different forms, depending on how they are used in sentences.

EXERCISE 6. SUFFIXES

In Reading 1, find examples of words that contain the suffixes that are listed in the chart below. From the examples, identify the part of speech created by each of the suffixes. The first one has been done for you.

Suffixes

Suffix	Meaning	Examples	Part of Speech
-able, -ible	capable of	*susceptible* *vulnerable*	adjective
-al	connected with		
-ance, -ence	instance of an action		
-ic	connected with		
-ion, -ation, -ition, -sion, -tion, -xion	the action or process of		
-ity	the quality or state of		
-ive	tending to; having the nature of		
-ly	in the manner of		
-ness	the quality, state, or character of		

EXERCISE 7. WRITING

1. Referring to the map on page 55, write your own overview of natural hazards in Canada. Consider using topic sentences to make your main ideas explicit to your reader.

2. Choose any country, excluding Canada, and give a general overview of the natural hazards that affect this country. Explain why this country is susceptible to each of the hazards that you discuss. Consider including topic sentences to make your main ideas explicit to your reader.

Reading 2—*Funnel Fury*

EXERCISE 8. PRE-READING DISCUSSION

This reading passage discusses tornadoes, or twisters. Before completing the scanning exercise, examine the picture shown above and discuss the questions below.

1. What do you know about tornadoes? Have you or has someone close to you ever experienced a tornado?

2. Many people are fascinated by tornadoes, and some even chase them as a hobby. What is it about tornadoes that makes them so fascinating?

EXERCISE 9. SCANNING

In the following reading passage, you will practise an important reading strategy called *scanning*. Scanning is used to search for specific information. When you scan, you have specific questions in mind, and you pass your eyes over the written text looking for the answers to these questions. When you scan, you do not read the entire text carefully; in fact, you ignore any information that is not directly related to your questions.

The following tips may help you scan efficiently.

1. Have a clear understanding of what you are looking for.

2. Look at the organization of the text and think about where the information is most likely to be found.

3. Use word clues to help you find the information. For example, if you are looking for a date, search for numbers; if you are looking for a name, look for capital letters. If you are looking for the of a process, look for such words as *first*, *second*, *next*, *then*.

4. When you think you've found the answer to your question, read around the informatio confirm that you have found what you are looking for.

Scan the reading "Funnel Fury" on pages 61 to 64 to answer the following questions.

1. Which parts of Canada are most frequently hit by tornadoes?
   _____

2. In an average year, how many tornadoes are seen in each of the following provinces?

   Ontario _____28_____   Alberta _____21_____

   Saskatchewan _____23_____   Manitoba _____13_____

3. Complete the following chart.

Type of Tornado	Wind Speed	Percentage of all Tornadoes	Consequences
weak			
strong			
violent			

4. a) Which Canadian tornado caused the highest number of casualties? _____

   b) Which Canadian tornado caused the second-highest number of casualties? _____

5. Which paragraphs explain how a tornado is formed? (Give the paragraph numbers only.)
   _____

6. What should you do if you see a tornado and you are in the following places?

   a) In a house

   _____

   _____

   b) In a mobile home

   _____

   _____

   c) In a car

   _____

   _____

Funnel Fury

[1] It is the most violent event in the atmosphere. It can blow buildings to pieces, topple trains from their tracks, and send trucks and cars cartwheeling across fields. Its timing is unpredictable, its course capricious. Yet for millions of North Americans, its prospect is a fact of life and its appearance a possible cause of death. It's the tornado, a violently rotating column of air that descends from a thunderstorm cloud and destroys what it touches.

[2] Tornadoes have been recorded virtually worldwide. In Canada, the southern prairies and southwestern Ontario are the areas most often hit. Ontario averages about 28 tornado sightings a year; Saskatchewan, 23; Alberta, 21; and Manitoba, 13, with the majority in Ontario occurring south of 45 degrees latitude. And their occurrence could potentially increase with climate change, says David Etkin, a tornado expert with the Atmospheric Environment Service who has compared tornado frequency with historical temperature trends. "With global warming, our climate would become more like that of the United States," says Etkin. "Increasing warmth would create more unstable air masses, a precondition for the formation of severe thunderstorms and tornadoes."

[3] Tornadoes usually occur in the late afternoon or early evening and, in Canada, most often in May, June, and July. They are a product of the same atmospheric instability that produces thunderstorms and cloudbursts, and are often triggered by the warfare between warm, moist air masses and cold, dry ones.

[4] Still, exactly why some storm clouds produce tornadoes is unclear. To whip winds up to 400 or 500 kilometres per hour is no small feat. Even for people who know tornadoes best, they remain a fascinating mystery. "It is remarkable," note storm chasers Richard Scorer and Arjen Verkaik in their book *Spacious Skies*, "that air can be made to move at such speeds over a small area."

[5] But move it does. A "weak" tornado with wind speeds as low as 65 kilometres per hour can break trees and lift the roofs off barns (thankfully three-quarters of tornadoes are weak). A strong one, blowing up to 330 kilometres per hour, can uproot trees, move cars and knock down houses. A violent one—and one in 100 is violent—with wind speeds above 330 kilometres per hour, brings total devastation. It produces the kind of wind that lifted an 18-tonne semitrailer off a highway near Plainfield, Illinois, in 1990 and bounced it 350 metres across a field.

[6] The Canadian tornado that caused the worst casualties struck Regina on 30 June 1912. Twenty-eight people died when a twister cut a five-block swath through the city centre. Two hundred others were injured, and 500 buildings destroyed. A close second was the Edmonton tornado of 31 July 1987, which killed 27 people, injured 300 and caused more than $250 million in damage. A series of tornadoes that hit Central Ontario, including Barrie, on 31 May 1985, killed 12, injured 300 and caused $100 million in damage.

[7] Two tornadoes touched down near Arthur and Williamsford, Ontario, on 20 April 1996, forcing the nearby Bruce Nuclear Station to temporarily shut down. Although the twisters only lasted a few minutes, they caused $2.8 million in damage to hydro lines and demolished or damaged

many barns and houses. No one was seriously hurt, though a 75-year-old man suffered a cut to his head when he was sucked out of his house and dumped in a field.

[8] One of the tornadoes damaged Lloyd and Hazel Hutchison's barn, left their farm fields strewn with wreckage, destroyed their woodlot, and ruined their son's house. "There was hail," said Hazel Hutchison, "and then our son, who was looking out the kitchen window, saw stuff flying in the air and yelled 'it's a tornado, get down to the basement.' All we could hear was a terrible roar. It lasted about two minutes."

[9] When they ventured out, the Hutchisons found one of their barn doors in a tree near the house. Someone's coat was hanging on a post. And the roof on their son's new brick house nearby had been lifted off and set down again, cracking the walls and shifting a steel beam in the basement.

[10] "But we were lucky," says Hazel Hutchison, a lifelong Arthur-area resident. "Our neighbours didn't have shoes on when they ran to the basement. When they came up, their house had been blown away. There was nothing left. They didn't even have shoes."

[11] Down the road, the twister took the roof off Bruce Eden's 100-year-old stone house and demolished his barn. Six cows inside died. Fields throughout the area were littered with lumber and sheet-steel roofing. Many area woodlots were destroyed, hardwoods broken or uprooted, and willow swamps levelled. Fences were a casualty, too. Corner posts, set five feet down and stoned in, were broken off.

[12] Tornadoes never used to cross Hutchison's mind. "It was something you saw on the news," she says. Then one struck in May 1985, wrecking homes and barns in the Arthur area before moving on toward Barrie.

[13] "It's a nice part of the country here, except for these episodes," says Hutchison. "I suppose not everybody finds it funny, but someone has put up a sign on the road at Bruce Eden's gate, 'Caution Tornado Crossing.'"

[14] Though tornado statistics in Canada are grim, they pale when compared to the carnage in the United States, particularly in the infamous, densely populated "Tornado Alley." Thousands have died in the stretch from Texas north through Oklahoma, Kansas, Missouri, Indiana, and neighbouring states, the setting for a staggering 100 to 150 tornadoes annually. There were 689 people killed by one or more twisters on 18 March 1925 (including 234 people in the town of Murphysboro, Illinois); 271 deaths on 11 April 1965; 307 on 4 April 1974, among other statistics. Over the past few years, there has been about a billion dollars a year in property damage. (It was also in Tornado Alley that a twister scooped up Dorothy and Toto and conveyed them to Oz, and there as well that special-effects thriller *Twister* was set.)

[15] In Tornado Alley and the tornado-prone areas of Canada, conditions are often just right for severe thunderstorms, which can produce heavy rain, hail, strong straight-line winds, and, once in a while, tornadoes. Warm, moist air from the Gulf of Mexico drifts north and encounters cool, dry air from the northwest. Sometimes the moist air gets trapped below the dry air until, on a hot day, it heats up and rises, bursting through the cool air and soaring in a mighty updraft that sometimes doesn't level off until 16 or 18 kilometres up. (The southern prairies and southern

Ontario have more tornadoes because they are generally more prone to the unstable air masses that create updrafts.) Of course, it's a lot colder at higher altitudes, so the moisture in the air condenses, causing a cloudburst or, sometimes, a hailstorm. Meanwhile, the thunderstorm clouds produce static electricity, which leads to lightning and thunder. All in all, a pretty wild show.

[16] Sometimes an updraft will start to rotate due to the same Coriolis force that causes tropical cyclones and water to swirl down a bathtub drain. If conditions are right, a large portion of the inside of a thundercloud—sometimes a 10-kilometre-wide core of it—will start to turn along with the updraft. This is called a mesocyclone. It is that big vortex that seems to trigger smaller, tighter vortices or funnel clouds at the base of the thundercloud. And if some mysterious conditions are just right, one or more of those funnels will start to grow downward, seemingly feeling its way like an elephant's trunk. If it hits the earth, it's a tornado.

[17] The funnel is usually visible because the swirling winds surround a low-pressure core, condensing water vapour into visible droplets. When the funnel hits ground, it often picks up dirt and debris making it yet more obvious and ominous. A rare but reportedly striking sight is a tornado over snow: the swirling funnel draws up some of the snow and turns a dazzling white.

[18] Tornadoes characteristically touch the earth intermittently, wreaking havoc in one spot, withdrawing into the parent cloud, then dipping down again elsewhere. The same cloud may produce a series of tornadoes. The 1925 twister that killed 689 people in the United States is thought to have been seven separate tornadoes over a 350-kilometre path. The one in 1974 that killed 307 may have been scores of tornadoes produced by the same storm system over a 16-hour period.

[19] The width of a tornado's path varies wildly, from just a few metres up to a monstrous 1 or 2 kilometres. As for wind speed, they start at about 65 kilometres per hour, but no one is sure of the maximum because taking a direct measurement is impossible. "By the time a tornado is on top of your equipment, you don't have your equipment any more," says meteorologist Etkin. Some feel tornadoes rarely top 400 kilometres per hour, others estimate they could reach 500 to 600.

[20] It is a sobering thought that global warming could put Canadians in the path of more tornadoes. In exploring the impact climate change is likely to have on the frequency of twisters in Western Canada, Etkin examined Environment Canada's archive of reported tornadoes. The archive, assembled by now-retired meteorologist Michael Newark, stretches back to 1792. Etkin concluded that tornado frequency is related to mean monthly temperatures. "There is some indication that the prairies could get more tornadoes," says Etkin. "On the other hand, some places may get less if climatic zones shift."

[21] The strange stories for which tornadoes are famous—straws driven into telephone poles; henhouses moved but the eggs uncracked; babies found unharmed in fields—could become even more plentiful and remarkable. During a tornado in April 1996 in southern Ontario, a wood stove was blown out of a house and set down upright in a neighbouring field, the fire still burning. But more often, tornadoes bring death and devastation. In 1987, a survivor in Edmonton reported, "My house was sitting up against a neighbour's house in 50 million pieces. There were a few dead people lying in the street."

[22] Which is why it's good to have a plan in case a severe thunderstorm becomes very dark and a wall cloud drops down from the base and begins swirling—and especially if you hear a roar like jet planes or locomotives, or the sky turns green. Choose a safe place ahead of time, preferably under a workbench or table in the basement. Alternatively, seek shelter in a small interior room, hallway or closet. Don't waste time trying to open windows to equalize the pressure between inside and outside.

[23] If you live in a mobile home, seek shelter elsewhere, preferably below ground. Failing that, crouch down in a ditch, depression, or culvert and protect your head with your hands. Get out of large halls or arenas. If you're in a car, don't try to drive to safety—you can't outrun a tornado. Get out of the car and move far enough away that it can't roll on you. If you're outside, lie in a ditch, cover your head, and stay put.

Source: Adapted from D. Lanken. "Funnel Fury." *Canadian Geographic*, 116, 4 (July/August 1996). Retrieved from Academic Search Premier (Accession Number 9607252440).

EXERCISE 10. COMPREHENSION CHECK

1. What is a tornado?

_____

2. David Etkin said that with climate change, the occurrence of tornadoes could increase. What is his reason for believing this?

_____

3. In paragraph 4, Richard Scorer and Arjen Verkaik are quoted as saying, "It is remarkable. . . ." What do they believe is "remarkable"?

_____

4. In paragraph 10, Hazel Hutchison is quoted as saying, "But we were lucky. . . ." What does she mean?

_____

5. In paragraph 13, to what does the phrase *these episodes* refer?

_____

6. What is the main idea of paragraph 14? What evidence does the writer use to support his main idea?

_____

7. Why is it difficult to measure the wind speed of a tornado?

_____

8. In paragraph 21, how many examples of strange tornado stories are given by the author?

_____

9. In paragraph 21, the writer uses the word "but." Writers use this word to contrast, or show the difference between two ideas. What two ideas is the author contrasting?

_____

Chronological Order

When describing a process or a series of events, writers often organize their texts according to the order in time at which specific steps or events occurred. That is, the event that occurred first is described first and the event that occurred second is described second, and so on. In paragraphs 15 and 16 of "Funnel Fury," the author describes the formation of tornadoes in some detail. Since a series of conditions is required for the formation of tornadoes, the author organizes his ideas in chronological order. That is, the condition that occurs first is described first, the condition that occurs second is described second, and so on.

EXERCISE 11. OUTLINING CHRONOLOGICAL ORDER

Outline the series of conditions that leads to the formation of tornadoes.

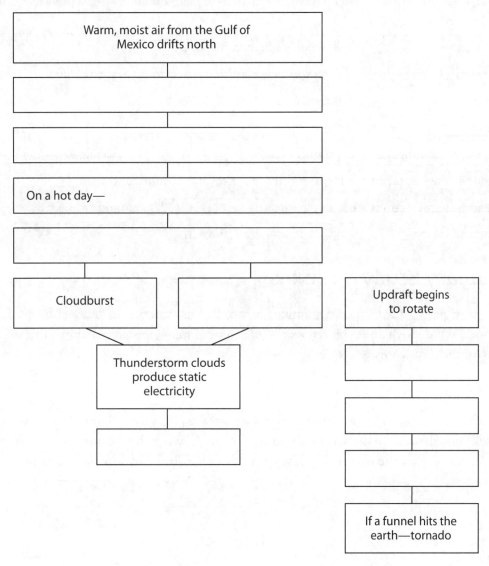

Exercise 12. Vocabulary in Context

1. In paragraphs 15 and 16, find synonyms for the following verbs.
    a) *to meet* (paragraph 15) _____
    b) *to break through suddenly* (paragraph 15) _____
    c) *to fly upwards* (paragraph 15) _____
    d) *to stop moving upwards* (paragraph 15) _____
    e) *to change from vapour to liquid* (paragraph 15) _____
    f) *to turn in a circle* (paragraph 16) _____
    g) *to cause* (paragraph 16) _____

2. Using the verbs you found in paragraphs 15 and 16, complete the following sentences. (One verb will have to be used twice.)
    a) The bubble _____ when I touched it.
    b) The bird _____ through the air as it returned to its nest to protect its young.
    c) Water _____ as it cools.
    d) She cannot eat chocolate because it sometimes _____ a headache.
    e) When people move to a new country, they _____ a new culture.
    f) After a plane has taken off, it gains altitude for several minutes and then _____.
    g) When water in a cup is stirred, it begins to _____ around.
    h) When a turbine _____, it generates power.

Vocabulary Study: Prefixes

Prefixes are word parts added to the beginnings of words. For example, in "Funnel Fury" the prefix *un* (meaning "not") is used with different root words (e.g., *unpredictable, unstable*). Adding this prefix changes the meaning of the root words.

Exercise 13. Prefixes

In the following table, examples of words that include prefixes are given. Some of these words are used in the article "Funnel Fury." In the second column of the table, write the meaning of each example word. Then, in column 3, note the overall meaning of each prefix. Information for the prefix *im* has been added for you.

Prefixes

Prefix	Example Words	Prefix Meaning
im-	*impossible* (paragraph 19) word meaning: not possible *immature* word meaning: not mature	not
in- (meaning #1)	*instability* (paragraph 3) word meaning: *insensitivity* word meaning:	
in- (meaning #2)	*interior* (paragraph 22) word meaning: *intake* word meaning:	
pre-	*precondition* (paragraph 2) word meaning: *prefix* word meaning:	
re-	*redo* word meaning: *redevelop* word meaning:	
tri-	*triangle* word meaning: *tricycle* word meaning:	
un-	*unpredictable* (paragraph 1) word meaning: *unstable* (paragraphs 2 and 15) word meaning: *unclear* (paragraph 4) word meaning: *uncracked* (paragraph 21) word meaning: *unharmed* (paragraph 21) word meaning:	

With the help of your classmates, fill in the meanings of any prefixes that you did not know. (See also the Appendix on page 244 for a more complete list of prefixes and their meanings.)

Exercise 14. Writing

Based on your analysis of paragraphs 15 and 16 in Exercise 11, describe the formation process of a tornado using your own words.

Remember to use signal words in your text to help the reader move from one step to the next. The signal words for chronological order include the following:

first	*second*	*third*	*next*
then	*after*	*finally*	*lastly*

⊢ Reading 3—*Avalanche Danger Scale* ⊢

Exercise 15. Pre-reading Discussion

The following two readings provide information about another natural hazard in Canada: avalanches. The first reading is a table published by the Canadian Avalanche Centre.

1. What is an avalanche?

2. Refer to the map on page 55. Where are avalanches a particular threat in Canada?

3. One expert, Chris Stetham, described the feeling of being in an avalanche in the following way: "The whole slope around you begins to move, it's rather like you're standing on a carpet that's suddenly pulled away, (Gzowski and Stetham, 1993). Using your own words, explain what Stetham means.

4. The word *backcountry* is often used in discussions about Canadian avalanches. What do you think is meant by this word?

Source: Chris Stetham, interviewed by Peter Gzowski, *Morningside*, CBC Radio, 10 November 1993, CBC Digital Archives, http://archives.cbc.ca/environment/natural_disasters/clips/9933/, modified 6 April 2006, retrieved 5 October 2011.

Many avalanches happen without anyone ever knowing. However, when they happen in areas where there are people, the effects can be disastrous. Because of the risks posed to people by avalanches, a warning system has been developed to let people who are travelling through mountainous backcountry know the level of avalanche risk.

The table below was published by the Canadian Avalanche Centre on its website. Study the table, and then answer the questions that follow, based on the information in the table.

⊢ Avalanche Danger Scale ⊣

North American Public Avalanche Danger Scale
Avalanche danger is determined by the likelihood, size and distribution of avalanches.

Danger Level		Travel Advice	Likelihood of Avalanches	Avalanche Size and Distribution
5 Extreme	4 5 ✕	Avoid all avalanche terrain.	Natural and human-triggered avalanches certain.	Large to very large avalanches in many areas.
4 High	4 5 ✕	Very dangerous avalanche conditions. Travel in avalanche terrain not recommended.	Natural avalanches likely; human-triggered avalanches very likely.	Large avalanches in many areas; or very large avalanches in specific areas.
3 Considerable	3 !!	Dangerous avalanche conditions. Careful snowpack evaluation, cautious route-finding and conservative decision-making essential.	Natural avalanches possible; human-triggered avalanches likely.	Small avalanches in many areas; or large avalanches in specific areas; or very large avalanches in isolated areas.
2 Moderate	2 !	Heightened avalanche conditions on specific terrain features. Evaluate snow and terrain carefully; identify features of concern.	Natural avalanches unlikely; human-triggered avalanches possible.	Small avalanches in specific areas; or large avalanches in isolated areas.
1 Low	1 ✓	Generally safe avalanche conditions. Watch for unstable snow on isolated terrain features.	Natural and human-triggered avalanches unlikely.	Small avalanches in isolated areas or extreme terrain.

Safe backcountry travel requires training and experience. You control your own risk by choosing where, when and how you travel.

Source: "Avalanche Danger Scale." Canadian Avalanche Centre, http://www.avalanche.ca/cac/bulletins/danger-scale, retrieved 5 October 2011.

Exercise 16. Comprehension Check

In the chart above, the column "Travel Advice" gives people travelling through backcountry instructions about what they should do to maximize their safety. First, underline what travellers are told to do in the "Travel Advice" column. (In some cases, this advice may not be directly stated but can be inferred.) Then, rewrite this advice using your own words in the chart below.

Danger Level	Travel Advice
extreme	
high	
considerable	
moderate	
low	

EXERCISE 17. COMPREHENSION CHECK

1. What factors do avalanche experts consider when determining the level of risk for a particular area?

   _____

2. Is it completely safe to travel through backcountry with a "Low" danger level?

   _____

3. Before people travel through backcountry areas, what should they do?

   _____

4. For whom do you think the "Avalanche Danger Scale" was created? Be prepared to explain your answer.

   _____

EXERCISE 18. VOCABULARY IN CONTEXT

One way that writers communicate the degree of possibility with which they believe an event will occur is through their choice of adjectives. In the column "Likelihood of Avalanches," the authors use adjectives to tell their readers the likelihood of an avalanche occurring at each danger level. The adjectives are listed below:

unlikely   *possible*   *likely*   *very likely*   *certain*

1. What degree of possibility is expressed by each of these adjectives? Write the adjectives in the chart below, placing each adjective in the slot that best represents the degree of possibility that it expresses.

An event will definitely occur.	_____
	_____
	_____
There is a 50 percent chance that an event will occur.	_____
	_____
An event will definitely not occur. There is a 0 percent chance.	

2. Circle the best answer for each of the questions below.
   a) What is the most frequent cause of avalanches in areas with a "Moderate" danger level?

   nature   humans   neither nature nor humans   both nature and humans

   b) What is the most frequent cause of avalanches in areas with a "Considerable" danger level?

   nature   humans   neither nature nor humans   both nature and humans

   c) What is the most frequent cause of avalanches in areas with a "High" danger level?

   nature   humans   neither nature nor humans   both nature and humans

   d) What is the most frequent cause of avalanches in areas with an "Extreme" danger level?

   nature   humans   neither nature nor humans   both nature and humans

Reading 4—*Snow Avalanches*

Reading 4 provides detail about the formation of avalanches. This reading is an excerpt from a book called *Environmental Hazards: Assessing Risk and Reducing Disaster* (4th ed.) by Keith Smith (2004). The writing style is more formal and technical than the style of the earlier readings in this chapter and is similar to the writing style in many university textbooks.

As you read the excerpt, think especially about the conditions that lead to the formation of an avalanche.

Snow Avalanches

[1] A snow avalanche results from an unequal contest between stress and strength on an incline (Schaerer, 1981). The strength of the snow pack is related to its density and temperature. Compared to other solids, snow layers have the ability to sustain large density changes. Thus, a layer deposited with an original density of 100 kg/m^3 may densify to 400 kg/m^3 during the course of a winter, largely due to the weight of over-lying snow, pressure melting and the re-crystallisation of the ice. On the other hand, the shear strength decreases as the temperature approaches 0°C. As the temperature rises further, and liquid melt-water exists in the pack, the risk of movement of the snow blanket grows.

[2] Most snow loading on slopes occurs slowly. This gives the snow pack an opportunity to adjust by internal deformation, because of its plastic nature, without any damaging failure. The most important triggers of pack failure tend to be heavy snowfall, rain, thaw or some artificial increase in dynamic loading, such as skiers traversing the surface. For a hazardous snow pack failure to occur, the slope must also be sufficiently steep to allow the snow to slide. Avalanche frequency is thus related to slope angle, with most events occurring on intermediate slope gradients of between 30–45°. Angles below 20° are generally too low for failure to occur and most slopes above 60° rarely accumulate sufficient snow to pose a major hazard. Most avalanches start at fracture points in the snow blanket where there is high tensile stress, such as a break of ground slope, at an overhanging cornice or where the snow fails to bond to another surface, such as a rock outcrop. The two main categories of snow pack failure are described in Box 7.1.

[3] All avalanches follow a path that comprises three elements: the *starting zone* where the snow initially breaks away, the *track* or path followed and the *run-out zone* where the snow decelerates and stops. Because avalanches tend to recur at the same sites, the threat from future events can often be detected from the recognition of previous avalanche paths in the landscape. Clues in the terrain include breaks of slope, eroded channels on the hillsides and damaged vegetation. In heavily forested mountains, avalanche paths can be identified by the age and species of trees and by sharp "trim-lines" separating the mature, undisturbed forest from the cleared slope. Once the hazard is recognized, a wide range of potential adjustments is available, some of which are shared with landslide hazard mitigation.

Box 7.1

How Snow Avalanches Start

Snow avalanches result from two different types of snow pack failure:

- *Loose-snow avalanches* occur in cohesionless snow where inter-granular bonding is very weak thus producing behavior rather like dry sand (Fig. 7.6A). Failure begins near the snow surface when a small amount of snow, usually less than 1 m³, slips out of place and starts to move down the slope. The sliding snow spreads to produce an elongated, inverted V-shaped scar.

- *Slab avalanches* occur where a strongly cohesive layer of snow breaks away from a weaker underlying layer, to leave a sharp fracture line or *crown* (Fig. 7.6B). Rain or high temperatures, followed by re-freezing, create ice-crusts that may provide a source of instability when buried by subsequent snowfalls. The fracture often takes place where the underlying topography produces some upward deformation of the snow surface, leading to high tensile stress, and the associated surface cracking of the slab layer. The initial slab which breaks away may be up to 10,000 m² in area and up to 10 m in thickness. Such large slabs are very dangerous because, when a slab breaks loose, it can bring down 100 times the initial volume of snow.

Avalanche motion depends on the type of snow and the terrain. Most avalanches start with a gliding motion but then rapidly accelerate on slopes greater than 30°.

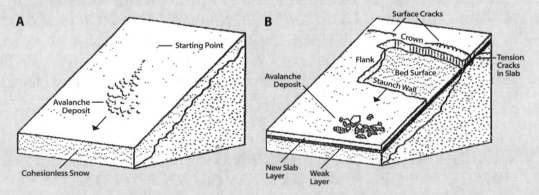

Figure 7.6 Two highly characteristic types of snow-slope failure. (A) the loose-snow avalanche; (B) the slab avalanche. Slab avalanches normally create the greater hazard because of the larger volume of snow released.

Reference:
Schaerer, P. A. (1981). Avalanches. In D. M. Gray and D. H. Male (Eds) *Handbook of snow* (pp. 475–518). Toronto: Pergamon.

Source: Smith K. (2004), *Environmental hazards: Assessing risk and reducing disaster,* (4th ed.) London: Routledge, 130–132.

EXERCISE 19. COMPREHENSION CHECK

1. With reference to paragraph 1, what two factors affect the strength of a snow pack?

_____

2. Find an example in paragraph 1 that shows how the density of a snow pack can change. Write "EX" in the margin beside that example.

3. In paragraph 1, the writer uses the transition phrase "On the other hand." Writers use this transition phrase to contrast, or show the difference between, two ideas. Which two ideas is the author contrasting?

_____

4. Why do many avalanches happen in March in British Columbia? (*Note:* The answer to this question is not directly stated in the passage but can be inferred from paragraph 1.)

_____

5. According to Smith, the author of this text, what are the most common triggers of avalanches?

_____

6. What conditions need to exist for most avalanches to occur?

_____

7. Many avalanches take place without anyone seeing them occur. How can avalanche experts tell where an avalanche has occurred?

_____

8. Rewrite the following sentence from paragraph 3 in your own words: "Because avalanches tend to recur at the same sites, the threat from future events can often be detected from the recognition of previous avalanche paths in the landscape."

_____

9. For paragraphs 1 to 3, add marginal notes that summarize the main idea of each paragraph.

10. Fill in the following chart, comparing loose-snow avalanches and slab avalanches.

	Loose-Snow Avalanches	Slab Avalanches
cause		
amount of snow that initiates the avalanche		
level of danger		

EXERCISE 20. COMPREHENSION CHECK

On page 65, you completed an outline showing the sequence of steps that lead to a tornado. Based on your understanding of Reading 4, "Snow Avalanches," complete the following on a separate sheet of paper:

1. Develop an original outline that shows the steps in the formation of an avalanche.

2. Compare your outline with the outlines of your classmates.

3. Revise your outline so that it includes any steps that you missed.

EXERCISE 21. VOCABULARY IN CONTEXT

The following sentences are taken from Reading 4. Choose the best meaning for the underlined word or words.

1. "A snow avalanche results from an unequal contest between stress and strength on an incline." (paragraph 1)

   stress
   a) volume
   b) physical pressure
   c) length

   incline
   a) slope
   b) mountain
   c) layer of snow

2. "The strength of the snow pack is related to its density and temperature." (paragraph 1)

   a) the extent to which something can melt
   b) the extent to which something can expand
   c) the extent to which something is packed together

3. "On the other hand, the shear strength decreases as the temperature approaches 0°C." (paragraph 1)

   a) gets far from
   b) gets close to
   c) goes below

4. "Most snow loading on slopes occurs slowly." (paragraph 2)

   a) falls
   b) decreases
   c) happens

5. "This gives the snow pack an opportunity to adjust by internal deformation, because of its plastic nature, without any damaging failure." (paragraph 2)

   a) to become lighter
   b) to change
   c) to break apart

6. "Angles below 20° are generally too low for failure to occur and most slopes above 60° rarely accumulate sufficient snow to pose a major hazard." (paragraph 2)

   a) small amounts of
   b) loosely packed
   c) enough

7. "Most avalanches start at fracture points in the snow blanket where there is high tensile stress, such as a break of ground slope, at an overhanging cornice or where the snow fails to bond to another surface, such as a rock outcrop." (paragraph 2)

   a) to attach
   b) to fall apart
   c) to break away

8. "All avalanches follow a path that comprises three elements: the *starting zone* where the snow initially breaks away, the *track* or path followed and the *run-out zone* where the snow decelerates and stops." (paragraph 3)

   comprises
   a) creates
   b) results from
   c) is made up of

   elements
   a) parts
   b) tracks
   c) levels

EXERCISE 22. WRITING A DESCRIPTIVE PARAGRAPH

Based on the original outline that you created showing the formation of an avalanche, describe how an avalanche develops using your own words and the vocabulary that you studied in this chapter.

EXERCISE 23. CRITICAL ANALYSIS

Think back to Reading 2, "Funnel Fury," and Readings 3 and 4 about avalanches, and discuss the following questions with your classmates.

1. To what extent are natural hazards random events?

2. How does human interaction with the environment create natural hazards?

Writing

Thesis Statements

A very important part of an essay is the thesis statement. The thesis statement tells the reader the main point or argument of the writer in one or two sentences; it also indicates the framework for the ideas in the essay. The thesis statement is usually placed at the end of the introduction, where it focuses readers before they read the body of the text. If there is no thesis statement, readers may feel lost as they progress through the text. That is, they may be trying to understand the writer's purpose instead of concentrating on the information used by the writer to justify or support the main idea.

Factors Involved in Shaping the Thesis Statement

Writing a thesis statement is one of the most challenging parts of essay writing. In academic settings, writers often consider the following factors as they draft thesis statements.

- **The Audience**

  In most academic situations, the audience is the professor. It is very important for the student writer to understand the expectations of the professor, especially those that are related to the purpose and direction of the paper. Some of a professor's expectations are stated explicitly in the written guidelines for assignments. Some of a professor's expectations are not stated explicitly but can be inferred from the way the professor presents information and discusses the topic in class.

- **The Student's Analysis of the Topic**

  In some academic assignments, students are asked to show that they understand a body of information or ideas. Often, however, it is important that the student provide a critical analysis of information or ideas; in this case, the student's analysis of the topic is essential and plays an important role in formulating the thesis statement.

- **The Available Material**

  Before writing a thesis statement, writers should carefully consider the information and ideas about which they have read. This is important because it is on the basis of the available information that the writer develops a point of view or position on a topic; it is this point of view that is expressed in the thesis statement.

In academic settings, writers often consider the following questions before they write thesis statements.

- What is the purpose of the assignment? To what extent is my own analysis important in fulfilling the requirements of the assignment?
- What content does my professor expect will be discussed in the paper?
- What is my position or point of view on the topic?
- What type of organization is expected?
- What major points will my essay cover?

Writing a Thesis Statement

To create a coherent essay, a writer needs to develop a point of view on the topic. It is not always possible to express a point of view clearly at the outset of the writing process. In fact, some writers do not write their thesis statements until they have written part of the body of the essay; they find out what they want to say in their essays as they write their essays. Once they have discovered their main points, they go back and revise what they have written to create a logical and coherent text. Other writers know what they want to say before they begin writing and express this in a thesis statement. Then they write the body of the essay.

Many writers use a combination of these two methods. They write a preliminary thesis statement before they write the body of the essay. Then they modify the thesis statement as they write the body of the essay.

For example, for an essay focusing on architect Frank Gehry, the original thesis statement was

> "The unique designs of Gehry's buildings, which incorporate a variety of shapes and materials, reflect both his philosophy of the modern city and his personal approach to dealing with his clients."

The thesis statement used in the final draft of this essay was

> "[Gehry's] architectural signature, which reflects his approach and philosophy, can be seen in the design of the Guggenheim Museum in Bilbao, Spain."

The writer modified the original thesis statement because, as she wrote her first draft, she decided that she wanted to use the Guggenheim Museum as the prime example of Gehry's work throughout the essay. Her thesis statement evolved as she wrote the body of the essay.

EXERCISE 24. ANALYZING THESIS STATEMENTS (A)

The following thesis statements were written for an essay about the flood of the Red River in Manitoba.

a) "The characteristics of the river and its surrounding landscape, along with unique weather conditions of the winter of 1996–1997, combined to make the flood of the Red River in 1997 the largest in Manitoba during the twentieth century."

b) "Events leading up to the crest of the Red River in Winnipeg triggered a series of powerful, personal emotions."

1. What is the difference in the emphasis of the two thesis statements?

2. How would each thesis statement be developed in an essay?

EXERCISE 25. WRITING ASSIGNMENT

Choose *one* of the topics below for your final essay in this chapter.

1. Describe a natural disaster that affected you or someone you know. Describe your reactions to the disaster or the reactions of others.

2. Choose one type of natural hazard that occurs or has occurred in Canada or another country (e.g., hurricanes or earthquakes). Describe the steps in the process that lead to the formation of this natural hazard with reference to such factors as landforms and weather conditions. (You may have to do some research.)

Remember, the thesis statement will most probably develop as you write your paper. Do not be concerned if the thesis statement is not exactly as you want it before you write the body. You can revise it throughout the writing process.

After You Write

After you have completed the first draft of your essay, take time to revise it. The following questions will help you.

1. Does your thesis statement express the main idea of your essay?

2. Does each paragraph focus on an idea that supports the main idea of the essay or the thesis statement?

3. Is each supporting idea thoroughly developed?

4. Does the conclusion make a logical and clear summary statement?

CHAPTER 4

Conflict Management: Different Roads to Justice

Introduction to the Chapter

Conflict and conflict resolution are important parts of life. In day-to-day life, we see conflict in many forms, from disagreements between children to conflicts between adults caused by serious crimes.

In this chapter, you will read about several methods of dealing with offenders and supporting victims of crime. The poem "Prison" expresses one inmate's response to life in prison. In "A Fable for Our Time," we read about a victim and an offender who come to understand each other's situations through mediation. Two articles called "14-Year-Old Finds Alternative to Court in Sentencing Circle" and "Conditional Sentences" describe two other approaches sometimes used within the Canadian justice system. Finally "Teaching Children How to Fight" explains a way of resolving conflict between children.

After you have read and discussed the readings, you will complete one of the following writing assignments:

1. In an essay, compare two of the approaches to justice about which you have read in this chapter.

2. In an essay, compare one of the approaches to justice described in this chapter with another approach with which you are familiar.

Reading 1—*Prison*

EXERCISE 1. PRE-READING DISCUSSION

Discuss the following questions before you read the poem.

1. What are your impressions of life in prison?

2. Using your own impressions of life in prison, complete the following sentence stem in as many ways as you can.

Prison is a place where _____

_____

_____

Prison

Prison is a Place

Where you exchange the dignity of,

Your name for the degradation of a number.

Prison is a Place

Where you live from visit to visit,

If you're fortunate enough to have a visitor.

Prison is a Place

Where you learn the counting of life,

You count the years, months, weeks, days,

hours, and even seconds.

Prison is a Place

Where you pray not to DIE.

Prison is a Place

Where the word Freedom can bring,

Tears of remembrance to

The meanest of cons, thieves, and killers.

Prison is a Place

Where you become mentally crippled,

Because responsibility is taken away from you.

Prison is a Place

Where you can hear the echo of,

Family and friends saying, "I told you so".

So please don't come to Prison,

For a life means nothing here,

"LIVE!"

Source: Anonymous. "Prison." *Inside the Walls: Writings from Stony Mountain Inmates.* 60.

EXERCISE 2. COMPREHENSION CHECK

1. Expressing the ideas of others in your own words is an essential skill in academic writing. After thinking carefully about what the writer of "Prison" is saying, rewrite the following lines from the poem, using your own words.

> **Example:** Original "Prison is a Place
> Where you exchange the dignity of,
> Your name for the degradation of a number."
>
> Paraphrase In prison, you don't have a name; you have a number. In giving up your name, you lose a sense of pride and dignity.

a) "Prison is a Place
    Where you live from visit to visit"

    _____

    _____

b) "Prison is a Place
    Where the word Freedom can bring,
    Tears of remembrance to
    The meanest of cons, thieves, and killers."

    _____

    _____

c) "Prison is a Place
    Where you become mentally crippled,
    Because responsibility is taken away from you."

    _____

    _____

d) "Prison is a Place
    Where you can hear the echo of,
    Family and friends saying, 'I told you so'"

    _____

    _____

2. Summarize the overall message of the poem.

    _____

    _____

3. What advice does the writer give to readers of his poem?

    _____

    _____

⊢ Reading 2—*A Fable for Our Time* ⊣

EXERCISE 3. PRE-READING DISCUSSION

Discuss the following questions before you read.

1. Have you ever had something of importance stolen from you? If yes, how did you feel?

2. How was the situation resolved?

3. In your opinion, what should the consequences be for a person who steals a wallet or a purse?

Exercise 4. Pre-reading Strategy—Skimming

1. The author of "A Fable for Our Time" integrates a fable (a traditional story) into her article. The fable, which is called "The Sun and the Wind," is printed in italics so that it stands out from the rest of her text. Read only the italicized print in the article below to discover the fable "The Sun and the Wind." What lesson or moral is taught in this fable?

2. Now read the boldfaced sections in the article. What do you think this article will be about?

⊣ A Fable for Our Time ⊢

[1] *The sun and the wind were having an argument. "Nothing is stronger than force," howled the wind. "I can make people do anything I want them to if I blow hard enough!"*

[2] *"Love is much stronger than force," smiled the sun. "When I shine warmly, people want to cooperate."*

[3] *"Non-s-s-sens-s-s-e!" hissed the wind.*

[4] *"Want to bet?" winked the sun.*

[5] *"Sure—sure—sure! I'll show you I'm right," whistled the wind.*

[6] *"All right," said the sun. "See that man down there?"*

[7] As Elaine walks out the double glass doors of the mall where she works, Dave speeds by on his motorbike, grabbing the purse from her shoulder. Elaine watches as her money, paychecks[1], and ID disappear down the road. Several hours later, Dave is caught while making a purchase with one of Elaine's checks.

[8] *"Yes," whirled the wind. "What about him?"*

[9] *"He is wearing a coat. I bet I can persuade him to take it off but you can't make him do it," grinned the sun.*

[10] At that point, Dave and Elaine enter a criminal justice system with the hopes of experiencing accountability, justice, and healing.

[11] *"Ho, ho, ho," roared the wind. "I'll show you! I'll show you!"*

[12] *"Very well," said the sun. "Go ahead!"*

[13] Dave is to blame for breaking a law and he must prepare himself to receive what he has coming. He must be punished so he will never commit such a crime again. He has hurt the state by his actions, so he must also be hurt. The attorneys[2] prepare themselves for the work ahead of them.

[14] *The wind blew hard. The man buttoned one of the buttons on his coat.*

[15] The police come and take Dave to jail for the night. He waits overnight for his parents to come and take him home. His family is called home from around the country.

---

[1] *Check* is the American spelling of *cheque*.

[2] *Attorney* is often used in the United States to refer to a lawyer.

As Elaine walks out the double glass doors of the mall where she works, Dave speeds by on his motorbike, grabbing the purse from her shoulder. Elaine watches as her money, paychecks, and ID disappear down the road.

Dave's friend who was involved in the offense is overlooked in the charges, leaving Dave to take full responsibility. Despite conversations with the friend's family, they are not willing to hold their son responsible. The police do not follow up with Dave's request that they talk with his friend. Dave becomes isolated and alienated from his friends and community as they discover what has happened.

[16] *The wind blew harder. The man buttoned another button on his coat.*

[17] Dave is formally charged with a felony status[3] crime. His attorney begins the preparations for the court proceedings. He explains that Dave will be looking at time in prison due to the severity of his crime and sentencing guidelines. He also explains that with "three strikes and you're out" legislation, he just received his first strike. He is a threat to society so he must be removed and taught a lesson. Dave begins to contemplate the humiliation and violence that exist within prison walls.

[18] Elaine no longer feels safe. Instead of keeping her purse beneath her cash register at work like she did for years, she now locks it in the store vault. She is fearful to walk alone to her car in the parking lot. Every day, she waits between the double glass doors of the mall, waiting for the parking lot to be empty of people before walking to her car. She mulls questions over in her mind—What did I do to deserve this? Is he waiting for me in the parking lot? Will he come to my house? She has lost her sense of security, even in those places with which she is familiar. Elaine is left with stereotypes and fears knowing that Dave is out there somewhere but not knowing anything about him.

[19] *The wind blew harder and harder. The man buttoned the third button on his coat.*

[20] Dave awaits his first court appearance with nervousness and fear, not knowing what will happen. A few days before the appearance, he receives notice that the date has been changed. He begins the wait for the second scheduled appearance. As time goes on, he becomes bitter with the system for taking away many of his privileges. He feels worthless for being the only person to have committed a crime in his family and for ruining their reputation. He is angry with the victim for being the source of his problems.

[21] Elaine also receives notice of the first court appearance. She asks for time off work to attend. She waits for most of the day before discovering that the date was changed but she was not notified. She asks for time off work again to attend court on the newly scheduled day.

Dave becomes isolated and alienated from his friends and community as they discover what has happened. Elaine asks: What did I do to deserve this? Is he waiting for me in the parking lot? Will he come to my house?

She waits all day for her case to be called. A young man sits beside her. She looks at him and recognizes Dave as the man who stole her purse. She stifles a scream and demands to change seats with the man beside her.

---

[3] *Felony status* is a legal term used in the United States, but not in Canada.

[22] Dave's case is finally called and processed but she is not called upon to speak. Throughout this process, Elaine has been ignored and left out. She is considered an unnecessary extra to the proceedings. In a time when she needed support and understanding, she was left alone to work through her fear and anger.

Both Dave and Elaine need a process which will help them work toward understanding, responsibility, and healing.

Her needs have not been met, let alone discussed.

[23] *The wind blew with all his might. The man turned up his collar and pulled his coat firmly around him.*

[24] Dave is ready to take what he has coming and prepares himself to spend several years in jail. He is humiliated and knows that when he leaves the courtroom that day, he will not see his family for some time and that he will live in a world of violence, manipulation, and fear.

[25] Elaine, furious with the lack of respect offered her throughout this ordeal, jumps up from her chair and yells, "He doesn't know what he has done to me. He needs to know what he has done!" The judge orders her to sit down or to be held in contempt and spend a night in jail. Elaine shakes her fist and shouts again, "He needs to know what he has done to me!"

[26] *The sun laughed. "Give up?" The wind was all out of breath.*

[27] *"All right. You try it," he sighed.*

[28] Both Dave and Elaine need a process which will help them work toward understanding, responsibility, and healing. Instead of broken laws and blame, justice involves broken people and relationships that need to be repaired. Instead of inflicting pain, there is a need for healing and restitution. Shalom provides the framework. Crime breaks the right relationships that we are called to live in. Justice is making things right. The essence of love replaces force and punishment.

[29] *The sun smiled warmly down on the man. The man looked up at the sun and unbuttoned one of the buttons on his coat.*

[30] The judge considers his options. Send Dave to jail and he will truly never know what exactly he has done to Elaine. Send Dave to jail and Elaine will never have the opportunity to say what happened to her or to feel that she played a role in justice. The judge postpones sentencing until Dave and Elaine have a chance to talk to each other. He refers them to the local Victim Offender Reconciliation Program (VORP).

[31] In a meeting led by a VORP volunteer, Dave and Elaine share their stories. Dave tells Elaine that he is a missionary kid who was born and raised in Japan. His family returned to the United States several months ago. He is having a difficult time making friends and adjusting to the North American way of life. While enrolled at the local community college, he formed a friendship with another guy who lived nearby. In order to fit in and maintain this friendship, Dave had agreed to steal the purse so the two men could buy compact discs and running shoes. They actually made several purchases before being caught. He admits that he knew what he did was wrong. He is embarrassed by what he did and is ready to take responsibility for it.

[32] Elaine then has the opportunity to tell her side of the story. She tells Dave that this was the third robbery in two months. Each robbery hurt their family financially and emotionally.

In a meeting led by a VORP volunteer, Dave and Elaine share their stories. They talk about making amends for what happened, and they discuss how things will be in the future.

In fact, due to Dave's actions, the family was not able to secure a bank loan to replace some of the goods lost in the first burglary. She tells Dave that in her purse that day was her husband's first paycheck after being unemployed for over two years. This check was now missing.

[33] She explains her fear of walking to her car alone and of leaving her possessions unattended. She recounts her fear when he sat next to her in court. She looks him square in the eye and says, "You need to know that there is someone in this world who is terrified of you."

[34] *The sun smiled still more warmly. The man unbuttoned another button.*

[35] Dave and Elaine talk about making amends for what happened. Elaine presents her monetary losses: the money in her wallet, the cost of replacing her identification and credit cards, the bank charges for the bad checks, and the two days of lost pay in order to attend the court proceedings.

The winds of "justice" are cold ones being blown on already cold and hurting people, offenders and victims alike. An alternative approach can warm victims and offenders, encouraging them to open themselves to restoration and healing.

Dave had already sold his motorbike and took on two jobs in order to pay her back. He pays half her losses at that time and agrees to pay the rest in one month. Dave further offers to talk with the appropriate bank personnel in order to explain that he is responsible for the actions that caused the bank loan to fall through.

[36] *The sun smiled even more warmly. The man unbuttoned the third button.*

[37] Dave and Elaine talk about how things will be in the future. Elaine asks Dave if she has to worry about him doing this to her again—would he ever be waiting for her in the parking lot? Dave assures her that he wouldn't. He tells her that now that he has listened to how his actions affected her, he better understands what he has done and would never do it again to anyone. He tells her that it really affected him to hear that someone is frightened of him and that he will not forget that.

[38] *His coat was flapping open. Now it was getting hot! The man took off his coat, hung it over his arm, and continued on his journey.*

[39] Dave and Elaine return to court for the sentencing hearing. Elaine arrives before Dave and waits for him so they can sit together in the courtroom. Dave shares with the judge what he heard from Elaine, explaining how his actions have hurt her. Elaine is then given time to talk. She tells the judge that she believes that Dave truly understands what he did and that his willingness to pay for the damages has helped her start to move on with her life. She further states that he has taken responsibility for his actions and that she has experienced justice. Dave leaves the courtroom that day with his family and Elaine, understanding what he has done and taking steps to make it right. Several weeks later, he makes the final payment to Elaine.

[40] *"Which is stronger, love or force?" asked the sun.*

[41] *The wind did not answer. He slid into a hollow to rest.*

[42] The wind presented Dave and Elaine with an option for justice that would have left them both alienated, excluded, and angry. Both would have continued to live in worlds of fear and pain: Dave in a world defined by punishment and Elaine in a private world of insecurity and loss. They would have walked away from the courtroom without having their needs met and without a feeling of resolution. The winds of "justice" are cold ones being blown on already cold and hurting people, offenders and victims alike.

[43] The sun offered Dave and Elaine the opportunity for justice, which empowered them to take control of their lives and to work together to repair the damage that had been done. Their needs became the priority, leading to a greater understanding of the offense and providing the framework for resolution. The sun warmed Dave and Elaine, encouraging them to open themselves up in order to experience restoration, healing, and thus true justice.

[44] *The sun smiled warmly and is still smiling today.*

Source: B. Toews, "A Fable for Our Time." *Conciliation Quarterly* 15, 3 (Summer 1996): 2–4.

EXERCISE 5. COMPREHENSION CHECK

1. In your own words, describe what happens to Dave in the legal system after he stole Elaine's purse.

   _____

2. How do Dave and Elaine feel during the court proceedings?

   _____

3. In your own words, explain the purpose of VORP.

   _____

4. How does Dave take responsibility for his actions after the VORP session?

   _____

5. How does Elaine's involvement with VORP help her?

   _____

6. In your opinion, is the story of Dave and Elaine true? Why or why not?

   _____

7. What is the wind compared to in this article?

   _____

8. What is the sun compared to in this article?

   _____

9. What parallels do you see between the story of the sun and the wind, and the story of Dave and Elaine?

_____

10. How does the author characterize the criminal justice system? (See especially paragraph 42.)

_____

11. How does the author characterize VORP? (See especially paragraph 43.)

_____

| Taking Notes

To help organize and remember important information in readings, it is sometimes helpful to create charts. Charts can be especially useful when you are making comparisons.

In this chapter you are reading about and ultimately comparing three systems of justice, one of which is the Victim Offender Reconciliation Program (VORP).

EXERCISE 6. COMPARISON CHART

Using your own words, fill in the column under VORP to help you remember some of the basic concepts behind this system of justice. (You will fill in the rest of the chart after you have completed Readings 3 and 4.)

	VORP	Sentencing Circles	Conditional Sentences
role of victim			
role of offender			
role of community			
underlying principles			

| Vocabulary Study: Collocations

Collocations are words that belong together. They are words that native speakers of English automatically use together. For example, what word do you use after the adjective _blond_? Many native speakers of English automatically add the word _hair_ to create the phrase _blond hair_. These two words naturally fit together. (Some words are not usually combined with other words. For example, the phrase _blond house_ sounds unusual.)

Many verbs and nouns have a strong collocational relationship in English. That is, they fit together naturally. For example, when native English speakers read or hear the verb _to inflict_ (which is used in Reading 2), many will automatically add the noun _pain_. This creates the phrase _to inflict pain_. It is important to be aware of and learn which words fit together in English so that when you speak or write, your meaning is communicated clearly and the flow of the language sounds natural.

EXERCISE 7. SCANNING FOR COLLOCATIONS

Scan Reading 2, "A Fable for Our Time," to discover some of the verb–noun collocations of English. Match each verb in column A with its collocation in column B.

A		B	
1.	*to break*	a)	a crime
2.	*to commit*	b)	a reputation
3.	*to be charged with*	c)	a scream
4.	*to mull over*	d)	a law
5.	*to ruin*	e)	amends
6.	*to stifle*	f)	a loan
7.	*to meet*	g)	a crime
8.	*to take*	h)	responsibility
9.	*to secure*	i)	a need
10.	*to make*	j)	a question
11.	*to take on*	k)	damage
12.	*to take*	l)	control
13.	*to repair*	m)	a job

On a separate sheet of paper, use the ideas in "A Fable for Our Time" to write sentences of your own that incorporate these collocations.

EXERCISE 8. VOCABULARY IN CONTEXT

For each of the underlined words in the following sentences, choose the most suitable definition from the list on page 90. Write the letter of the word in the space provided.

> **Example:** At that point, Dave and Elaine enter a criminal justice system with the hopes of experiencing accountability, (e) justice, and healing.

1. Dave becomes isolated and alienated (   ) from his friends and community as they discover what has happened.

2. His attorney (   ) begins the preparations for the court proceedings.

3. Dave begins to contemplate (   ) the humiliation (   ) and violence that exist within prison walls.

4. Throughout this process, Elaine has been ignored (   ) and left out.

5. Elaine, furious (   ) with the lack of respect offered her throughout this ordeal, (   ) jumps up from her chair and yells, "He doesn't know what he has done to me. He needs to know what he has done!"

6. Instead of broken laws and blame, (   ) justice involves broken people and relationships that need to be repaired.

7. The judge postpones (   ) sentencing (   ) until Dave and Elaine have a chance to talk to each other.

8. The wind presented Dave and Elaine with an option for justice that would have left them both alienated, excluded, (   ) and angry.

Definitions:

a) a very difficult or painful situation

b) to think about

c) very angry

d) to feel alone for a long time

e) accepting responsibility for one's own actions

f) not included

g) the feeling that one's position in life is very low

h) giving a penalty for a crime

i) saying that someone has done something wrong

j) to put off until a later time

k) not included

l) lawyer

EXERCISE 9. CRITICAL ANALYSIS

Discuss the following questions with your classmates.

1. The writer of "A Fable for Our Time" works with VORP. To what extent is bias evident in her article?

2. To what extent do you agree with Toews's bias?

3. When Dave went to VORP, he had the opportunity to talk about the circumstances in his life around the time of his offence. To what extent should an offender's circumstances be considered after he or she commits a crime?

4. In the poem "Prison," the writer says that prison makes people "mentally crippled" because it takes responsibility away from them. In "A Fable for Our Time," Dave has the opportunity to take responsibility for his actions. Why is the idea of responsibility so important to the writers of these two texts?

EXERCISE 10. WRITING

1. Retell the story of "The Sun and the Wind" in your own words.

2. Do you know of another fable that teaches a lesson similar to that of "The Sun and the Wind"? Write the story in as much detail as you can. Share it with your classmates.

3. Using the descriptions offered by Toews, explain the differences between court proceedings and VORP.

Readings 3 and 4 describe two different approaches to sentencing individuals who have committed crimes. One of these approaches is the sentencing circle and the other is the implementation of conditional sentences. Half of your class should focus on Reading 3 and the related exercises, and half of your class should focus on Reading 4 and the related exercises.

After you have finished the exercises, you will explain the information and ideas from your reading to a partner who has not read your article.

Reading 3—*14-Year-Old Finds Alternative to Court in Sentencing Circle*

EXERCISE 11. PRE-READING DISCUSSION

Choose a leader from among your classmates who are reading "14-Year-Old Finds Alternative to Court in Sentencing Circle." The leader should lead a brief discussion of the pre-reading questions provided below.

1. A 14-year-old girl confronts another girl at school who has been harassing her younger sister. This starts a fight, and the other girl gets hurt. In your opinion, who should determine the punishment for the girl who initiated the fight?

2. In your opinion, what should the consequences be for the girl who initiated the fight?

14-Year-Old Finds Alternative to Court in Sentencing Circle

Face-to-face acknowledgment, handshake, even shame may help girl to stay out of trouble in the future, Anthony Reinhart writes.

[1]   In late afternoon on a grey winter day, the corridors of the Etobicoke Civic Centre seem like the last place to find a bright idea.

[2]   Drab and dim, the sixties-era municipal building near Highway 427 and Burnhamthorpe Road exudes just a touch more charm than a nursing home stricken with the Norwalk virus.

[3]   Still, to the 14-year-old girl awaiting her fate in Committee Room 1, it's far better than the courthouse. The girl is here to answer to an assault charge, but in a process that will spare her a criminal record, guilty though she is.

[4]   It's called a sentencing circle, and by the time it's over in a couple of hours, the girl will have owned up to her actions, albeit grudgingly, apologized to her victim face to face, and perhaps been shamed enough by the proceedings to keep her away from committing crime in the future.

[5]   Her chances look good, if she's anything like the hundreds of young offenders who have attended similar sessions as an alternative to court trials since they began in Scarborough two years ago as a way to reduce backlogs in the youth courts.

[6]   The sessions are run by a program called PACT, which stands for participation, acknowledgment, commitment and transformation. Participants, usually first-time offenders charged with relatively minor crimes, admit guilt and agree, in consultation with their victims, to atone for their actions, usually through apologies, counselling and community service.

[7]   While statistics show that 43 per cent of young offenders in Canada typically offend again within a year, PACT claims a repeat-offence rate of just 5 per cent.

[8]   And at $500 per session, funded by private donations, the program comes cheaper than a $2,000 court case, which can lead in turn to even more expensive consequences, such as time in custody.

[9]   PACT's success, hailed by the assistant Crown attorney who runs Scarborough's youth court, led to the program's expansion to Etobicoke just before Christmas.

[10]   On its face, the program appears soft compared with a court hearing. It takes place in a carpeted meeting room, with chairs arranged in a circle for the accused, the victim, their families and the two casually dressed PACT officials who conduct the session, a far cry from the courtroom, with its prisoner's box, imposing judge's bench and lawyers' tables on opposing sides.

[11]   But before long, you see that PACT probably works for that very reason: It's up close and personal, and there's nowhere to hide.

[12]   In this case, the girl was charged last fall after she went to a school to confront another girl for harassing her little sister.

[13]   Heated words led to a fight that left the victim, slightly younger, with minor leg injuries.

[14]   As the session begins, volunteer facilitator Neil Webster lays out the ground rules, all of which are broken at some point: "One person speaks at a time. No interrupting. 'I don't know' is not an acceptable answer, unless it's the absolute truth."

[15]   The accused goes first, offering an account that paints her actions as neutral at best.

[16]   "I told her to stay away from my sister. Then her friends came and everybody came," she says, flanked by the same sister, their mother and a family friend.

[17]   "I got pushed, I fell on her, I ripped my pants; she pulled my hair. I fell on [the victim] and we both got hurt."

[18]   Visibly angered, the victim, clearly no shrinking violet, offers a different version.

[19]   "Before we fell to the ground, she kicked me," she says, seated next to her mother. "Then everybody started pushing and we fell to the ground."

[20]   For the rest of the session, Mr. Webster and a fellow PACT worker nudge the two girls closer to agreement on the facts, and the accused, in particular, toward accountability for instigating the fight.

[21]   The girls' mothers weigh in with their feelings of fear, concern and shame over what happened.

[22]   Still, when the time comes for the girl to make restitution, she only offers to "stay away from her, and not to have any conversation with her."

[23]   Mr. Webster is not impressed: "I think they're going to want more than that, and I think more than that is appropriate," he says.

[24]   The victim's mother suggests anger-management counselling and written apologies to her daughter and to the school where the fight took place.

[25]   The accused girl, bolstered by her own mother, relents. An agreement is printed out, the girl signs it and the session ends.

[26]   When Mr. Webster suggests a handshake, the two girls lean forward in their chairs and briefly clasp hands.

[27]   Their smiles are brief and lukewarm, but there are smiles nonetheless.

[28]   As the girls and their families rise to leave, PACT co-founder Dave Lockett, a Toronto business-man, is not completely convinced of the girl's remorse.

[29]   Mr. Lockett, who runs a transportation company, has seen far more contrition at previous sessions, and says this girl came dangerously close to having her case handed back to the courts.

[30]   Still, PACT's track record, after more than 500 cases in Scarborough, gives him encouragement.

[31]   "I firmly believe this offender will come out of this a hell of a lot better" than she would have from court, he says, because she got to see how her actions affected others, and because the victim had a say in the consequences.

[32]   And that's likely to stick with her far longer than anything a brief, sterile hearing before a judge would have offered.

Source: "14-year-old finds alternative to court in sentencing circle" Reinhart, Anthony. *The Globe and Mail* [Toronto, Ont]
20 Jan 2004: A.10

EXERCISE 12. COMPREHENSION CHECK

1. In a one-line statement before beginning the article, the author writes, "Face-to-face acknowledgment, handshake, even shame may help girl to stay out of trouble in the future." What is shame? How can it help someone stay out of trouble?

_____

2. The girl has been charged with assault. What does that mean?

_____

3. Why did officials in Scarborough, Ontario, begin to use sentencing circles?

_____

4. Based on the details of this story, summarize how the sentencing circle works. Be sure to use your own words.

_____

_____

5. If the sentencing circle process is successful, will the girl have a criminal record? Why is this important?

_____

_____

6. If the sentencing circle is not successful, what will happen to the girl who initiated the fight?

_____

_____

7. Does the author of the article believe that the sentencing circle is a "soft" form of justice? Support your response to this question with evidence from the text.

_____

_____

EXERCISE 13. VOCABULARY IN CONTEXT

In groups of three, discuss any important words in this reading that are unfamiliar.

EXERCISE 14. MAKING COMPARISONS

Fill in the chart in Exercise 6 on page 88 with information on sentencing circles.

EXERCISE 15. DISCUSSION

In groups of three or four, discuss your answers for the Comprehension Check and check the information that you have added to the chart. Then discuss the following questions.

1. What is your opinion of the consequence for the girl who initiated the fight?

2. What is your opinion of the process involved in sentencing circles?

EXERCISE 16. SHARING YOUR INFORMATION

Your instructor will now pair you with one of your classmates who has not read "14-Year-Old Finds Alternative to Court in Sentencing Circle." Using what you have learned from the article, explain in as much depth as you can how a sentencing circle works.

⎯⎯| **Reading 4**—*Conditional Sentences* |⎯⎯

EXERCISE 17. PRE-READING DISCUSSION

Choose a leader from among your classmates who are reading "Conditional Sentences." The leader should lead a brief discussion of the following pre-reading questions.

1. What is the meaning of the word *condition*? Brainstorm examples of how this word could be used in a variety of contexts.

2. Before reading the passage from beginning to end, read the title and the subheadings to get a sense of the overall direction of this text. What does the passage discuss?

3. In the context of the justice system, what do you think a "conditional sentence" is?

Conditional Sentences

What is a conditional sentence?

[1]   When a court finds a person guilty of a crime, the person may be sentenced to time in prison or, in certain circumstances, may be allowed to serve the sentence in the community. This is called a conditional sentence.

[2]   During a conditional sentence, the offender is supervised and must follow the rules set by the judge or risk going to prison.

When is a conditional sentence possible?

[3]   A judge can give an offender a conditional sentence when:

- the *Criminal Code*[1] does not set a minimum prison term for the offence;
- the judge decides that the sentence should be less than two years;
- the judge setting the sentence is convinced that allowing the offender to remain in the community is not a danger to the public; and
- the judge is convinced that a conditional sentence is consistent with the purposes and principles of sentencing set out in the *Criminal Code*.

The judge has the authority to decide on the appropriate punishment for the offender and could decide to send an offender to prison even if a conditional sentence is possible.

What types of conditions can a judge set?

[4]   All conditional sentences have the following conditions. The offender must:

- keep the peace and be of good behaviour;
- go to court when required;
- report to a criminal justice system supervisor regularly;
- stay in the area under the court's authority and get written permission to travel outside this area; and
- tell the court or criminal justice system supervisor before moving or when changing jobs.

[5]   In addition to these conditions, a judge can tailor the conditions to the needs of the offender, the victim and the community by setting other conditions that the offender has to follow. For example, a judge might require the offender to:

- pay the victim restitution;
- make other reparations to the victim or to the community;

---

[1] The Canadian *Criminal Code* lists most of the actions or behaviours that are considered crimes by the Government of Canada.

- participate in a treatment program (for example an alcohol, drug or anger management program);
- provide support for any dependents (such as a child or spouse);
- do up to 240 hours of community service work; or
- respect a curfew, for instance by staying at home except to go to work or to approved activities, such as a treatment program or community service.

As well, a judge could prohibit an offender from:

- using alcohol or drugs, and
- possessing a gun, rifle or other weapon.

[6] The Supreme Court of Canada decided several cases involving conditional sentencing. The Court has made it clear that conditional sentences should generally include punitive conditions that restrict an offender's liberty, such as house arrest. The Court has said that a conditional sentence is a punishment, which also promotes a sense of responsibility in the offender and has the objectives of rehabilitation and reparation to the victim and the community.

What happens if the offender does not follow the conditions in the sentence?

[7] A conditional sentence is a prison term that the offender is allowed to serve in the community, according to the set conditions. If the offender does not follow the conditions, he or she will be brought back to court and the judge can order the offender to serve the rest of the sentence in prison.

Can a victim of the crime have a say in court?

[8] Yes. A victim can prepare a victim impact statement, describing the harm done and the loss suffered. Although the victim impact statement should not include the victim's views on a punishment, it may help the judge to decide on appropriate conditions to include in a conditional sentence, if a conditional sentence is being considered.

[9] A judge must take a victim impact statement into account when deciding on the appropriate punishment for an offender.

Source: Department of Justice Canada, Policy Centre for Victim Issues. "Conditional Sentences." Government of Canada, http://dsp-psd.pwgsc.gc.ca/Collection/J2-197-2001E.pdf, retrieved 5 October 2011.

EXERCISE 18. COMPREHENSION CHECK

1. The first two paragraphs explain what a conditional sentence is. In your own words, what is a conditional sentence?

_____

2. What do you think is meant by "house arrest" in paragraph 6?

_____

3. Based on the details of this reading, summarize how conditional sentencing works. Be sure to use your own words.

_____

_____

4. If an offender does not follow the requirements set out in a conditional sentence, what could the consequences be?

_____

_____

5. What is the author's position on conditional sentences? In other words, does the author support or not support the use of conditional sentences? Support your response to this question with evidence from the text.

_____

_____

EXERCISE 19. VOCABULARY IN CONTEXT

In groups of three, discuss any important words in "Conditional Sentences" that are unfamiliar.

EXERCISE 20. MAKING COMPARISONS

Fill in the chart in Exercise 6 on page 88 with information on conditional sentences.

EXERCISE 21. DISCUSSION

In groups of three or four, discuss your answers for Exercise 18 and check the information that you have added to the chart. Then discuss the following questions.

1. The use of conditional sentences in Canada is controversial. Why do you think they are controversial?

2. Do you believe there are situations in which conditional sentences are appropriate instead of prison sentences? Be prepared to explain your answer.

EXERCISE 22. SHARING INFORMATION

Your instructor will now pair you with one of your classmates who has not read "Conditional Sentences." Using what you have learned from the article, explain in as much depth as you can how a conditional sentence works.

EXERCISE 23. APPLYING WHAT YOU HAVE LEARNED

Read the following case studies. Decide which approach to justice (i.e., use of the court system resulting in a prison sentence, a mediation system like VORP, a sentencing circle, or the court system resulting in a conditional sentence) you believe is the most appropriate for addressing each situation. Be prepared to explain your point of view.

1. A 19-year-old female is caught shoplifting a pair of pants and a sweater from a local store. The woman has been caught shoplifting clothing once before when she was 16.

2. A 24-year-old male is charged after speeding in his car through a school zone and hitting a child who was crossing the road. The driver was going 15 kilometres over the speed limit. After spending a little time in the hospital, the child fully recovered. The driver has no previous speeding tickets and has been in no other accidents.

⊣ **Reading 5**—*Teaching Children How to Fight* ⊢

EXERCISE 24. PRE-READING DISCUSSION

1. How did you learn how to resolve conflict as a child?

2. When you were in your early years at school, what methods did teachers use to resolve disputes between students?

The following article by Ron Kraybill discusses the ways in which parents and teachers can help children learn "how to fight."

⊣ Teaching Children How to Fight ⊢

[1]   How adults respond to disagreement among children profoundly shapes the attitudes and skills which children will bring to conflict in later years. Consider a typical feud between Johnny and Susie:

[2]   Daddy, who is reading the newspaper, notes that a storm is brewing in the playroom over who gets to play with the blocks. The storm gets noisier, and finally, when several thumps and a thud signify sharp escalation, Daddy rushes to intervene. "Johnny, Susie, what's going on in here?" he inquires sharply. Each child responds with an accusing tale of woe. Daddy reflects for a moment—after all, he wants to be fair and wise—and then instructs: "OK, each of you will get your turn to play with the blocks. Johnny, you may play first; Susie, you go find something else to do for 10 minutes. Then, Susie, when the big hand on the clock gets up to the "nine" you can come and play with the blocks for awhile." Relieved to have peace restored, Daddy returns to his newspaper.

[3]   What's wrong with this intervention? After all, Daddy has terminated the feud, and has provided a fair, impartial, and practical solution!

[4]   The problem is that *Daddy* has taken responsibility for resolution on *his* shoulders. The children are learning that the way to solve conflict is to go to Daddy, or someone bigger and stronger than you, who imposes an answer. No need for the parties to a dispute to take responsibility for listening to each other, expressing their own wishes in a helpful fashion, or jointly attempting to find a solution that is acceptable to both.

[5]   In our society, Johnny and Susie have grown up, but they still believe the way to solve conflicts is to go to someone bigger and stronger who imposes a solution. When neighbors have a dispute, do they get together and talk things through? Often not. Increasingly, Americans hire an attorney and go before a judge, a "big Daddy in black" who will render a decision.

[6]   Parents and teachers can teach children to develop skills and be responsible for resolving many of their own disputes. A veteran schoolteacher in Oregon told me several years ago how she teaches children that *they* are accountable for working out differences:

[7]   Johnny and Susie are squabbling, so teacher intervenes—someone needs to break the cycle of escalating anger. Then, however, teacher instructs the children, "I want each of you to make a request of the other child, or say what you would like the other child to do." She would give the children a minute to prepare their requests, or even help them to prepare if necessary. But when the children were ready, they stated their requests *directly to the other child.*

[8]   The teacher's second instruction then was, "Now, I want each to say or do something in response that will help solve this or help make you friendly again." As before, she gave the children a minute to prepare their response, or helped them individually if necessary. But again, when ready, the children responded directly to each other.

When my brother hit me, *by Emily Hofer*

[9]   The teacher reported that the first time or two children experienced this process, they reacted with puzzlement and required considerable coaching. Most children have never experienced anything like this before: One of my friends was amused by his five-year-old daughter, who burst out laughing in the middle of her tears when he said he'd like her to tell her younger brothers what she wants them to do that will make her and them happy. This seemed like an interesting game to Katie! Children often react with surprise, but quickly master this procedure. My Oregon teacher friend found that soon little coaching on her part was necessary and before long she would observe children using the same procedure on their own on the playground.

[10]   If adults focus their authority on guiding children through a process of creating their *own* solutions to conflict, children readily learn conflict management skills of their own. When adults simply impose solutions on children, we deprive them of the primary learning laboratory for developing lifelong skills in peacemaking which every human needs for successful relationships. How we solve children's conflicts profoundly molds how the world conflicts of tomorrow will be resolved.

Source: R. Kraybill, "Teaching Children How to Fight". *Conciliation Quarterly 4,* 1 (March 1985): 8–9. © Mennonite Conciliation Service, Akron, PA.

EXERCISE 25. COMPREHENSION CHECK

1. State the writer's main idea in your own words.

   _____

   _____

2. How does the father described in the article resolve the dispute between the two children?

   _____

   _____

3. How is the way in which the dispute in paragraph 2 was settled similar to the way in which many adults resolve their disputes?

   _____

   _____

4. Outline the steps in paragraphs 7 and 8 that the teacher uses to settle an argument between two of her students.

   _____

   _____

5. What is the crucial difference between the ways in which the teacher and the father handled the disputes?

   _____

   _____

6. In the author's opinion, whose method was better, the father's or the teacher's? Why?

   _____

   _____

EXERCISE 26. VOCABULARY IN CONTEXT

In this exercise, you are given six sentences from the article, with one or more words underlined in each. Choose the best meaning for each word or phrase from the list of definitions.

1. "The storm gets noisier, and finally, when several thumps and a thud signify sharp escalation, Daddy rushes to intervene." (paragraph 2)

   escalation
   a) rapid development
   b) going out
   c) decreasing disagreement

   to intervene
   a) to choose a side
   b) to take action
   c) to tell someone to stop

2. "After all, Daddy has terminated the <u>feud</u>, and has provided a fair, <u>impartial</u>, and practical solution!" (paragraph 3)

feud
a) continuing argument
b) physical fight
c) problem

impartial
a) subjective
b) objective
c) self-interested

Note: The common meaning of *feud* is a bitter, prolonged, and often violent quarrel between families or clans.

3. "The children are learning that the way to solve conflict is to go to Daddy, or someone bigger and stronger than you, who <u>imposes</u> an answer." (paragraph 4)

a) makes something happen based on authority
b) suggests gently
c) offers

4. "No need for the <u>parties</u> to <u>a dispute</u> to take responsibility for listening to each other, expressing their own wishes in a helpful fashion, or jointly attempting to find a solution that is acceptable to both." (paragraph 4)

parties
a) good times
b) judges
c) people or groups

a dispute
a) a disruption
b) a final agreement
c) a disagreement

5. "Johnny and Susie are <u>squabbling</u>, so teacher intervenes—someone needs to break the <u>cycle</u> of escalating anger." (paragraph 7)

squabbling
a) pushing
b) arguing
c) hitting

cycle
a) a series that repeats itself
b) a round shape
c) a line

6. "If adults focus their <u>authority</u> on guiding children through a process of creating their *own* solutions to conflict, children readily learn conflict management skills of their own." (paragraph 10)

a) energy
b) time
c) power

EXERCISE 27. VOCABULARY EXERCISE

One way to remember new words is to organize them graphically. You can organize them in any way you like; the main thing is that your graph should show the relationships that you see between the meanings of the words.

A sample diagram for the words from Exercise 8 is shown below.

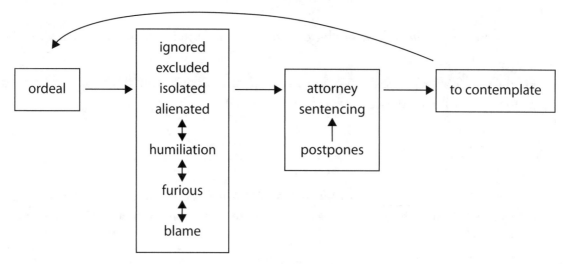

Organize the words in the list below into a diagram that will help you to remember the meanings of the words.

impartial	*parties*	*to impose*
authority	*intervention*	*cycle of escalating anger*
dispute	*feud*	*squabbling*

When you have finished your diagram, compare it with those of other students. Explain why you designed it the way you did.

Note: This exercise is based on the exercise "Charting Words" suggested by John Morgan and Mario Rinvolucri in *Vocabulary* (Oxford University Press, 1986) 80–81.

EXERCISE 28. CRITICAL ANALYSIS

Discuss the following questions with your classmates.

1. According to the author of "Teaching Children How to Fight," "When adults simply impose solutions on children, we deprive them of the primary learning laboratory for developing lifelong skills in peacemaking." (paragraph 10) To what extent do you agree with this statement?

2. The author maintains that it is best for the people involved in a dispute to find their own solutions. Are there ever times when someone "bigger and stronger" is needed to intervene in disputes? In which situations?

3. The author describes a judge in the legal system as "a big Daddy in black." (paragraph 5) To what extent do the alternative sentencing systems that you have discussed in this chapter (i.e., VORP, sentencing circles, conditional sentences) rely on "a big Daddy"?

Writing

Comparison

In many situations, an effective way of making a point is to show similarities and differences between two or more ideas or objects. One common reason for making a comparison is to show that one thing is superior to another.

The author of "Teaching Children How to Fight" uses a comparison to help the reader understand his main point that adults should help children learn how to settle their own disputes. He compares two situations in which adults intervene in conflicts. His two situations, or examples, are chosen carefully in that they demonstrate two very different ways of intervening in conflicts between children.

EXERCISE 29. SUMMARIZING MAIN IDEAS

To fully understand the organization of the author's comparison, summarize the main idea of each paragraph in a phrase of three to six words.

Paragraph 1:

General introduction—adults shape children's perspectives on conflict.

Paragraph 2:

Example 1— _____

Paragraph 3:

_____

Paragraph 4:

_____

Paragraph 5:

_____

Paragraph 6:

_____

Paragraph 7:

Example 2— _____

Paragraph 8:

_____

Paragraph 9:

_____

Paragraph 10:

_____

Notice that after the author has given each example he also provides an analysis of the weakness or strength demonstrated in the example. A simple outline of his article might look like the following.

> **Main idea**
>
> Example 1 + Analysis
>
> **Transition** to second example: "Parents and teachers can teach children to develop skills and be responsible for resolving many of their own disputes."
>
> Example 2 + Analysis
>
> **Conclusion**

The author's analysis is integrated into the comparison so that by the time the reader gets to the conclusion, he or she can already predict what the author's conclusion will be.

Notice, too, how the author restates his main idea just before he begins his second example, not only to provide a transition between the two examples, but to remind the reader of his main point.

Organizational Patterns for Comparison

In general, there are two ways of organizing a text in which a comparison is made. These are shown below.

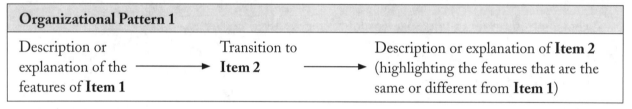

Organizational Pattern 1		
Description or explanation of the features of **Item 1**	Transition to **Item 2**	Description or explanation of **Item 2** (highlighting the features that are the same or different from **Item 1**)

Organizational Pattern 2		
Comparison of one feature of **Items 1 and 2**	Comparison of another feature of **Items 1 and 2**	Comparison of another feature of **Items 1 and 2**

The author of "Teaching Children How to Fight" uses the first organizational pattern, discussing one example fully and then moving on to another.

EXERCISE 30. ANALYSIS

In "A Fable for Our Time," the writer uses a complex comparison structure to make her point that programs such as the Victim Offender Reconciliation Programs (VORP) offer more satisfying *processes* and *outcomes* than does the legal system.

1. Skim through "A Fable for Our Time." Which organizational pattern does the writer use for her comparison?

_____

2. Find the paragraph or paragraphs that act as a transition between Toews's discussion of the legal system and her discussion of VORP. What is the specific purpose of this transition?

_____

3. Underline the following sentence structure within the transition: Instead of X, Y.

4. Examine paragraphs 42 and 43 of "A Fable for Our Time." How does Toews conclude her article?

Transitional Phrases for Comparison

The authors of "Teaching Children How to Fight" and "A Fable for Our Time" use few transitional phrases in making their comparisons. Instead, they carefully structure their texts so that the comparisons are clear. However, a variety of transitional words and phrases can be used to show that a comparison is being made.

To Show Differences	To Show Similarities
Instead of X, Y	Just like X, Y
Unlike X, Y	Like X, Y
X. However, Y	X. Likewise, Y
X. On the other hand, Y	X. Similarly, Y
In contrast, Y	Both X and Y
To compare, Y	

EXERCISE 31. WRITING

Complete *one* of the following assignments.

1. In an essay, compare two of the approaches to justice about which you have read in this chapter.

   or

2. In an essay, compare one of the approaches to justice described in this chapter with another approach to justice with which you are familiar.

In this essay, you will select and integrate information from at least one of the readings in this chapter. In other words, you will paraphrase some of what you have read. Therefore, before you begin to write, read the section below.

Paraphrasing

To paraphrase is to take an idea or a fact that someone else has expressed and put it into your own words. In a second language, paraphrasing can be quite difficult since it requires changes to sentence structures and vocabulary. An idea is not expressed in your own words if the vocabulary or sentence structure is copied from the original source.

Example:	Original	"If adults focus their authority on guiding children through a process of creating their *own* solutions to conflict, children readily learn conflict management skills of their own."
	Faulty paraphrase	When adults focus on leading children through a process in which they create their own solutions to problems, children learn to manage their own conflict.

Faulty paraphrase	Children learn conflict management skills if adults focus on guiding them through a process of creating solutions to conflict.
Adequate paraphrase	Adults can help children learn to settle their disputes themselves.

Notice that in the two faulty paraphrases, the basic sentence structure of the original is retained. In a paraphrased text, both the vocabulary and the sentence structure should be different from the original.

Although paraphrasing can be very challenging, you do have the ability to paraphrase. At the beginning of this chapter, you paraphrased the ideas from the poem "Prison," and earlier in this chapter, you paraphrased the information in an article for your classmates.

EXERCISE 32. PARAPHRASING (A)

Compare sentences (a) to (e) with the original excerpts from "A Fable for Our Time" shown below. Put a check mark beside the most adequate paraphrases.

1. Original excerpt: "The wind presented Dave and Elaine with an option for justice that would have left them both alienated, excluded, and angry. Both would have continued to live in worlds of fear and pain: Dave in a world defined by punishment and Elaine in a private world of insecurity and loss."

_____ a) The legal system presented Dave and Elaine with an option for justice that would have left them both alienated, excluded, and angry.

_____ b) The traditional legal system gave Dave and Elaine an option for justice that left them feeling alienated, excluded, and angry. If they had experienced only the legal system, they both would have lived in worlds of fear and pain.

_____ c) If Dave and Elaine had experienced only the traditional justice system, they both would have felt isolated and angry.

_____ d) If Dave and Elaine had experienced only the traditional justice system, they would both have continued to live in worlds of fear and pain.

_____ e) After experiencing the traditional justice system, Dave and Elaine were both left with negative feelings. Both felt angry and isolated from their communities.

2. Original excerpt: "Both Dave and Elaine need a process which will help them work toward understanding, responsibility, and healing. Instead of broken laws and blame, justice involves broken people and relationships that need to be repaired."

_____ a) In "A Fable for Our Time," both parties needed a process that would help them work toward understanding, responsibility, and healing. Justice involves broken people and relationships that should be mended.

_____ b) In "A Fable for Our Time," both parties needed a process that would help them rebuild their own lives and restore the relationship that had been broken.

_____ c) Dave and Elaine require a process that will allow them to understand, take responsibility, and heal themselves.

_____ d) In situations where justice has not been served, for example, in the case of Dave and Elaine, individuals need a process that allows them to understand what has happened, to take responsibility, and to heal themselves.

_____ e) Justice involves hurting people and relationships that need to be fixed instead of a focus on broken laws and blame.

Plagiarizing

Plagiarizing is the act of taking another person's words or ideas and not giving that person credit. In other words, it is a type of theft—intellectual theft. In some of the sentences in the last exercise, strings of words were taken from the author of "A Fable for Our Time." Quotation marks were not used to show that these strings of words came from the original text. This is considered plagiarism.

Plagiarism is a very serious offence. A student who plagiarizes may be given a failing grade on a paper or in a course or, in the most serious cases, may be expelled from a university or college. Ask your instructor how plagiarism is defined at your institution and what the consequences are.

To avoid plagiarism when you are paraphrasing, change the sentence structure and vocabulary from the original text. (You must also give the source from which you take information; the procedures for doing this will be discussed in detail in Chapter 10.)

EXERCISE 33. PARAPHRASING (B)

Paraphrase the following excerpt from "Teaching Children How to Fight."

> "When adults simply impose solutions on children, we deprive them of the primary learning laboratory for developing lifelong skills in peacemaking which every human needs for successful relationships. How we solve children's conflicts profoundly molds how the world conflicts of tomorrow will be resolved."

After You Write the Essay

After you have completed the first draft of your essay about justice, spend some time revising your essay. The following questions will assist you:

1. Does your thesis statement express the main idea of your essay?

2. Does each paragraph focus on an idea that is related to the main idea or thesis statement?

3. Is each supporting idea developed in enough depth that your reader will understand your point?

4. Are ideas from other sources adequately paraphrased?

5. Does the conclusion make a logical and clear summary statement? Will it be satisfying for the reader?

CHAPTER 5

Crossing Cultures: The Challenge of Adjustment

Introduction

> Culture regulates our lives at every turn. From the time we are born until we die there is, whether we are conscious of it or not, constant pressure upon us to follow certain types of behavior that others have created for us.
>
> —*Clyde Kluckhohn*

Since we live our own culture daily, we become as comfortable in it as fish in water. We know our culture intrinsically. When we leave our own culture and go to another for a while, it doesn't matter how excited we are to leave our country, we find it difficult to understand and adjust to this different culture and the behaviour of the people. When we are asked about our own culture, we often find it very difficult to answer. What then are the challenges we face in crossing to another culture? And what can we do to adjust well?

In this chapter you will read about the stages of adjustment, which describe the ideas of Pierre Casse, a world-renowned writer on cross-cultural training. You will also read a personal story of one person's immigration to Canada. Finally, in "Seeing Through the Rules" you will learn about the cultural values of Canada's Aboriginal people.

The main writing task in this chapter is an essay about the process of adjusting to a new country and a different culture.

Reading 1—*Culture Shock and the Stages of Adaptation*

(mid)

EXERCISE 1. PRE-READING DISCUSSION

Discuss the following questions before you read.

1. When we visit another culture or country, we generally have expectations of what it will be like. What did you expect before you came to Canada?

2. What surprises did you encounter in Canada?

3. How did you adapt to your new experiences?

4. What would newcomers not understand or have difficulty adapting to in your country?

Taking Notes from Readings

When taking notes from a reading, you are really focusing on the reading process. It is essential to concentrate on main ideas and supporting details. Taking notes helps you to define the topic, note the important points and supporting details, remember the material much more accurately, and organize the main ideas or points in the reading.

One way to take notes on a reading is by asking and then answering questions. This process helps you better understand the text. Exercise 2 provides a model for this process.

EXERCISE 2. NOTE-TAKING

Take notes as you read the following piece, "Culture Shock and the Stages of Adaptation," by answering the following questions.

Paragraph 1:   What do people have to do when they travel to another country?

Paragraph 2:   What is culture shock? What are the causes and effects?

Paragraph 3:   What are the general stages of culture shock according to anthropologists?

Paragraph 4:   What does Pierre Casse say is important about culture shock?

Paragraph 5:   Summarize Casse's four stages in paragraphs 5 to 10.

Culture Shock and the Stages of Adaption

[1]   Every person has a culture that has been acquired from his or her own cultural group. People tend to regard their own culture as correct and often use its standards to judge those from other cultures. Each society tries to pass its culture on to its children. When someone travels to another country and encounters people from the new culture, he or she must immediately make adjustments to function well in that society; people pass through a number of stages as they try to adjust.

[2]   Problems of personal adjustment to a foreign environment are referred to as "culture shock," a common experience for a person learning a second language in a new culture, for instance. It is usually brought on by the sudden loss of familiar surroundings. The effect that culture shock has on an individual ranges from mild irritability to deep psychological panic and crisis. Culture shock is associated with feelings of estrangement, anger, hostility, indecision, frustration, unhappiness, loneliness, homesickness, and even physical illness. The person undergoing culture shock views this new world out of resentment and alternates between being angry with others for not understanding and being filled with self-pity.

[3]   Anthropologists agree that individuals adjusting to a new culture pass through several stages: Stage 1 (also known as the honeymoon stage) is the stage of happiness or euphoria over the newness of the surroundings. Stage 2, culture shock, emerges as the individual begins to feel more and more cultural differences. In this stage the individual is deeply disenchanted and in a state of crisis. In stage 3 the person begins, slowly but surely, to accept and adjust to the differences in thinking and feeling that surround him or her. The person then begins to become empathic with those in the new culture. Stage 4 represents recovery, either adaptation or assimilation. In this stage the person feels confident in the new person he or she has become. This last stage is re-entry into the new culture.

[4]   Pierre Casse (1981) has provided a model of the culture-shock process, summarized in the diagram "The Culture-Shock Process," shown on page 111. It is important to note that (a) the process is different for each person, and (b) people's reactions vary broadly. However, a pattern does emerge that should be considered when trying to adjust to another culture.

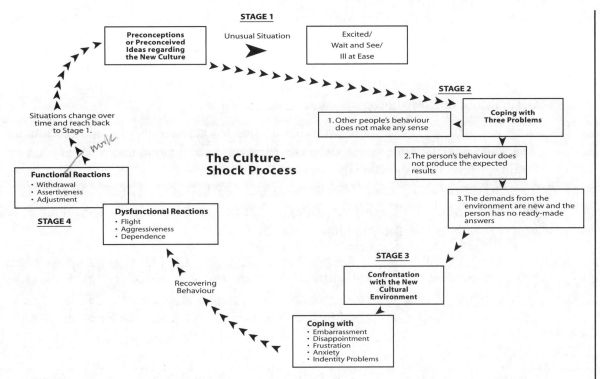

The Culture-Shock Process

STAGE 1

Preconceptions or Preconceived Ideas regarding the New Culture → Unusual Situation → Excited/ Wait and See/ Ill at Ease

Situations change over time and reach back to Stage 1.

STAGE 2

Coping with Three Problems

1. Other people's behaviour does not make any sense

2. The person's behaviour does not produce the expected results

3. The demands from the environment are new and the person has no ready-made answers

STAGE 4

Functional Reactions
• Withdrawal
• Assertiveness
• Adjustment

Dysfunctional Reactions
• Flight
• Aggressiveness
• Dependence

Recovering Behaviour

STAGE 3

Confrontation with the New Cultural Environment

Coping with
• Embarrassment
• Disappointment
• Frustration
• Anxiety
• Indentity Problems

Source: Pierre Casse, *Training for the Cross-Cultural Mind: A Handbook for Cross-Cultural Trainers and Consultants*, 2nd ed. (Society for Intercultural Education, Training and Research, 1981, p. 88).

[5]   Casse then presents four stages.

[6]   Stage 1: First contact. Preconceived ideas have a tremendous impact on the way people react when joining a new cultural environment. They always exist. The higher the expectations, the more the chance people have to be disappointed.

[7]   According to Casse, the first reactions have been identified by psychologists as spread on a spectrum that goes from being excited to ill at ease, with a sort of "wait and see" position in between. The reactions depend on the individuals, their personalities, and their cultural backgrounds. Someone can be at the beginning of the joining process and become very upset after a while. Another individual can remain cool and just curious during the entire adjustment. The very nature or expression of the excitement and uneasiness will also vary from one culture to another.

[8]   Stage 2: The first attempt to adjust. After the initial reactions, the individual makes his or her first attempt to adjust to the new cultural setting. This is the stage in which the person first experiences culture shock. He or she is immediately confronted with three problems:

1.   From the environment in the new culture, the person receives demands on his or her behaviour for which, in most cases, there is no ready-made answer. The situation can indeed be embarrassing since the person does not know what to say or how to respond effectively to the new cultural environment.

2.   The second problem is characterized by the fact that the person is now called upon to change existing behavioural patterns or create new ways of coping. However, the individual's

behaviour does not deliver what it was intended to do. In other words, the reactions from the environment are not quite as expected.

3. The third problem is related to the fact that the newcomer tries to observe and understand what is going on in the new social system he or she now belongs to, and it seems to the individual that what people do does not make any sense.

[9] Stage 3: Confrontations creating stress. In this stage the person slowly but surely begins to adjust. The confrontation with the new cultural setting can lead to emotional reactions that are by all means healthy. They signal to the individual the need for further action in order to "survive." These reactions can sometimes become too extreme and lead to what psychologists call an identity problem. The individual feels (very strongly) that he or she has to prove something not only to other people but also mainly to himself or herself.

[10] Stage 4: Coping with stress. In this stage, people who experience some kind of anxiety have three options to recover or control the situation. The positive or negative feelings the person experiences in each option depend on the degree to which the person enters into the situation. When a person is overinvolved, even healthy, functional reactions become dysfunctional. Also, even in each unadapted reaction, there is something positive. Nevertheless, the reactions are either functional or dysfunctional. Functional reactions include withdrawing, becoming assertive, or adjusting. Dysfunctional reactions include fleeing, becoming aggressive, or giving up. Casse (1981) reiterates the proviso that (a) what is good and functional for one individual may not be so for another, (b) the three options can be used alternatively, and (c) what is functional in one situation may be dysfunctional in another. (pp. 82–87)

[11] Finally, a person successfully moving from one stage to another has, one way or another, adapted to the new culture. They can once again feel positively about themselves and their environment, and participate effectively in society.

Source: Based on Pierre Casse, *Training for the Cross-Cultural Mind: A Handbook for Cross-Cultural Trainers and Consultants*, 2nd ed. (Society for Intercultural Education, Training and Research, 1981).

EXERCISE 3. COMPREHENSION CHECK

1. Who experiences culture shock?

_____

2. What causes culture shock?

_____

3. List the effects of culture shock.

_____

_____

4. The following four questions refer to Casse's stages as seen in the diagram.

   a) At what stage does a person manifest a set of emotional reactions that lead to an identity problem?

   _____

   b) The person behaves as he or she did in his country of origin, and this leads to problems. At what stage does this happen?

   _____

   c) What stage allows the person to adjust in a positive or negative way?

   _____

   d) Which of Casse's stages is the "honeymoon stage"? Why do you think it is called that?

   _____

5. Do you agree with the quotation from Clyde Kluckhohn at the beginning of the chapter? Explain your answer.

   _____

EXERCISE 4. USING YOUR KNOWLEDGE TO IDENTIFY THE STAGES

State which stage of culture shock is represented in each situation described below. Discuss your answers with a classmate.

1. Nathan, a Canadian, was so excited about living in Zimbabwe that he sent postcards home every day so that his friends and relatives would realize what a fantastic place he was living in. _____

2. Shon became so homesick that he felt he could not go to classes. Instead he stayed home, watched TV, and dreamed of going home and being with his family and friends. _____

3. Suzhen finally accepted that she had to invest more time and effort in improving her English to excel in her graduate classes at a university in Canada. _____

4. Paula and Fred are Canadians who took an assignment to teach abroad. They decided that it would be a friendly gesture to invite their fellow teachers to a potluck dinner. To their surprise their colleagues did not respond favourably to the invitation. Only one or two teachers came, but even they seemed uncomfortable, because in their country it was not customary to ask guests to bring food to a party.

   _____

5. After living in Brazil for a year and trying to fit in, Ruth, who is Canadian, shouted angrily at Richard (a Brazilian), who once again arrived at the tennis lesson without a tennis racquet and had to borrow hers. _____

6. Phyllis recently returned home to Canada from Sudan where she had taught English for three years. She is critical now of the narrow-mindedness and strange behaviour of the people in her hometown.

   _____

EXERCISE 5. VOCABULARY STUDY: PROVERBS

Here are some proverbs and sayings from Canadian culture. After reading and discussing them, add some on each subject from your own culture.

1. Time: Time is money.

   _____

2. Space: I don't want to step on her toes.

   _____

3. Absence: Absence makes the heart grow fonder.

   _____

4. Friendship: She wears her heart on her sleeve.

   _____

5. Putting off: A stitch in time saves nine.

   _____

6. Intimacy: Three is a crowd.

   _____

7. Agreements: Don't count your chickens before they're hatched.

   _____

EXERCISE 6. VOCABULARY IN CONTEXT

A. Write a synonym for each vocabulary word from Reading 1. You may need to look up the words in a dictionary or thesaurus.

   estrangement (paragraph 2) _____

   resentment (paragraph 2) _____

   euphoria (paragraph 3) _____

   disenchanted (paragraph 3) _____

   empathic (paragraph 3) _____

   assimilation (paragraph 3) _____

   functional (paragraph 10) _____

   dysfunctional (paragraph 10) _____

B. Complete each blank in the sentences below with one of the vocabulary words above.

   1. Jennifer worked very hard to win the special scholarship, and when she finally learned that she had won, she was in a state of _____.

   2. John was away from his family so often because of job obligations that he sometimes had feelings of _____ from them when he attended special events at his children's schools.

3. Ken felt _____ toward a colleague who he thought did not do his share of the work.

4. When the computer was no longer _____, Sharon decided it was time to buy a new one.

5. After living in the country for six years, Sarah knew the language and the way things worked. Now she wanted to become a citizen because, for her, _____ had occurred.

6. After being away from her friends and family for three months, Michiko found herself depressed and unhappy in her new country. She did not want to leave her apartment or attend classes. She had become _____.

7. Diogo hoped that the teacher would be _____ when she learned the reason for his absence from the test.

8. After Serge had been in Canada most of the cold winter, he became _____ _____ with living and holidaying in this country.

Exercise 7. Vocabulary Words Describing a State

The reading "Culture Shock and the Stages of Adjustment" contains many words that describe a positive or negative psychological state. Find the words in the reading that describe positive and negative states. List them under the appropriate headings.

> **Example:** Positive   Negative
>   empathic   panic

Exercise 8. Writing

1. Using the words you identified in Exercise 7, write a description of a person you know who has crossed cultures and experienced culture shock. Give the effects of positive or negative behaviour that you have observed.

2. Summarize Reading 1 using the notes you took in Exercise 2. Before you complete this exercise, you may want to review the information on writing a summary introduced in Chapter 1.

Exercise 9. Critical Analysis

Discuss the following questions with your classmates.

1. "Culture regulates our lives at every turn. From the time we are born until we die there is, whether we are conscious of it or not, constant pressure upon us to follow certain types of behavior that others have created for us" (Clyde Kluckholm).

   How does culture regulate our lives? Discuss what types of behaviour would be impolite in your country? Describe what the effects are if a person behaves contrary to cultural norms.

2. Have you experienced any of the stages of culture shock described in the reading? Explain your answer.

Reading 2—The Long and Winding Road to the Top

EXERCISE 10. PRE-READING DISCUSSION

Discuss the following questions before you read.

1. Give reasons why you think people move to another country. Provide examples from your experience.
2. What do you think would be the most difficult aspects of moving to another country?
3. Which is the more challenging when moving to another country: learning the culture or learning the language? Explain your answer.
4. Relate any success stories you may know regarding immigration.

EXERCISE 11. SCANNING FOR INFORMATION

1. In what country was the author educated?

   _____

2. What is his profession?

   _____

3. After he came to Canada, what was his first job?

   _____

4. What did he expect would happen as soon as he arrived in Canada? What actually happened?

   _____

5. How long did it take the writer to achieve his goal in Canada? What did he end up doing?

   _____

The Long and Winding Road to the Top

[1] Born in Kenya, I went to England for post-secondary education and I graduated with honours in Law from the University of Reading. After returning to Kenya, I practised law with one of the best firms in Nairobi and early in my career, established a reputation in banking-and-insurance related litigation. I was head of the litigation department in the firm and had five lawyers working under me. Four years later, I became a partner in the firm.

[2] Life should have been wonderful, but I could never come to terms with the corruption that existed in every aspect of life in Kenya. In Kenya, a bribe is known as "chai" or tea. The traffic

policeman, the immigration officer, the court clerk; it seemed that everywhere I went someone wanted chai. It was well known in the legal community which judges were corrupt, and if your case was listed for hearing before a particular judge, you either tried to have the case adjourned or advised your client to go and "negotiate" with the judge. The highest bidder would win! When I realized I was becoming a part of that system, my wife and I decided that it was time to immigrate.

[3] The application was a breeze. Within months, we were called for the interview. The visa officer asked why I was giving up a successful career in Kenya to immigrate to Canada. He wondered if I knew how difficult it would be to find employment as a lawyer in Canada. At the time, I did not realize the importance of that question. I had done my homework and knew the process that would be involved in getting my Canadian accreditation. I had emailed my resumé to several employment agencies and had received some favourable replies from agencies that led me to believe that they would be able to place me with a law firm as a paralegal or a law clerk soon after I arrived.

[4] With a false sense of confidence, I landed in Canada in July 2002. The encouraging employment agencies now, surprisingly, found me either over-qualified or lacking in Canadian experience. I cannot tell you how many people I asked, "How can I have Canadian experience? I am a new immigrant!" Bills had to be paid and daycare for our two year old was a drain on our savings. My wife, Jumana, was the executive assistant to the president of an international corporation in Kenya, but here she happily took a job as a customer service representative at an electronics shop. As for me, my first Canadian work experience was at a discount department store.

[5] Everyone around us, especially other new immigrants in our apartment building, had the same negative outlook. They told us about people who were also well educated, as a doctor for instance, and had been in Canada for ten years working as a cashier at the local drug store. And they told about a teacher who is now babysitting the neighbourhood kids. When I was growing up, my father would tell us, "You can wash anything off your hands, except blood." In this way, he taught us not to be ashamed of doing any kind of work, so long as it was legitimate and did not hurt anyone else.

[6] One day, our outlooks completely changed. I heard my wife tell our daughter, "You can wash anything off your hands, except blood." And, at that point, it was like the light came into our lives. Until then we had felt short-changed by the Canadian immigration system. Because we needed someone to blame, we blamed the system. The system was not fair. The complaints were many. However, I soon remembered that nobody brought me here; it was my own decision. Nobody promised to give me a job as soon as I landed. In fact, I knew from the start that I needed to re-qualify as a lawyer working in Canada. Therefore, my wife and I made a list of what our goals were and how to achieve them. I knew that I had to go back to school since I had invested too much in being a lawyer to let that go.

[7] I wrote to the Law Society and applied to have my qualifications assessed. Their accreditation committee informed me that I would have to sit for eight exams to re-qualify to Canadian standards. We engaged in back and forth communication and eventually, the Law Society reduced the requirement to three papers—Canadian Constitutional Law, Administrative Law, and Taxation—and I received a handwritten note from the Chair of the accreditation committee that these were the basic three papers that all Canadian law students must complete!

[8]	A mistake that many newcomers make is in the kind of jobs they apply for. When I first landed in Canada my resumé was impressive, but it got me no interviews. Now my wife and I looked at our resumés from the point of view of potential employers. I realized that even I would not want to hire a law clerk who told me in his resumé that he had been the head of a litigation department in a large law firm in Kenya. I would not want to invest time, energy, and money in training that person for fear that they would "jump ship" at the first opportunity. I realized the employers were not being unfair as they were doing what any reasonable person in their place would do.

[9]	In addition, we avoided the "negative people" or the "put-me-downers" as my wife called them. When our neighbours asked us how we were doing, we truthfully told them that we were happy because

- we had decided to immigrate to Canada and we were here;
- we had a home and food on the table;
- we had employment, maybe not in our own fields, but it paid the bills;
- we were healthy and safe; and
- we were doing what we needed to do to re-qualify and to better ourselves.

[10]	After a couple of months at the store, I was overjoyed when I got a temporary assignment at a bank's mortgage centre, as a customer service representative on the lawyer's helpline. So when mortgage instructions were sent out to the lawyer and he did not understand certain conditions, he would call the lawyers' helpline and speak to me. Furthermore, I used the time between calls to study for my exams.

[11]	My supervisor at the bank was very supportive and encouraged me to apply for other positions within the bank. As a result, I slowly progressed within the bank. My wife also made progress. She gave up her permanent position at the electronics store she worked at to take on a temporary assignment at a college. This turned into a permanent position as well and opened the door for future advancement in the college.

Advice for Others

[12]	Be prepared to take risks. Set your goals and then work toward them. What I find is that many immigrants get comfortable and do not want to risk losing that comfort to aim higher. Many complain about lack of opportunities for skilled professionals. I would not be telling the truth if I told you that my journey was easy. It was not. Having practised as a lawyer, it was difficult to "go back to the books." On the weekends and after work, I had errands to run, chores to do and wanted to spend time with my growing family. But I had my wife encouraging me, insisting that I go to the library every Saturday to study.

[13]	Once I completed my accreditation process with the Law Society, I applied for positions with law firms. I targeted the smaller law firms because at this point in my life, the hands-on experience was more valuable than a higher salary. Knowing I would have to start from the bottom of the ladder, I applied for the position of law clerk. I told the interviewer that he would get a qualified lawyer for the price of a law clerk. I kept my expectations low and did not ask for unrealistic salaries because of my experience as a lawyer. Instead, I told my potential employer what my goals were and that I was working toward my Canadian qualification. My honesty paid off since I soon

found employment as a real estate clerk at a law firm. I articled with the same firm and upon completion of my Bar exams, I was called to the Bar of Ontario in June 2007—four years, 11 months and 12 days after I immigrated to Canada.

[14]   Following my call to the Bar of Ontario, I joined Aylesworth, a Bay Street firm, as an associate in its Financial Institutions and Real Estate Practice Group. Building on my Bay Street experience, I founded RealCorp Law Professional Corporation in April 2011 and my practice now focuses on Real Estate Law, Corporate Law, and Estate Law. People I know are telling me that I am lucky, after all I got a job with a Bay Street law firm. And to them, I say it is not luck. It was positive thinking, a supportive family, and hard work. We made many sacrifices and kept our focus on our goal. We listened to ourselves, not to the put-me-downers. We reminded ourselves constantly of why we were here and we made the extra effort to enjoy what we had. And we are teaching our daughters that you can wash anything off your hands, except blood.

Source: Adapted from Shaffiq Dar, "The Long and Winding Road to the Top." *Canadian Newcomer*, http://www.cnmag.ca//issue-25/601, retrieved 4 July 2011.

EXERCISE 12. COMPREHENSION CHECK

1. a) What major factors caused the author to move to Canada?

_____

_____

   b) What effects did his leaving Kenya have?

_____

_____

2. Define *chai* as the author uses it and state the effects of using chai.

_____

_____

3. What indirect warning did the visa officer give with his question at the interview?

_____

_____

4. In paragraph 4, the author speaks of "a false sense of confidence." What were the effects of this false confidence?

_____

_____

5. What was the outlook of other immigrants the author met?

_____

_____

6. What is the meaning of "You can wash anything off your hands, except blood"?

_____

_____

7. For the following statements, indicate the cause or effect.

a) Cause: "... we had felt short-changed by the Canadian immigration system." (paragraph 6)
List three effects of the author feeling short-changed.

_____

b) "I knew that I had to go back to school. . . ." (paragraph 6)
What caused him to make this decision?

_____

c) "Now my wife and I looked at our resumés from the point of view of potential employers." (paragraph 8)
What caused them to take this step?

_____

d) What were the effects of the author taking a temporary assignment at a bank?

_____

8. "People I know are telling me that I am lucky, . . ." but he believes that it is not luck. In what way is his success more than luck? (paragraph 14)

_____

9. What were the causes of the author's success?

_____

_____

Vocabulary in Context

Context clues help you figure out the meaning of unfamiliar words or idioms without using your dictionary. In university classes, you will be reading many long, complicated passages that contain a number of complex words and expressions. Guessing from context helps you to understand what you read and to read faster. It also helps you remember the words, make logical connections, and infer meaning. These are all skills that good readers have acquired.

There are four types of context clues:

1. words with a similar meaning

2. words used in contrast

3. definitions

4. general context

Exercise 13. Using Context Clues

A. The sentences below are taken from Reading 2. For each underlined word, choose the best definition from the list of words below the sentence. If the underlined word is unfamiliar, try to use context clues to guess the meaning.

1. "... but I could never come to terms with the corruption that existed in every <u>aspect</u> of life...." (paragraph 2)

   a) part or piece
   b) modern or stylish
   c) final or conclusive

2. "... my wife and I made a list of what our goals were and how to <u>achieve</u> them." (paragraph 6)

   a) negate
   b) succeed
   c) complete

3. "... I had <u>invested</u> too much in being a lawyer to let that go." (paragraph 6)

   a) resisted
   b) contributed
   c) managed

4. "I wrote to the Law Society and applied to have my qualifications <u>assessed</u>." (paragraph 7)

   a) evaluated
   b) permitted
   c) defended

5. "I would not want to invest time, energy, and money in training that person for fear that they would '<u>jump ship</u>' at the first opportunity." (paragraph 8)

   In your own words, give the meaning of *jump ship*.

   _____

6. "... I was overjoyed when I got a <u>temporary</u> <u>assignment</u> at a bank's mortgage centre...." (paragraph 10)

   Define *temporary:*_____

   Define *assignment:*_____

7. Write a synonym for the underlined words and expressions. "I <u>targeted</u> the smaller law firms because at this point in my life, the <u>hands-on experience</u> was more valuable than a higher <u>salary</u>." (paragraph 13)

   targeted (v): _____

   hands-on experience (noun phrase): _____

   salary (n): _____

8. "We made many sacrifices and kept our focus on our goal." (paragraph 14)

   a) We learned a lot.
   b) We gave up a lot.
   c) We chose carefully.

9. The word *immigrate* appears in the reading in various forms and performs various functions. Give the sentence from the reading in which the words below are used and the part of speech for each word, and then use each word in a sentence. The first one is done for you as an example.

   Example: a) *immigrate*

   From the reading: "The visa officer asked why I was giving up a successful career in Kenya to immigrate to Canada." (paragraph 3)

   Part of speech: verb

   Sentence: Although my father wanted to immigrate to Canada, my mother was not so sure because she found it difficult to leave behind her extended family.

   b) *immigrants*

   From the reading: _____

   Part of speech: _____

   Collocations: _____

   Sentence: _____

   c) *immigrated*

   From the reading: _____

   Part of speech: _____

   Collocations: _____

   Sentence: _____

   d) *immigration*

   From the reading: _____

   Part of speech: _____

   Collocations: _____

   Sentence: _____

B. Write synonyms for the underlined words.

   1. "The application was a breeze." (paragraph 3) _____

   2. "In this way, he taught us not to be ashamed of doing any kind of work, so long as it was legitimate and did not hurt anyone else." (paragraph 5) _____

3. "Now my wife and I looked at our resumés from the point of view of potential employers." (paragraph 8) _____

4. "Many complain about lack of opportunities for skilled professionals." (paragraph 12) _____

| Writing Style |

A writer may choose among different strategies to address an issue and an audience. The choices the writer makes reveal his or her writing style. Writing can change in its organization, its sentence structures, how formal it is, and the choice of words used—all dependent on the writer's purpose and audience.

The article "The Long and Winding Road to the Top" is written in newspaper or journalistic style. Often newspaper articles are written in short paragraphs, use personal information, use direct quotes, and may contain slang or idioms used in everyday speech. Additionally, they frequently contain just one sentence per paragraph. Newspaper articles are written this way to make their point and to reach their audiences quickly and succinctly.

In contrast, the purpose of academic writing is to inform the audience fully on topics that may be higher level or complex. To express the ideas well, the writer uses more formal words, complex sentence structures, and complete paragraph development.

EXERCISE 14. IDENTIFY WRITING STYLES IN READINGS 1 AND 2

In pairs or small groups, discuss the answers to the following questions. First you should answer the questions for Reading 1 and then answer the same questions for Reading 2.

1. Why was the article written? Give its purpose.

2. Who is the audience the writer had in mind?

3. Is the organization journalistic or academic in style? Explain your answer and give examples.

4. Is the language formal or informal? Give examples.

EXERCISE 15. WRITING

> **Words That Indicate Cause and Effect**
> Cause: *because, since, for, due to*
> Effect: *as a result, consequently, therefore, thus, so, accordingly*

Interview an immigrant to Canada about his or her experiences and then write a report for your school newspaper. Why did this person immigrate, that is, what were the causes? What were the effects on his or her life or family? Be sure to use complete paragraphs. You may use the words in the box to indicate cause and effect.

Reading 3—*Seeing Through the Rules*

EXERCISE 16. PRE-READING DISCUSSION

A. Discuss the the following questions before you read.

1. Give an example of an incident when you did not know what was going on because of a cultural misunderstanding.

2. Describe an occasion when you tried to show respect, but your action was misinterpreted and taken the wrong way.

3. What examples can you give of Aboriginal cultural behaviour?

B. Preview before you read.

1. What information do you obtain from the title?

2. After quickly scanning the article, can you guess what the main idea might be?

3. What support does the author provide in the form of details or examples?

Seeing Through the Rules

[1] Every culture has its rules, spoken or unspoken. When two cultures meet, misunderstandings may arise because each is working with its own set of rules, not understood by the other.

[2] A Mohawk band once hosted a sporting tournament to which they invited a group of James Bay Cree. The Mohawk, who were an agricultural people long before contact with Europeans, had developed a custom of always setting out considerably more food than their guests could consume. In this way they demonstrated both their wealth and their generosity. The Cree, however, had a different custom. A hunter-gatherer people for whom scarcity was a daily fact, their custom involved always eating everything that was set before them. In this way they demonstrated their respect for the successful hunter and for the hunter's generosity.

[3] Needless to say, a problem arose when these two sets of rules collided. The Cree, anxious to show respect, ate and ate until they were more than a little uncomfortable. They considered the Mohawk something akin to gastrointestinal sadists intent on poisoning them. The Mohawk, for their part, thought the Cree ill-mannered people intent on insulting Mohawk generosity.

[4] What is of interest in this story is not simply the collision of social customs. That might well be expected. The significant point is that each group believed that the other was *intentionally* being insulting and disrespectful when, in fact, each group had been going to great pains (especially the Cree!) to show exactly the opposite. The problem was that each group could see the other only through its own rules, could interpret the behaviour of others only from within its own perspective.

[5] Acts are never merely acts. They are also signals of attitude. Those signals, however, are often culture specific. When individuals see the acts, but their signal-content is misinterpreted, it is

impossible to avoid forming inaccurate interpretations of others. Until we understand what particular acts *mean* to the other, we will continually ascribe motivations and states of mind that are well off the mark. As in the Cree–Mohawk situation, the two groups will go away believing that the other was deliberately trying to insult them.

[6]   An encounter in a court of law on a remote reserve in northwestern Ontario offers another illustration. A community Elder had been of invaluable assistance by advising the court on appropriate sentences for each offender. After the session, the Crown attorney went up to him, looked him straight in the eye, shook his hand, and told him, in effusive terms, how much the Elder's contribution was appreciated.

[7]   In doing so, the attorney made two basic errors. First, he failed to recognize that for the people of that reserve, verbal expressions of praise and gratitude are considered embarrassing and impolite, especially in the presence of others. The proper course is to quietly ask the person to *continue* making his contribution next time around.

[8]   Second, looking someone straight in the eye, at least among older people in that community, was rude. It sent a signal that you consider that person in some fashion inferior. The proper way to send a signal of respect was to look down or to the side, with only occasional glances up to indicate attention. The attorney had been trying to say one thing, but had done so in a way that conveyed exactly the opposite. To his great relief, he was later assured that the man had probably not taken offence; he knew, after all, that a great many non-Aboriginal men simply hadn't learned how to behave in a civilized fashion!

[9]   When told that sustaining direct eye contact was frequently considered rude, the attorney was swamped with memories of countless Aboriginal victims and witnesses who, almost without exception, had taken the witness stand and refused to look anyone in the eye. Instead, they alternated between staring off into the distance and giving only the most fleeting of glances. In doing so, they had meant to send messages of attention and respect. The messages received by court personnel, however, were exactly the opposite ones. Within the non-Aboriginal culture (and especially the culture of the courtroom) individuals are trained to see such behaviour as evasive. When people won't hold eye contact their words are discounted, and it is often concluded that they are insincere and untrustworthy as witnesses. The attorney wondered how many true stories had been dismissed simply because Aboriginal people had been seen through the lens of another culture. Because Aboriginal people's attempt to show respect had been seen through the lens of another culture, the effect was that the actions had been entirely misinterpreted.

[10]   In his book *The Politics of Experience*, Scottish psychiatrist R.D. Laing said, "Until you can see through the rules, you can only see through the rules." We can interpret that proposition in this way: until you realize that your own culture dictates how you understand everything you see and hear, you will never be able to see or hear things in any *other* way. The first step in coming to terms with people of another culture, then, is to acknowledge that we constantly *interpret* the words and acts of others and that we do so subconsciously but always in conformity with the way that our culture has taught us is the "proper" way. The second step involves trying to gain a conscious

understanding of what those culture-specific rules might be. Until that happens, it is impossible for us to admit that our interpretation of the behaviour of someone from another culture might be totally erroneous.

[11]   These stories illustrate that it is commonplace for signals to be misread when Aboriginal and non-Aboriginal people meet, commonplace for each of us to hear things that the other never intended, and commonplace to go away with entirely mistaken impressions. We are not aware that we act within conventional sets of rules ourselves. We assume instead that the way we behave, express ourselves, and interpret others is the way all people do it. It seems that all cultures operate with this myopia, not even suspecting that others may have developed very different rules.

[12]   What the two stories illustrate is that both groups in a meeting of cultures have an obligation to *expect* difference, to expect that our interpretations of the other's words and acts are liable to be incorrect. Above all else, whenever we find ourselves beginning to draw negative conclusions from what the other has said or done, we must take the time to step back and ask whether those words and acts might be open to different interpretations, whether that other person's actions may have a different meaning from within his or her cultural conventions.

[13]   This, then, is the nature of the task at hand: learning to go beyond what we think we see and hear to ask what a person from a different culture and with a different sense of reality is truly trying to tell us.

Source: Adapted from Rupert Ross, "Seeing Through the Rules." In *Dancing with a Ghost: Exploring Aboriginal Reality* (McClelland & Stewart, 2006). Used by permission, McClelland & Stewart, Inc. The Canadian Publishers.

EXERCISE 17. COMPREHENSION CHECK

1. Why did the Mohawk provide more food than their guests could eat?

2. In what way did the Cree show respect for the hunter?

3. Writers often use irony to make their point. An ironic situation is one in which what is expected to happen is very different from what actually happens. Give two examples of ironic situations in "Seeing Through the Rules." Describe how each incident is ironic.

4. What is significant about the story of the Mohawk and Cree?

5. What were the errors the Crown attorney made in complimenting the Elder?

6. In paragraph 9, how did the attorney apply what he learned about direct eye contact?

_____

7. In your own words, write the meaning of the following sentence from paragraph 10. "The first step in coming to terms with people of another culture, then, is to acknowledge that we constantly *interpret* the words and acts of others and that we do so subconsciously but always in conformity with the way that our culture has taught us is the 'proper' way."

_____

8. In paragraph 13, line 1, what does "this" refer to?

_____

EXERCISE 18. CRITICAL ANALYSIS

Discuss the following questions with your classmates.

1. What is the value of writing such an article as "The Long and Winding Road to the Top"? What is the author's purpose for writing? What does the author gain in writing about his experiences? What do you as a reader gain in reading about his experiences?

2. The first people in Canada are sometimes known as Aboriginal peoples or as First Nations. What do you know about the lives and values of Aboriginal people in Canada? What contributions can you name that Canada's Aboriginal people make to this country? In what way is traditional Aboriginal culture similar to your own?

EXERCISE 19. VOCABULARY IN CONTEXT

The following words are all found in "Seeing Through the Rules." Use the italicized vocabulary words to complete both parts A and B.

A. By guessing from context or by using a dictionary if necessary, find a synonym for each of the words.

myopia (paragraph 11): _____

hosted (paragraph 2): _____

commonplace (paragraph 11): _____

collided (paragraph 3): _____

erroneous (paragraph 10): _____

effusive (paragraph 6): _____

proposition (paragraph 10): _____

sustaining (paragraph 9): _____

evasive (paragraph 9): _____

swamped (paragraph 9): _____

B. Complete the sentences with the most suitable vocabulary word.

1. To be successful, a radio talk show needs to be _____ by a good interviewer.

2. The newspaper reported that several different groups of people _____ over the businesses proposed for their area. Fortunately, they were able to come to a compromise.

3. The parents were _____ in their thanks to the doctor who saved their child's life.

4. Jennifer, who has been working overtime for two weeks, says that _____ this pace is quite impossible.

5. After we put an advertisement in the paper to sell our car, we were _____ with calls from people who were interested in buying it.

6. Four candidates for city council answered questions from the audience at last night's meeting. To the annoyance of the audience, all the candidates were often _____ in their answers.

7. Riding on the train in Europe, the two Canadian girls received an unexpected _____ from a well-dressed gentleman.

8. James was accused of stealing money from the school travel funds, but he said that the accusation was completely _____.

9. Something that is quite _____ in one country may be unknown in another.

10. Someone with _____ can be said to see only the obvious and not what lies beneath the surface.

EXERCISE 20. ESSAY ORGANIZATION

"Seeing Through the Rules" is organized to present the author's views regarding the rules we follow in our own culture and how we apply these rules to other cultures that we encounter. This exercise will help you examine, and thus better understand, the organization of "Seeing Through the Rules." In pairs or groups, look back at the reading and answer the questions that follow. When you have completed the exercise, discuss your answers with the class.

Paragraph 1: What is the thesis statement?

State thesis statement:

_____

In your own words paraphrase the thesis statement.

_____

Paragraph 2: The author relates a story of two different cultures: the Mohawk and the Cree. Why is this effective? How does it relate to the thesis?

Effective story:

_____

Relationship to thesis:

_____

Paragraph 3: What problem is identified? What are the causes and effects?

Problem identified:

_____

Causes:

_____

Effects:

_____

Paragraphs 4 and 5: What can we learn that is significant and ironic?

Significant lesson:

_____

Ironic:

_____

In paragraph 2, and again in paragraph 6, the writer begins by giving information about cross-cultural misunderstandings. How are the "culture bumps" in paragraphs 2 and 6 similar, and how are they different?

Similar:

_____

Different:

_____

Paragraphs 7 and 8: What are the two basic errors the writer notes? State the causes and the effects.

Two errors:

_____

Causes:

_____

Effects:

_____

Paragraph 9: How does the author widen our understanding about eye contact?

Understanding widened:

_____

_____

Paragraph 10: How does the author connect new information with research or previously known information?

Connections:

_____

_____

Paragraph 11: How are we *as readers* led to believe that we are included and can learn from this reading?

How we are included:

_____

_____

Paragraphs 12 and 13. Conclusion: What does the author say we need to learn?

Conclusion:

_____

_____

─────────┤ **Writing** ├─────────

Exercise 21. Essay Writing

Write an essay on one of the following topics. Exercise 20 allowed you to examine the structure of a cause-effect article in detail. This examination of a model can instruct you as you write your own essay.

1. "Culture regulates our lives at every turn. From the time we are born until we die there is, whether we are conscious of it or not, constant pressure upon us to follow certain types of behaviour that others have created for us" (Clyde Kluckhohn).

    Describe how culture affects your life. From your own culture, give examples of ways in which you are compelled to behave and what the effects are on you.

2. For most people it is difficult to immigrate to another country. Write an essay describing the causes and effects of immigrating to another country. Suggest what can be done to help immigrants adapt.

3. Look back at the readings on crossing cultures in this chapter and select the information that you think is useful to know before immigrating to Canada. Then write an essay or newspaper article about your findings.

Revising Checklist

When you have finished writing the draft of your essay, consider the following questions:

1. Has the thesis been clearly stated?

2. Has the thesis been supported? How?

3. Are the causes and effects clearly stated?

4. How has the information been organized?

5. Does each paragraph have a clear subject?

6. Have you used connectors to help the reader make the transition from one idea to the next?

7. How have you concluded?

CHAPTER 6

Concerning Community

Introduction to the Chapter

In this chapter you will examine the idea of community, including NIMBYism, which is derived from an acronym Not in My Backyard. It refers to those individuals who might welcome a new development or project, but object if it is too near their own home. The chapter also focuses on the attempt to preserve the distinctiveness of a community, the natural benefits of our backyards, and the idea of friendship in community. In Reading 1 Siri Agrell writes about what Canadians believe makes a good community. Reading 2 is an extended definition of NIMBYism, its meaning, and use. In Reading 3 David Suzuki explains how NIMBYism can be viewed positively and enhance community. Finally, in Reading 4 Dr. Beverley Fehr provides an extended definition of friendship, an important aspect of our lives.

In this chapter, it is important to understand the conventions of writing extended definitions as you will be asked to write extended definitions on various topics.

Reading 1—*What Makes a Canadian Community Great?*

EXERCISE 1. PRE-READING DISCUSSION

1. Who makes up your community? How do you define community?

2. In what way has your community changed since you came to Canada?

3. How important is community? Is it necessary for everyone to be part of a community?

4. What does your upbringing teach you about community? To what extent do you follow this teaching?

What Makes a Canadian Community Great?

[1] When Kerry Jang was growing up, his community was defined by boundaries. His East Vancouver neighbourhood was the indisputable territory of the working class, his Chinese heritage a classification no one seemed willing to hyphenate, even though his parents were second-generation Canadians. "I think their community was pretty much defined by the Chinese community in Vancouver," he says. "It was very much just keep your head down." Since then, his world and the notion of community have expanded exponentially. For Mr. Jang, like most Canadians, the term has taken on connotations beyond ethnic background or physical environment, and now refers to the banding together of like-minded individuals. But fundamentally, it's still about where we live.

[2] Now 49, Mr. Jang still lives in East Van, where gentrification has created an urban mosaic of different types, colours, classes and castes. Like his neighbours and his neighbourhood, he defies easy categorization. He is a psychiatrist and city councillor, an activist and a father. But when he

talks about community now, it isn't about boundaries, but about how to make where he lives even better. "People confuse neighbourhood engagement with NIMBYism," he says. "The big change in Vancouver that I've seen is that people are actually more involved in solving a problem instead of just opposing something."

[3] Fifteen years ago, a Harvard academic named Robert Putnam wrote about the death of community in an essay called "Bowling Alone," later expanded into a much discussed book. In it, he cited American statistics that showed a drastic and steady decline in participation at the neighbourhood level. People weren't joining their local choral societies and football clubs any more, he found, and they weren't voting or canvassing for votes, reading their local paper or volunteering at the neighbourhood school. There was no longer a sense of community beyond the actual physical lines that separate one neighbourhood from another.

[4] Across Canada, it's hard to imagine that anyone is still bowling alone. In the time since Mr. Putnam's findings were published, the urban tide has turned, at least up here, and created a flood of interest in all things local. Recently, when the *Globe and Mail* asked readers to nominate the best communities in Canada, no one sent us messages about fancy houses or high-tech infrastructure, or places they are living out their comfortable lives in isolation.

[5] People who brag about their neighbourhoods today talk about a place where people know one another, where they are loved. These are places, we are told, where you can walk to the bookstore and the grocery store, to your kid's school and your own office. These are places where green space is not just found around the large "P" marking the nearest multistorey parking lot, but where a connection to nature is part of the urban plan. These places are easy to get around, but are not one size or one style. Some are urban, some are rural and some occupy the tree-lined spaces in between. In these communities there is a mix of people of different backgrounds, different ages, different jobs, all of whom take part in the same rituals, from summer festivals to evening strolls.

[6] Julia Deans, chief executive officer of CivicAction, Toronto's city-building organization, remembers growing up in a time when community development was dominated by wealthy, Anglo-Saxon families such as the Bassetts and Eatons. "They really led the community investment and put in place some of the big institutions that have served us as a community since," she says. Now, she sees the city's institutions being built by people with such names as Singh and Chang, reflecting a changing population and its needs. "We're building a new kind of community that equally reflects where the new power and leadership fits," she explains.

Walkability Is Key

[7] Even if Canadian communities are populated by a different mix of people today, what those people want has not changed, says John Tory, a former Toronto mayoral candidate and Civic Action chair. "If I go back to thinking about what mattered when I was a little boy, it was the park at the end of our street, where we had a hockey rink in the winter, and the local churches, where we had Cub Scouts, and the public school where I went," he says. "If you think about what was important, it was that sense that you lived in a safe place with nice places to go and play. I don't think it's much different now."

[8] What has changed, says Ken Greenberg, an urban planner and author of *Walking Home: The Life and Lessons of a City Builder*, is the map of where those places can be found. Gone is the idea that quality neighbourhoods must be built around large suburban yards or that anywhere worth living has a two-car garage. "There's a big difference between passing someone in the driving lane of an arterial and passing them on the sidewalk, where you make eye contact," he explains. Today, the focus in urban planning boils down to one word: walkability. A strong community is one where you can walk to all the things you need: the grocery store, school, public park and pub, whether you're in the heart of the city or a small town. "To me, the key is to have that combination of things in close proximity and in variety, not to have things that are homogeneous," Greenberg says.

[9] Lenore Swystun, a Saskatoon-based community planner and urban consultant, believes the country is also shifting back to a sense that neighbourhoods must include a shared outdoor space where communing with nature and one another goes hand in hand. "Whether you're in an urban environment or a remote rural environment, that call back to the natural landscape is very profound," she says. "It's going back home, so to speak."

Community Is Inclusivity

[10] But in Canada, building a real sense of community will always be more complicated than marking off green space and strolling to the local farmer's market. Where we live is all tangled up with who we live among, and for neighbourhoods to work, everyone must be welcome to participate.

[11] Leslie Spillett of the Winnipeg-based, First Nations non-profit Ka Ni Kanichihk says her group is trying to build a sense of community that allows native people to feel good about who they are while also bonding them to the rest of the country. "For me, healthy community is being fully accepted for everything we have brought to this country and what we continue to contribute, but also fully accepting ourselves as well," she says.

[12] In Nova Scotia, 24-year-old Swantje Jahn is trying to make her city more accepting of new-comers through her work as the community engagement co-ordinator for the Halifax Refugee Clinic. The office helps about 25 new arrivals each year, many of whom were persecuted, and arrived with no real experience of what a home can be. The city is too small to have ethnic enclaves, says Ms. Jahn: "There is no Chinatown here." And so she works to create new communities by introducing her clients to the people of Halifax and vice versa. Next week, she will hold a baby shower for a newcomer from Iraq, the gifts provided by local moms motivated by a shared experience that transcends nationality. "We have so many differences, but at our core, we all want the same thing: We all want to belong," Ms. Jahn says. "That's what community is."

What are some great recent initiatives in community planning?

[13] **Greeting Fluency:** How often do you say good morning to your neighbours? Ever do it in their native tongue? This initiative of former Vancouver mayor Sam Sullivan and his organization, Global Civic, encourages citizens to learn a few words of greeting and has identified nine basic phrases, such as "'hello," "thank you," and "how are you?" Greeting Fluency provides instructional

videos in Cantonese, Punjabi and Tagalog, and is meeting provincial education officials in a bid to bring the program into schools. Mr. Sullivan says that anyone who makes the effort is "really showing respect"—and will see how difficult it is for "people coming here and learning English."

[14] **Awesome Cities:** Created in Boston in 2009, the Awesome Foundation awards monthly $1,000 grants to neighbourhood projects and their creators. Chapters have sprung up in Toronto, Ottawa, Kitchener-Waterloo, Edmonton, Montreal, and Calgary. Awesome Calgary was founded by Lori Stewart, a former eBay executive who worked on Mayor Naheed Nenshi's election campaign. Last month, her group heard pitches on projects ranging from an outdoor demo space for a local circus school to a poetry event and a community walk. The budding acrobats and jugglers won out.

[15] **Project Neutral:** In Toronto, two neighbourhoods are vying to become carbon neutral. The pilot program is pitting Riverdale against the Junction (in the friendliest way possible) to see which community can be the first to drastically reduce its carbon footprint. A project of the Greater Toronto CivicAction Alliance, the project hopes that neighbourhood allegiances can be used to get people involved in making a radical change.

[16] **Sustainable subdivisions:** With just 400 residents, Hafford, Saskatchewan, is a small town with big ambitions. Located near the Redberry Lake Biosphere Reserve, the community developed a plan in 2007 to become one of the most sustainable towns in Canada. The off-grid community is the first in the province to have a growth boundary. "We don't need to grow, we want to nurture that small sense of place," said Lenore Swystun, the community planner who helped develop Hafford's sustainability plan with funding from the Federation of Canadian Municipalities. "It's a visionary community."

Source: S. Agrell. "What Makes a Canadian Community Great?" *Globe and Mail* (30 June 2011). http://www.theglobeandmail.com/news/national/time-to-lead/what-makes-a-canadian-community-great/article2082694/, retrieved 17 October 2011.

EXERCISE 2. COMPREHENSION CHECK

1. What is the function of the question in the title of Reading 1?

_____

_____

2. In paragraph 1 and 2, we learn that Jang's idea of community has expanded. What was his idea of community and how has it changed?

_____

_____

3. From the following quote, what can you deduce Jang means by "NIMBYism"? "'People confuse neighbourhood engagement with NIMBYism,' he says. 'The big change in Vancouver that I've seen is that people are actually more involved in solving a problem instead of just opposing something.'" (paragraph 2)

_____

_____

4. Paraphrase the following sentence from paragraph 4. "In the time since Mr. Putnam's findings were published, the urban tide has turned, at least up here, and created a flood of interest in all things local."

_____

_____

5. What do modern communities have that makes them desirable places to live?

_____

_____

6. In building a modern community, how have the investors changed? Why has there been a change?

_____

_____

7. Write a short summary of Reading 1 in which you answer the question in the title: What makes a Canadian community great?

_____

_____

_____

Vocabulary Study: Defining

Authors use definition to make clear the meaning of a word, an object, or an abstract concept. Definition is used to explain something in detail. Defining is often required in science and textbooks where specialized vocabulary is used. And when writers want to define a word directly, they may use one of the following words or phrases:

means	_can be defined as_
_is_	_refers to_
describes	_consists of_

Formal definitions, particularly scientific definitions, are written in the following way.

Definition = Term + verb + class + distinguishing characteristics

Example: A chair + is + class + description

A chair is furniture that is used to sit on.

Example: Pump + refers to + class + description

Pump refers to a device that raises, transfers, or compresses fluids.

Example: Friendship + describes + class + description

Friendship describes a state in which one person is attached to another by affection.

Example: Community + consists + class + description

A community consists of a group of people with common interests who live in close proximity.

Exercise 3. Vocabulary in Context

With a partner, find words that are unfamiliar to you in Reading 1, then write a formal definition for each word you identify. Follow the examples presented on page 137.

Extended Definitions

Formal definitions of concrete words, as in the examples on page 137, are often short and to the point. The short definition reduces the subject to its most important characteristics. The advantage of the short definition is that it provides a precise meaning for a word, one that is readily understood by both readers and writers. Concrete words, such as *table*, *orange*, or *pencil*, can be defined simply and in a straightforward manner.

However, the more abstract a word is, the more difficult it is to define it simply. When writers want to define an abstract, controversial, or complex idea, a short definition is often too limiting. Words such as *friendship*, *community*, *personality*, *conformity*, or *government* cannot be adequately defined in a word, phrase, or sentence. Such words require an extended definition.

An extended definition may begin similarly to a formal definition, but it contains much more information. Extended definitions can vary in length from a paragraph or two to an entire essay. In the reading "Extended Definition of NIMBY," the author needed to write a short essay to define NIMBYism adequately. Whether an extended definition is a paragraph in length or longer, it uses techniques of support similar to an essay. It begins with a formal definition that is then extended with facts, examples, research, description, physical detail, or personal experience.

⊣ Reading 2—*Extended Definition of NIMBY* ⊢

Exercise 4. Thinking about the Topic before You Read

1. What is an acronym?
2. Give examples of acronyms that you are familiar with. Which one appeals to you most and why?
3. Why do you think acronyms are used?

⊣ Extended Definition of NIMBY ⊢

[1]   NIMBY (N) is an acronym which means Not In My Back Yard. Its component parts include: NIMBYism (N), NIMBYies (pl), and NIMBYists (N). It is sometimes written in capital letters (NIMBY) and sometimes in lower case letters (nimby) corresponding to a person's preference.

[2]   According to the *Oxford Advanced Learner's Dictionary*, NIMBY is a disapproving or humorous term that is used to refer to a person who claims to be in favour of a new development or project, but objects if it is too near their own home. In other words, it is fine for the project or development to exist in someone else's community but not in the NIMBY's community.

[3] The term NIMBY is usually applied to opponents of a development, implying that they have narrow, selfish, or myopic views. Its meaning is often negative. The opponents may be more affluent people who are afraid that the facilities built might attract "undesirable" people. The term has been applied in debates over developments in diverse situations, including, but not limited to, the following: building new roads, airports, shopping centers, nuclear waste sites, wastewater treatment plants, landfills, sewage plants, prisons, halfway houses, subsidized housing for poor people, supportive housing for mentally ill people, and homeless shelters for people without a home.

[4] A current example of NIMBYism is that of a small town in central BC which decided to move its transfer station (waste system) to an area further out of town. They may have chosen this area because it can accommodate their needs for more space while still being relatively close to town. However, on the way to the new transfer station, there is a large electronics business which employs 200 people from the small town. This business believes that having a waste disposal station so near its site will be bad for their business and will discourage potential new business partners. Their attempt to stop the move of the transfer station into their area was to encourage employees to sign a petition opposing the transfer station, and for the CEO to write a letter and make a presentation to the town council. The electronics company does not oppose the idea that the transfer station should move out of town, they just don't want it in their backyard.

[5] In her research on NIMBYism, Liza Jimenez (2005) found that common NIMBY arguments for opposing a project include: fears for personal safety, property devaluation, and neighbourhood degradation. As well, common factors that influence opposition are size of the proposed facility, clientele, the consultation process, and the particular neighbourhood. She explains that long-term residents and those who attended planning meetings are most likely to hold NIMBY attitudes, and pose the most resistance. New residents, she found, normally are not as likely to hold NIMBY attitudes and may also not be as aware of the plans for that community.

[6] Thus it is evident that NIMBYism can include a wide range of issues in society and it appears to be a way for some people to believe they can safeguard their community.

Reference:
Jimenez, L. (2002) From NIMBY to YIMBY: Understanding Community Opposition to Special Needs Residential Facilities in Vancouver (Master's Thesis). Retrieved from http://www.sfu.ca/mpp-old/pdf_news/Capstone/Liza%20Jimenez%20capstone.pdf.

EXERCISE 5. ANALYZING: EXTENDED DEFINITION OF NIMBY

Study the extended definition of NIMBY and determine whether it has the characteristics commonly found in extended definitions as shown in the chart below. Complete the chart with the relevant information.

Characteristics of Extended Definitions	Examples from Reading 2
formal definition	
facts	
examples	
research information	
description	
physical details	
personal experience	

EXERCISE 6. WRITING AN EXTENDED DEFINITION

Write an extended definition of community from the information provided in Reading 1, "What Makes a Canadian Community Great?"

Reading 3—*A New Kind of NIMBY: Nature in My Backyard*

EXERCISE 7. PRE-READING DISCUSSION

1. What comes to mind when you hear the phrase *nature in my backyard*? What does it include?

2. Many people grow gardens in their backyards, but some people would like to keep chickens and bees as well. What is your opinion?

3. What benefits of having nature in our backyards can you identify?

EXERCISE 8. SCANNING THE READING FOR INFORMATION

Scan Reading 3 by David Suzuki for the answers to the questions that follow.

1. According to Suzuki, how can NIMBY "arise"?

_____

2. What is the new kind of NIMBY that Suzuki proposes?

_____

3. Where does Suzuki think we should begin the change he proposes?

_____

4. What is Suzuki most enthusiastic about?

_____

A New Kind of NIMBY: Nature in My Backyard

[1] On reading about the growing resistance to a mega-quarry being proposed for Southern Ontario, I had an epiphany about the media's use of the term NIMBY, for "not in my backyard." It's normally used to describe grassroots efforts to block everything from landfills and windmills to big-box stores, and bike lanes. NIMBYism has taken on a negative association, often implying naive or parochial resistance to projects that challenge the status quo in a community.

[2] But NIMBYism isn't always bad. Although it can arise out of fear of something new or different in a community, it can also be the result of genuine concern for the local environment. I'd like to propose a new kind of NIMBY, one that is positive and reflects a true sense of caring for our communities. Let's go green and say yes to Nature in My Backyard.

[3] A good place to start recognizing this new NIMBYism would be literally in our backyards. That means encouraging more home veggie and herb gardens, more native plants that support birds, bees, and butterflies, and more backyard composters for fruit and veggie scraps and yard clippings.

[4] Next, we can bring Nature in My Backyard-ism to the neighbourhood. Our municipal parks are undoubtedly important green spaces, but they are often seen as an afterthought, especially when overzealous municipal leaders want to cut spending. Let's rethink urban parks as places that provide more than just a space to play sports or sit on a bench.

[5] Our local parks provide a variety of essential services that we take for granted. For instance, trees clean and cool our air, absorb pollutants, store and filter rainwater, reduce noise, add colour, absorb and store carbon, and are home to many species of insects, birds, and other critters. Add up the benefits that local parks provide. You might be surprised. The city of Philadelphia found that investment in its park system returned a net increase in economic wealth of more than $700 million each year.

[6] At the regional level, the new NIMBYism could be directed toward wrapping "greenbelts" around our sprawling urban areas. Protecting the farms, fields, forests, and wetlands around our urban areas is an investment that will pay huge dividends. The internationally renowned 1.8-million-hectare Ontario Greenbelt is estimated to provide the Golden Horseshoe region with more than $2.6 billion in economic benefits each year, and it serves as a bright green example of how we can protect and restore nature in the backyards of an entire region.

[7] But perhaps the most exciting Nature in My Backyard campaign is an effort to establish Canada's first urban National Park in the Rouge Valley, at the east end of Toronto. Parks Canada is celebrating the 100th year of our magnificent National Parks system. I can think of no better way

to commemorate this milestone than to bring nature to urbanites. Imagine a National Park that is accessible by public transit for millions of city dwellers, including huge and diverse populations of new Canadians.

[8]   I encourage citizens across the country to join me in celebrating the new NIMBY and saying yes to nature in our backyards, neighbourhoods, and communities. It will be an important reminder that nature isn't a destination; it is literally in our backyard.

Rouge Valley

Source: Excerpted from David Suzuki. "A New Kind of NIMBY: Nature in My Backyard." http://www.davidsuzuki.org/blogs/science-matters/2011/06/a-new-kind-of-nimby-nature-in-my-backyard/, 8 June 2011, retrieved 3 August 2011.

EXERCISE 9. COMPREHENSION CHECK

1. The meaning of NIMBY includes, literally, your own backyard. However, Suzuki writes about a National Park that clearly cannot be in someone's backyard. How far, do you think, "in my backyard" extends?

    _____

2. "But NIMBYism isn't always bad." (paragraph 2) When is NIMBYism positive?

    _____

3. What four-step process does Suzuki outline regarding the new NIMBY?

    1._____

    2._____

    3._____

    4._____

4. What benefits does a local park provide?

    _____

    _____

5. What is unique about the proposed park in the Rouge Valley at the edge of Toronto?

    _____

    _____

EXERCISE 10. VOCABULARY IN CONTEXT

1. Suzuki writes about different kinds of parks. Provide the meaning of each.

   a) municipal parks_____

   b) urban parks_____

   c) local parks_____

   d) national parks_____

2. "NIMBYism has taken on a negative association, often implying <u>naive or parochial</u> resistance to projects that challenge the <u>status quo</u> in a community." (paragraph 1)

   Choose the best meaning of the underlined words in the quotation.

   naive or parochial

   a) immature and narrow-minded resistance
   b) never open-minded resistance
   c) infamous resistance

   status quo

   a) alternative ideas
   b) the way things are now
   c) new ways of seeing

3. "Our local parks provide a variety of essential services that we <u>take for granted</u>." (paragraph 5) What is the meaning of this idiom?

   Choose the best meaning of the underlined words in the quotation.

   a) are used to
   b) underestimate the value of
   c) do not care about

4. Write a definition of the word *regional*.

   _____

5. "... including huge and <u>diverse</u> populations of new Canadians." (paragraph 7) Choose the best meaning for the underlined word.

   a) varied
   b) common
   c) similar

Reading 4—*Friendship*

EXERCISE 11. PRE-READING DISCUSSION

Discuss the following questions before you read.

1. What do you most appreciate about your friends?
2. Do you have the same relationship with your friends as you have with your family?
3. How are your friends part of your community?
4. In what ways do you rely on your friends?

Friendship

[1] Friendships are a kind of interpersonal relationship. They differ from other relationships, such as familial or marital relationships, in that they are highly voluntary. Friendships are characterized by intimacy, trust, loyalty, caring, enjoyment of one another's company, and the provision of practical and emotional support. Friends regard one another as equals and are committed to the continuation of the relationship.

[2] When Sapadin (1988) asked adults living in major US cities to complete the sentence, "A friend is someone . . .", the most frequent responses were

- with whom you are intimate
- you can trust
- you can depend on
- with whom you share things
- who accepts you
- with whom you have a caring relationship
- with whom you are close
- you enjoy.

[3] There are different kinds of friendship, ranging from acquaintances, to casual friends, to close friends. These can be differentiated in terms of the extent to which they exemplify each of the friendship characteristics listed above. To take intimacy as an example, one generally does not have an intimate relationship with an acquaintance. Conversations tend to be nonpersonal. However, if both people begin to reveal more personal, intimate information about themselves, the relationship evolves to the casual friendship stage. In this process where friends reveal more and more intimate information about themselves, the relationship progresses to the level of a close friendship. Thus, friendships progress from acquaintance to close friendship when the individuals engage in greater intimacy, loyalty, trust, commitment, and so on.

[4] Friendships have been affected by the development of computer-mediated communication such as email, chat rooms, and text messaging. Although people are relying on the Internet to form friendships, most friendships are still formed face-to-face (Fehr, 2008). Recent research shows that people find their offline friendships to be more satisfying and of higher quality than their online

friendships (Bane, Cornish, Erspamer, & Kampman, 2010; Buote, Wood, & Pratt, 2009). However, there is controversy over whether people who have low social skills and are socially isolated are better off now because they can form friendships online. The concern is whether this makes things worse because now there's no reason for these people to develop the required skills to form friendships in the real world.

[5] It is thought that friends serve three major functions in our lives (Solano, 1986). First, friends meet our material needs and provide various kinds of help and support. Second, friends meet our cognitive needs; they provide intellectual stimulation through shared experiences and activities, as well as through the lively exchange of ideas. Finally, friends meet our social-emotional needs through the provision of love, warmth, and esteem. Given these benefits of friendship, it is not surprising that people regard friends as a primary source of joy and meaning in their lives.

References:
Bane, C. H., Cornish, M., Erspamer, N., & Kampman, L. (2010). Self-disclosure through weblogs and perceptions of online and 'real-life' friendships among female bloggers. *Cyberpsychology, Behavior, and Social Networking, 13*(2), 131–139.
Buote, V. M., Wood, E., & Pratt, M. (2009). Exploring similarities and differences between online and offline friendships: The role of attachment style. *Computers in Human Behavior, 25*(2), 560–567.
Fehr, B. (1996). *Friendship processes*. Newbury Park, CA: Sage.
Fehr, B. (2008). Friendship formation. In S. Sprecher, A. Wenzel, & J. Harvey (Eds.). *Handbook of relationship initiation* (pp. 29–54).
Sapadin, L.A. (1988). Friendship and gender: Perspectives of professional men and women. *Journal of Social and Personal Relationships, 5*, 387–403.
Solano, C.H. (1986). People without friends: loneliness and its alternatives. In V. J. Derlega & B. Winstead (Eds.), *Friendship and social interaction* (pp. 227–246). New York: Springer-Verlag.

Source: Beverley Fehr, from *Friendship Processes* (Sage, 1996); updated and adapted by the author in 2011.

EXERCISE 12. COMPREHENSION CHECK

1. According to Dr. Fehr, friendship, family, and marriage are all relationships. How is friendship different from family and marriage relationships?

_____

_____

2. What are the predominant characteristics of friendship?

_____

_____

3. What role does intimacy play in friendship?

_____

_____

4. Summarize the different levels of friendships.

_____

_____

5. Paraphrase the following two sentences from the reading: "However, there is controversy over whether people who have low social skills and are socially isolated are better off now because they can form friendships online. The concern is whether this makes things worse because now there's no reason for these people to develop the required skills to form friendships in the real world." (paragraph 4)

_____

_____

EXERCISE 13. VOCABULARY IN CONTEXT

A. The words below were taken from Reading 4, "Friendship," by Dr. Beverley Fehr. Write a formal definition for each of the words as outlined earlier (i.e., term + class + description). Since the author has attempted to make the meaning clear in the reading, try to deduce the meaning from the context first before you consult a dictionary.

> *interpersonal*   *acquaintance*   *computer-mediated*   *controversy*

B. The following words are defined in the reading in paragraph 5. Provide the meanings.

1. *material needs* _____

2. *cognitive needs* _____

3. *social–emotional needs* _____

EXERCISE 14. SUMMARIZING

Answer the following questions on a separate sheet of paper.

In the essay "Friendship," the author carefully develops the definition. In a sentence or two, give the main idea that the author is expressing in each paragraph. Finally, write a summary from the information you gleaned.

Exercise 15. Analyzing

Analyze Dr. Fehr's extended definition, "Friendship," and determine the techniques of support she used. In the box below, write the appropriate information for each category that is applicable.

Defining words used	
Examples given	
Facts provided	
Description included	
Research employed	
Physical details provided	

Exercise 16. Conduct a Survey

1. Following a class discussion, ask students in your class to complete this sentence from the reading: "A friend is someone who. . . ."

2. After that, survey other classes in your school by having them complete the same statement.

3. Then survey your friends and have them complete the statement.

4. Next, classify the responses you collected according to the major functions—material, cognitive, or social-emotional—as shown in Reading 4, "Friendship." (paragraph 5)

5. Finally, report to your class on your findings.

Exercise 17. Critical Analysis

Discuss the following questions with your classmates.

1. There is great opportunity to form friendships online. What do you see as the pros and cons of this phenomenon?

2. In our daily lives, we have come to believe that communities have responsibility for the welfare of individuals. In your opinion, whose responsibility is it to make communities safer, more livable, more beautiful, and more just? Give reasons, examples, personal experience, or facts to support your opinion.

Writing

EXERCISE 18. WRITING

Think of your own friendships and what they bring to your life. Write about your closest friendship and what that person means to you. Do your friendships fit with the characteristics or major functions outlined in Reading 4?

EXERCISE 19. WRITING AN EXTENDED DEFINITION

Write an extended definition of *one* of the following words. Remember that extended definitions begin with a formal definition, which is then extended with facts, examples, research, description, physical detail, or personal experience.

community	*entrepreneur*
friendship	*marriage*
etymology	*racism*
	happiness

After You Write

After you have completed the first draft of your extended definition, you should spend some time revising. The following questions will assist you.

1. Does your first paragraph contain a thesis statement and a formal definition of your topic?

2. Have you used description and physical details to make your extended definition interesting and easier to understand?

3. Have you provided examples, facts, or further research to give credibility to your extended definition?

4. Are your paragraphs well developed and do they follow logically?

CHAPTER 7

Ethical Issues: What Are the Boundaries?

Introduction to the Chapter

Almost every day, people everywhere have to make moral decisions. These decisions—all ethical decisions—could be about taking performance-enhancing drugs or about the way we treat animals for scientific purposes or whether we should end a life early or some other issue. Often we learn about ethical issues from newspapers or from radio or television. And often they affect us personally or professionally. The readings in this chapter concern ethical and moral choices. Reading 1 defines ethics and shows how ethical decisions concern us in sports for instance. Reading 2 examines the argument regarding ending a life early (assisted suicide and euthanasia) and examines what the law allows. Finally Reading 3 discusses the best way to train doctors when they need to learn new and difficult medical procedures.

As a writing assignment you will be given a choice of topics and asked to write an argumentative essay.

Reading 1—*Ethics and Integrity: Personal and Professional*

EXERCISE 1. PRE-READING DISCUSSION

Discuss the following questions before you read.

1. What does "moral choice" mean to you?

2. Give an example of a moral choice you have had to make.

3. What ethical choices do you think athletes have to make?

Ethics and Integrity: Personal and Professional

[1]   Basically, ethics has to do with moral choices—deciding what is the right or wrong thing to do in situations that have an effect on ourselves and those around us. Whether you decide to go for coffee or study is not typically a moral decision. However, if you really need to study for an important exam, which could determine whether or not you pass the course, ethical considerations do creep into this decision. Let's say your parents are supporting you while you attend university. By focusing on other activities at the expense of studying, you could be hurting your parents in that they have made sacrifices so that you could receive an education, and you are not doing your part in the process.

[2]   Integrity has to do with the seriousness with which you adhere to your moral principles. If your moral principles include not hurting your parents and fulfilling your part of a deal, then you will avoid the temptation to do something other than study for an important exam. People with little integrity seem to easily compromise their moral principles when they find themselves in situations where they are tempted to do so.

[3]   What are the vulnerabilities that exist for students? Probably the most obvious one is to commit some form of academic dishonesty, i.e., cheating on an exam or plagiarizing a term paper. When you cheat on an exam or plagiarize a paper, you hurt yourself as you are not demonstrating your awareness of a body of knowledge and without this background knowledge, you will not be able to extend the practice of academic pursuits. You also hurt the professor who was operating within a relationship of trust with his or her students.

[4]   Whether you are an athlete on a university team, a participant in intramural or recreational sports, or someone who works out to improve physically, you will most likely have to make some ethical decisions regarding your involvement in sport. One of the most common decisions athletes have to face is whether or not to take performance-enhancing drugs. This decision is not only a concern of elite athletes. The temptation to "bulk up" is a concern not only for the recreational weightlifter, but also for those participating in many sports at all levels. What are the ethical issues involved in taking performance-enhancing drugs?

[5]   When you take performance-enhancing drugs, you hurt yourself, you hurt other people, and you hurt the practice of sports. First, there are the health risks. If the drugs you take are dangerous to your health, you may hurt yourself. And you potentially hurt those who care for you, in the event that you suffer physical harm from taking these drugs. Also, if you play sports at a high level and are caught taking a drug which is banned in your sport, you could suffer fairly severe penalties which could hurt you as well as the people who have supported you in your involvement in sport. Finally, not only will you hurt your family and friends by taking performance-enhancing drugs, but you will also hurt your competitors. If you take drugs and your competitors don't, an element of unfairness has been added to the game. It is even possible that your competitors feel that they have to take drugs to compete with you, and they may feel they are being coerced into taking drugs, even if they would prefer not to.

[6]   As well as hurting your family and competitors, by taking performance-enhancing drugs, you are also hurting the practice of sport. Sport is often perceived as an opportunity to test one's abilities against people with similar skills. If you play simply to win, it will be difficult to persuade you not to use performance-enhancing drugs. However, if you participate in sports to improve your skills, there is a good reason not to take the risks involved when using performance-enhancing drugs; the reasons being, these drugs do not improve your skill level. They may increase your strength and speed, but they will not improve your technique. With the added strength or speed or both, you may increase your chances of winning but that does not mean that you are the more skilled player. Arguably, playing "drugged" changes the nature of the competition. The focus should remain on the athlete's ability to perform and not on how his or her body can perform with drugs. Thus, if we want sports to remain a competition between people to determine who is the most skilled, we must refrain from using performance-enhancing drugs.

[7]   Examples from two areas of your lives— academic and sporting—have been shared. The ethical principles you hold and the integrity with which you hold them affect not only you, but the people around you, as well as the practices of academic as well as sporting pursuits.

Source: Written by Dr. Sheryl Bergmann Drewe, University of Manitoba.

EXERCISE 2. COMPREHENSION CHECK

1. Answer true or false.

   Choosing where to go for a holiday is usually a moral decision. _____

2. Answer true or false.

   Concentrating on other activities when you should study affects only you and has no effect on anyone else. It is not a moral decision. _____

3. In your own words, write the meaning of the following terms.

   ethics: _____

   integrity: _____

   academic dishonesty: _____

4. Complete the sentence.

   When you commit academic dishonesty, you _____.

5. Paraphrase the following quotation: "When you cheat on an exam or plagiarize a paper, you hurt yourself as you are not demonstrating your awareness of a body of knowledge and without this background knowledge, you will not be able to extend the practice of academic pursuits." (paragraph 3)

   _____

   _____

   _____

6. According to Reading 1, what is one of the most important ethical decisions an athlete has to make?

   _____

   _____

7. In paragraph 5 the author says, ". . . they may feel they are being coerced into taking drugs." What is a synonym for *coerced*? Who does *they* refer to?

   coerced: _____

   they: _____

8. What effect does taking illegal drugs have on the personal and professional life of an athlete?

   _____

   _____

   _____

9. How is it possible to "hurt" the sport? What is a synonym for *hurt* as used in this reading?

   _____

   _____

EXERCISE 3. VOCABULARY IN CONTEXT

In paragraphs 4, 5, and 6 the author uses vocabulary that especially relates to sports. Study those paragraphs and find the words and phrases pertaining to sports. Define those that are not familiar to you. Try to find the meaning from the context before looking them up in the dictionary or asking someone else. Several of the words and phrases have been identified below.

Example: *Intramural* refers to sports that are played within a community or an institution, such as a university.

Example: *Recreational sports* are engaged in by most people for their own enjoyment and edification. The participants are not part of an elite team, such as might go to the Olympic Games, for instance.

EXERCISE 4. UNDERSTANDING THE STRUCTURE OF THE READING

Reading 1 is an argumentative essay in which the author puts forward a position on the topic and then provides points to support the argument. An argumentative essay has a specific structure and understanding that structure will help you in writing your own argumentative essay.

Complete the chart below. First determine what the thesis statement is. In other words, what is the author trying to persuade us to think? Then write short answers to the questions. Finally determine whether the author has supported her thesis statement well. If yes, how does the author do it?

Thesis statement:
Paragraph 2: How does the idea of integrity support the thesis?
Paragraph 3: What are the vulnerabilities for students?
Paragraph 4: What are the ethical issues in sport?
Paragraph 5: What are the effects of taking drugs?
Paragraph 6: What are the effects of drugs on sports?
Paragraph 7: What does the author conclude?

List five points of support that the author provides for the thesis statement. How can you categorize these points, that is, as examples, descriptions, facts, personal experience, or research?

1. _____

2. _____

3. _____

4. _____

5. _____

What is the author's position on the topic? Support your answer.

_____

_____

EXERCISE 5. WRITING

Write a letter to a friend in which you give your opinion about performance-enhancing drugs. Use 10 or more sports-related words and phrases you have learned. Be sure to support your opinion.

⊣ Reading 2—*The Fight for the Right to Die* ⊢

EXERCISE 6. PRE-READING DISCUSSION

Discuss the following questions before you read.

1. Have you any experience with someone who died? Explain.

2. Sometimes patients in hospitals are kept alive by machines. In your opinion, who has the right to turn off a machine when the patient is too sick to make the decision?

3. Most people avoid thinking of death, especially about helping someone end their life. Just thinking about it causes anxiety. Give your opinion of those (doctors or others) who help people end their lives to escape extreme pain and suffering.

4. In the country you are from, what is the "right" thing to do in such situations?

5. Complete this sentence: "What I dread most in my life is. . . ."

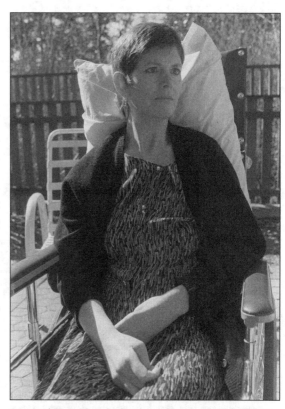

Sue Rodriquez fought for the right to assisted suicide.

EXERCISE 7. VOCABULARY TO KNOW BEFORE YOU READ

The following words are found in paragraph 1 of Reading 2. Study them in context and write the meaning on the line.

1.

Parliament:_____

legislators:_____

Supreme Court:_____

2. Use the three words in the following sentences.

   a) The highest court in the land, the _____, rejected their appeal to have the charges dropped concerning income tax evasion.

   b) When the _____ were asked to vote on the law, it was clear from the close count that they were divided on the issue.

   c) The members of _____ in Ottawa represent the people of Canada.

The Fight for the Right to Die

If I cannot give consent to my own death, whose body is this? Who owns my life?

—*Sue Rodriguez*

[1]   In Canada, as in most countries, assisted suicide is illegal but there is growing debate about changing the law in many parts of the world. In 1992, Sue Rodriguez forced the right-to-die debate into the spotlight in Canada. She was suffering from Lou Gehrig's disease, which is a debilitating and fatal illness. In a video statement played to members of Parliament, Rodriguez asked legislators to change the law that bans assisted suicide. She also fought the law that prohibits assisted suicide all the way to the Supreme Court of Canada, but she lost. Although the Supreme Court of Canada ultimately ruled against Rodriguez, her struggle did help to galvanize the public. Soon after the Supreme Court ruling, Rodriguez committed suicide with the help of an anonymous doctor.

Differences between Assisted Suicide and Euthanasia

[2]   Assisted suicide occurs when a person, typically someone suffering from an incurable illness or chronic intense pain, intentionally kills him or herself with the help of another individual. For example, a doctor may prescribe drugs with the understanding that the patient plans to use them to overdose fatally. Or a doctor may insert an intravenous needle into the arm of a patient, who then pushes a switch to trigger a fatal injection.

[3]   Euthanasia differs from assisted suicide in that someone other than the patient ends the patient's life as painlessly as possible. Euthanasia may be active, such as when a doctor gives a lethal injection to a patient. It can also be passive, in cases where a physician does not resuscitate a patient whose heart has stopped. As well it can happen when a doctor removes life-support equipment.

When Assisted Suicide Became a Legal Issue

[4]   Philosophers have contemplated the concept of "a good death" since ancient times. However, individual choice over dying only surfaced in intense public debate in the 1970s. Until then, anyone found guilty of attempted suicide in Canada, and in many other countries, could face jail time. However, the federal government decriminalized attempted suicide in 1972.

[5]   The legal right to refuse medical treatment emerged at the same time as technological advances in medicine allowed doctors to keep patients alive longer. A series of court cases in the 1970s won a mentally competent person the right to refuse medical intervention; this is a view now widely accepted. The debate over patient autonomy now centres on issues of active euthanasia and assisted suicide. It is those patients who live in chronic intense pain or with a degenerative or terminal illness such as multiple sclerosis, AIDS, or Alzheimer's disease who fight for the right to die.

Why It Is an Issue

[6]   People who want assisted suicide to be legalized believe that individuals should be able to control the time and circumstances of their own death. Some argue that actively causing one's own demise is no different from refusing life-saving treatment.

[7]   Opponents fear that vulnerable individuals may be coerced into assisted suicide to ease the financial burden of caring for them. They also worry that assisted suicide could ease pressure to provide better palliative care and find new cures and therapies. Some religious opponents argue that God, not humans, should decide the time for death. And many medical professionals maintain it is never morally permissible for doctors to help kill a patient.

The Law in Canada

[8]   The Criminal Code of Canada outlaws suicide assistance with penalties of up to 14 years in prison. However, opponents have recently challenged the law's constitutionality in court. The Rodriguez case was the most famous. The 42-year-old BC woman asked the Supreme Court of Canada to be allowed to kill herself with a doctor's help. Another woman, Chantal Maltais, also became famous when she committed suicide by hanging herself. She argued that the ban on assisted suicide violated the Constitution by curbing her rights of personal liberty and autonomy guaranteed in the Charter of Rights and Freedoms. The court rejected her argument and ruled that society's obligation to preserve life and protect the vulnerable outweighed her rights. However, several judges did suggest that Canada's laws might need to be changed to help people like Maltais and Rodriguez.

The Law in the United States

[9]   Both Canada and the United States have long outlawed assisted suicide, charging people who help others kill themselves with murder, manslaughter, and other offences. However, in the United States, there are three states where assisted suicide is sanctioned: Oregon, Washington, and Montana.

[10]   Many US states have introduced specific laws prohibiting assisted suicide after Dr. Jack Kevorkian and others pushed the debate into the public spotlight in the 1990s. Kevorkian, a retired Michigan pathologist, loudly advocated a person's right to die and invented an instrument that lets patients inject themselves intravenously with a lethal amount of potassium chloride. Police charged him in the deaths of a number of people, but juries repeatedly let him off until 1999, when he was jailed for second-degree murder after helping a terminally ill patient die. Kevorkian was released from jail in June 2007 and said he had no regrets about conducting the assisted suicide.

[11]   Oregon is the first state with a law that specifically allows physician-assisted suicide. Oregon's Death with Dignity Act was approved by voters in 1994, but blocked for three years by critics who challenged its constitutionality in the US Supreme Court. Oregon won, but again came under attack by the then US Attorney General, who threatened to revoke the licenses of doctors who assisted suicides. The law was upheld by the US Supreme Court in January 2006. The state's strict rules governing assisted suicides stipulate that the patient must have been declared terminally ill by two physicians and must have requested lethal drugs three times, including in writing.

[12]   Washington too allows assisted suicide. It adopted a ballot measure based on the Oregon law called Initiative 1000 during the November 2008 election.

[13]   In December 2008, a Montana judge overturned that state's law prohibiting doctor-assisted suicide in a ruling on a case involving a man with terminal cancer. However, since then, Montana has moved to sanction and make legal assisted suicide.

Where Euthanasia and Assisted Suicide are Legal

[14]   In addition to three American states, only three countries have authorized assisted suicide openly, legally and strictly regulated: the Netherlands, Belgium, and Switzerland.

[15]   The Netherlands introduced specific legislation to legalize assisted suicide and active euthanasia in 2002. The Dutch laid out narrow guidelines for doctors which include the following: The patient, who must be suffering unbearably and have no hope of improvement, must ask to die. The patient must clearly understand the condition and prognosis, and a second doctor must agree with the decision to help the patient to die.

[16]   Belgium legalized euthanasia in 2002, and the laws seem to encompass assisted suicide as well. Two doctors must be involved, as well as a psychologist if the patient's competency is in doubt. The doctor and patient negotiate whether death is to be by lethal injection or prescribed overdose.

[17]   Switzerland has allowed physician- and non-physician-assisted suicide since 1941. Three right-to-die organizations in the country help terminally ill people by providing counselling and lethal drugs. Many foreigners come to Switzerland from countries where assisted suicide is illegal in order to end their lives. Researcher David Wood (2011) writes that "recently, the Swiss have had to look at restricting foreign access to its Dignitas assisted-suicide program in the face of its growing international popularity. They don't want to become a suicide tourism destination. Since 1998, almost 1000 terminally ill people have left their homelands, where

assisted suicide is illegal, to be provided with a means to end their lives." He goes on to say that after strict medical protocols, the person is handed a lethal barbiturate, which is consumed with family present.

[18] Elsewhere, many countries seem to show slow movement toward legalizing assisted suicide and euthanasia, including

- Luxembourg, where legislation that would have permitted euthanasia was lost by a single vote in March 2003.

- Britain, where legislation that would have legalized assisted suicide for the terminally ill was defeated in the House of Lords in May 2006.

[19] The debate continues regarding how best to assist the terminally ill and how best to accommodate their last wishes, especially where it concerns assisted suicide. At this time, the laws in Canada and many countries around the world are not accommodating of the personal wishes of those who choose to end their life.

Sources: Adapted from "The Fight for the Right to Die." CBC News, http://www.cbc.ca/news/canada/story/2009/02/09/ f-assisted-suicide.html, retrieved 17 August 2011; and D. Wood, "The Fight to Die." The Tyee, http://thetyee.ca/ News/2011/07/13/FightToDie/, 13 July 2011, retrieved 8 October 2011.

EXERCISE 8. COMPREHENSION CHECK

1. What is the function of the quotation at the beginning of Reading 2?

   _____

2. What is meant by giving "consent to my own death"?

   _____

3. In your own words, state the difference between assisted suicide and euthanasia.

   _____

   _____

4. Why did assisted suicide become a legal issue?

   _____

5. What problems exist for Switzerland, where assisted suicide is legal?

   _____

6. Answer true or false to the following questions.

   a) For most of us, it is not difficult to know what we believe about assisted suicide or euthanasia.

      _____

   b) If assisted suicide becomes legal, the concern is that this will remove the initiative to provide better palliative care and find new cures and therapies. _____

7. Where is assisted suicide legal?

_____

8. Why do you think assisted suicide has been legalized in some countries and several states but not in others?

_____

EXERCISE 9. VOCABULARY IN CONTEXT

Collocations: Find the following medical-related collocations in Reading 2. Study them in context and guess their meanings. Write your guesses on the lines.

assisted/committed suicide:

_____

_____

intense/chronic pain:

_____

_____

incurable/degenerative illness:

_____

_____

medical intervention:

_____

_____

life-support equipment:

_____

_____

EXERCISE 10. USING COLLOCATIONS

Complete each sentence with the correct form of one of the collocations above.

1. The patient could not breathe on his own; he needed _____.

2. Sue Rodriguez wanted to be allowed _____ to end her life from _____ and _____ pain.

3. When a person has _____, it is thought that they have brought a long-term solution to a short-term issue.

4. HIV/AIDS is an _____ and _____ illness.

5. Because the accident was so serious, the occupant of the vehicle required _____ _____ to survive.

Mapping Information

By mapping information, it is possible to show relationships between the topic and its related ideas. Mapping shows visually how a reading passage is organized and how ideas are connected. It is a map of the concepts, the ideas, and the supporting information. You may use circles, boxes, or lines for mapping the information.

EXERCISE 11. UNDERSTANDING ORGANIZATION

Reading 2, "The Fight for the Right to Die," can be mapped according to the main ideas in the author's argument. It is also possible to include the position, whether pro or con, that the author is taking in the idea of assisted suicide. In a small group or with a partner complete the following questions.

1. Choose the thesis statement or main argument from those listed here.

   a) Doctor-assisted suicide should be allowed because doctors don't break the law when they help patients.
   b) Sue Rodriguez committed suicide with the help of a doctor; therefore, she was breaking the law.
   c) In Canada, as in most countries, assisted suicide is illegal but there is growing debate about changing the law in many parts of the world.
   d) Assisted suicide should never be allowed because it is morally wrong to many people.

2. What is the issue as outlined in paragraph 1?

   _____

3. What is the difference between assisted suicide and euthanasia?

   _____

4. Identify the salient points that led to assisted suicide becoming a legal issue.

   _____

   _____

5. What are the pros and cons of the issue?

   _____

   _____

6. Summarize the law regarding assisted suicide in Canada, in the United States, and in the world.

   _____

   _____

7. What is the conclusion?

   _____

   _____

EXERCISE 12. MAPPING

Map the article from the information you gathered by answering the questions in Exercise 11. Follow the guide below.

```
┌─────────────────────────────────────────┐
│              Paragraph 1                 │
│     Introduction: background provided    │
│  _____    │
│  _____    │
│  _____    │
└─────────────────────────────────────────┘
                    ▼
┌─────────────────────────────────────────┐
│            Thesis statement              │
│  _____    │
└─────────────────────────────────────────┘
                    ▼
┌─────────────────────────────────────────┐
│          Paragraphs 2 and 3              │
│   Define assisted suicide and euthanasia.│
│  _____    │
│  _____    │
└─────────────────────────────────────────┘
                    ▼
┌─────────────────────────────────────────┐
│          Paragraphs 4 and 5              │
│  Describe why assisted suicide is a legal│
│      issue and what prompted this.       │
│  _____    │
│  _____    │
│  _____    │
└─────────────────────────────────────────┘
                    ▼
┌─────────────────────────────────────────┐
│              Paragraph 6                 │
│   Give arguments for and against (pro    │
│      and con) assisted suicide.          │
│  pro: _____    │
│  _____    │
│  con: _____    │
│  _____    │
└─────────────────────────────────────────┘
                    ▼
```

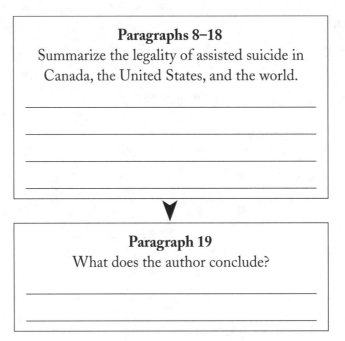

Paragraphs 8–18
Summarize the legality of assisted suicide in
Canada, the United States, and the world.

_____

_____

_____

_____

▼

Paragraph 19
What does the author conclude?

_____

_____

EXERCISE 13. DEBATE

First, in groups of four or five, share your opinions with other students and complete a group list outlining the arguments for and against assisted suicide. You may answer these questions in your groups: What is your instinctive response to assisted suicide and the right to die? Are you for or against it? Give reasons. Then, share the information with the class. Each group presents its list of pros and cons to the class. This list may be recorded on the board in a pro/con chart.

Finally state whether any of the points made you rethink your initial reactions or whether any of the points made you change your mind.

EXERCISE 14. SUMMARY WRITING

From your concept map or outline, write a summary of Reading 2.

EXERCISE 15. CRITICAL ANALYSIS

Discuss the following questions with your classmates.

1. Imagine you are a talented athlete who has just signed up with a coach who has a reputation of being able to take athletes to the Olympic Games. After observing you perform, the coach tells you that if you want to be ready for the Olympics, you will need a miracle. Athletes on your own team and others tell you that you should take performance-enhancing drugs, as other athletes do. What would you do? Give reasons for your decision.

2. Your father is 90 years old. He has just undergone hip surgery, which is healing quite well, but he has pneumonia and an infection. He cannot get out of bed, feed himself, speak, hear, or see very well. He is suffering as he struggles to survive. The hospital where he is staying has put him on oxygen and is feeding him intravenously. Do you ask the doctor to stop all assistance, or do you do whatever is possible to keep him alive? Give reasons for your answers.

Reading 3—*Medical Ethics: A Ghastly Way to Practice*

EXERCISE 16. PRE-READING DISCUSSION

Discuss the following questions before you read.

1. Identify some moral or ethical issues doctors have to deal with.
2. How do you think doctors learn to do the complicated medical procedures they have to perform?
3. What is your opinion of practising on animals? Give reasons.
4. Do you think it is proper for medical students to practise on human beings? Give reasons.

EXERCISE 17. SCANNING FOR INFORMATION

1. As a member of the trauma team, what was Dr. Meyers meant to do?

   _____

2. What did Dr. Meyers do when the patient died?

   _____

3. After the nurse walked in on Dr. Meyers and the student, what did she do?

   _____

4. What does Dr. Pat Melanson say is the tricky part?

   _____

5. Why did doctors stop practising on animals?

   _____

6. What are two current ways for doctors to practise and learn?

   _____

Medical Ethics: A Ghastly Way to Practice

[1] Dr. Christine Meyers, a young emergency-medicine resident at Montreal General Hospital, saw opportunity in death. She was a member of a trauma team that had tried and failed to revive an elderly surgical patient. As soon as he died, she called over a medical student and together they began a central-line insertion into a large blood vessel in the man's upper chest.

[2] This is a last-ditch procedure normally reserved for trauma victims on the brink of death. But in this instance, the medical student and Dr. Meyers were the only ones to benefit: They got a chance to practice a difficult procedure on someone who couldn't be injured by a mistake.

[3] Not everyone felt that their medical education trumped the fact that they were messing about with a dead person without permission. A veteran nurse walked in on them and objected. "Don't you realize the patient is dead?" Dr. Meyers recalls her saying. "I said, 'I think it's better for the

[3] medical student to learn this procedure on someone who can't be harmed rather than doing it for the first time on a patient who is alive.' The nurse felt what I was doing was inherently disrespectful."

[4] The nurse reported the incident to the hospital's ethics board. A hearing was held in April, and the board decided that Dr. Meyers's action was inappropriate. "The non-physician members of the board were pretty outraged," she recalls.

[5] Dr. Meyers was in one of the grey areas of medical ethics: How does a resident learn without practicing? How do you teach someone the hundreds of life-saving techniques used in an emergency department? Dr. Meyers and many others believe that acquiring experience by practicing on the newly dead—before they've become rigid with rigor mortis—is the best way to spare future patients from the mistakes of insufficiently prepared doctors. But every dead body is someone's mother or father, offspring, or sibling. It can be daunting for young residents to have to get consent from families for such procedures.

[6] This issue has been debated in the bioethics journals for years: Is it the best way for students to learn? What are the alternatives? Should hospitals have policies? Should family consent be required? There are no easy answers.

[7] What has evolved in the absence of a national protocol in the United States and Canada is passive acceptance—a belief that families would agree if we asked them so why bother them while they are grieving. A 1989 survey of 919 US hospitals found that 54 percent had practiced on the newly dead and just 3 percent of those hospitals had a policy requiring family consent. The issue is sufficiently hot that an episode of a medical television series featured two doctors practicing an intubation on a newly dead patient when the family walked in.

[8] In Montreal's teaching hospitals, it is not a question of whether the practice occurs but how often. The medical community is sharply at odds.

[9] Clinical ethicist Dr. Eugene Bereza of the Royal Victoria Hospital says he was appalled when he learned of the Meyers incident: "Doctors don't have a monopoly on making these decisions," he says. "Society never said to the medical profession, 'Forget about what we think.' Society never said, 'On issues that society is really uptight about, go ahead and disregard us.'"

[10] Dr. Pat Melanson, an emergency and critical-care specialist, says he has never practiced on the newly dead but he's seen it done several times. A teaching doctor at McGill Medical School, he says he thinks it's probably a good way to learn. But the consent issue is tricky: "It would be useful, strictly from the point of view of overall benefit, to allow residents to perform these skills on the newly dead. I think there are other ways to do it, but I'm not sure they're ideal. On the other hand, I do find the procedure somewhat distasteful."

[11] In a very informal survey, Dr. Meyers polled 32 emergency department physicians and found that more than 60 percent admitted to practicing on newly dead people. Only 3 percent had acquired family consent; most felt it was wrong not to.

[12] It isn't just emergency residents who are affected. Veteran physicians also need to practice seldom-used skills. For example, emergency-medicine physicians should be proficient at hundreds of

lifesaving techniques, including open-heart massages, central-line insertions and alternative forms of ventilation, including cricothyroidotomy, in which a tube is inserted into the trachea via a hole in the neck. Dr. Meyers hasn't done any of these in her three years of training. Someday, she says, she could be called upon to use those skills. Even Dr. Melanson is concerned about his skills, long ago honed in the cadaver lab and the intensive-care unit. "I've done many cricothyroidotomies but I haven't done one in three years. So the next time I have to do one, will I have the level of confidence I had before?"

[13] Dr. Kenneth Iserson, an Arizona surgeon who's written extensively in support of practicing on the newly dead, argues there is an ethical imperative because it provides the best training ground. He says society, by seeking perfection in its doctors, has implicitly given its consent.

[14] If the autonomy of the dead is so important, what about the rights of the living Dr. Meyers wonders? Any time a person is anesthetized for surgery, he or she runs a risk of having the intubation done by a medical student who has never done it before. And sometimes, doctors keep patients alive in order to practice resuscitation techniques. Doctors who spoke of this said it's hard to judge sometimes whether resuscitation is done for the sake of experience or whether it is a resident's final desperate attempt to save a life.

[15] These are all practices that blur the informed-consent and autonomy rules that guide doctors. "My position is that it shouldn't be done surreptitiously," says Dr. Melanson. "It should be out in the open. And if the resident has discomfort approaching the family, then I think that tells you something about how much they think the benefit will be."

[16] So what are the alternatives? There is an ever changing need to examine more ethical ways of doing things.

- When Dr. Melanson took an advanced trauma life-support course, they used animals that had been killed for the sole purpose of being practiced on. Animal rights activists have effectively eliminated that avenue. These days, his students use pig tracheas, leftovers from the local butcher. But pig and human throats aren't identical.
- During his training, Dr. Bereza recalls an excruciating two hours during which he and a classmate practiced IV insertion on each other.
- Paying volunteers is another option, but that has drawbacks. Some techniques are simply too painful and mutilating.
- Using plastic models is a clean solution, but has obvious drawbacks—no blood, no pressure.
- Doctors can visit a cadaver lab, but tissue changes soon after death. Using virtual cadavers is also an option, but the limitations are evident.
- Dr. Bereza says he understands the need for training, but he vehemently opposes any action without family consent. "You'd be surprised at how many people are willing when approached properly," he says.
- The Medical Secretariat of the Ontario Ministry of Health (2004) advises that video capacity has greatly increased the ease of difficult procedures such as intubations, especially in the operating room and in training students. Supervisors can assess students more easily by visualizing the procedure.

- Robots are used to perform difficult procedures. In 2011, a robot operated by remote control was introduced by Dr. Thomas M. Hemmerling of McGill University Health Centre and his team. Dr. Hemmerling performed the world's first robotic intubation in a patient at the Montreal General Hospital.

[17] In conclusion, Dr. Meyers has been asked to sit on the committee studying the issue. She would like to see the matter put into the public forum for no other reason than to let the public know what is happening. Then when a doctor comes looking for consent, it won't be such a shock.

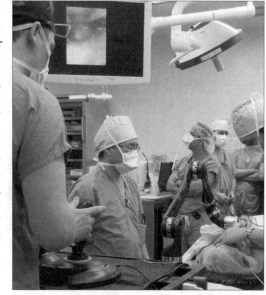

Source: Adapted from Charlene Sadler. "A Ghastly Way to Practice."
Globe and Mail 6 June 1998. D5; and Medical Advisory Secretariat,
Ontario Ministry of Health "Video Laryngoscopy for Tracheal Intubation. An Evidence-Based Analysis." Ontario Health Technology Assessment Series 2004: 4, 5. http://www.health.gov.on.ca/english/providers/program/mas/tech/reviews/pdf/rev_vidlaryng_050104.pdf. Retrieved 8 August 2011.

EXERCISE 18. COMPREHENSION CHECK

1. In paragraph 2 you read, "They got a chance to practice a difficult procedure on someone who couldn't be injured by a mistake." Who are "they?" What procedure was practised?

_____

2. In paragraphs 2 and 3 the author uses some informal language; in academic English, more formal language is usually the norm. Identify the informal words, give their meanings, and substitute more formal synonyms.

_____

_____

3. Why did the nurse report the case to the ethics board?

_____

4. What is the ethical issue in this instance?

_____

5. What does Dr. Eugene Bereza believe families of the dead patient would do if a medical student practised on their relative?

_____

6. What policy do most hospitals have regarding practising on newly deceased patients?

_____

7. Does ethicist Dr. Bereza agree with Dr. Meyers? Give support for your answer.

_____

8. Why do some doctors practise on newly dead people without the consent of the deceased person's relatives?

_____

9. What are some modern ways that doctors can practise and learn? And, what are the limitations?

_____

_____

10. What do you think should be the policy for doctors who must practise difficult procedures?

_____

Exercise 19. Vocabulary in Context

A. Medical Terminology

Reading 3 contains many medical terms. Try to guess from the context what the underlined terms mean, before consulting a dictionary or discussing with your instructor.

1. "She was a member of a trauma team that had tried and failed to revive an elderly surgical patient. As soon as he died, she called over a medical student and together they began a central-line insertion into a large blood vessel in the man's upper chest." (paragraph 1)

   trauma team: _____

   revive: _____

   central-line insertion: _____

2. "Dr. Meyers and many others believe that acquiring experience by practicing on the newly dead—before they've become rigid with rigor mortis—is the best way to spare future patients from the mistakes of insufficiently prepared doctors." (paragraph 5)

   rigid with rigor mortis: _____

3. Give the meaning of _cricothyroidotomy_ as defined in paragraph 12.

   _____

4. Give the meaning of the underlined words. "Even Dr. Melanson is concerned about his skills, long ago honed in the cadaver lab and the intensive-care unit." (paragraph 12)

   cadaver lab: _____

   intensive-care unit: _____

5. Provide a formal definition of intubation (paragraph 14) and resuscitation. (paragraph 14)

   intubation: _____

   resuscitation: _____

B. Vocabulary: Completing Sentences

The following words are from "Medical Ethics: A Ghastly Way to Practice." Choose the word from the list that best fits into the blank spaces in the sentences. It may be necessary to change the form of the word.

Vocabulary words:

trauma, revive, last-ditch, brink, veteran, inherently, daunting, distasteful, proficient, implicitly, excruciating, mutilating, vehemently

a) The family was _____ opposed to using the patient for medical practice.

b) Jason demanded that he be compensated for the _____ he suffered in the accident. His girlfriend was so severely injured that she could not be _____ by the medics at the scene.

c) The engineer, a person _____ and respected in his profession, said that because of the extreme cold in Canada the foundations of buildings would predictably crack. These cracks do not represent any _____ danger to the soundness of the structure.

d) During the war, the victims suffered _____ pain as was evident from their _____ bodies.

e) The princess was annoyed by the media's unending interest in every facet of her life. She found their pictures of her on private family occasions extremely _____.

f) The police made one more _____ effort to find the missing man.

EXERCISE 20. CRITICAL ANALYSIS

In small groups, discuss the ethical issues that follow.

1. Suppose your sister, brother, or another relative died soon after a car crash. The doctor comes to the waiting area just before the relative dies to tell you that death is near and then asks if student doctors may practise a difficult procedure on your relative immediately after death. How would you react? What would you say? Explain.

2. Imagine that a good friend of yours enjoys hunting. He invites you to go along, all expenses paid of course, to hunt bear. But it is not bear-hunting season, and the particular bears your friend is after are on the endangered species list. Do you go hunting? Give reasons for your answers.

EXERCISE 21. MAPPING THE AUTHOR'S ARGUMENT

> 1. State the main argument about using newly dead patients for medical professionals to practise on.
>
> _____
>
> _____
>
> _____

▼

2. Present pro arguments (arguments in favour of the practice).

_____

_____

_____

3. Present con arguments (arguments against the practice).

_____

_____

_____

4. State the author's conclusion.

_____

_____

_____

Exercise 22. Summary Writing

Write a summary using the information in the mapping chart.

Writing

Exercise 23. Writing an Argumentative Essay

Choose one of the following topics for your essay assignment.

1. Doctors have the right and the power to attach a Do Not Resuscitate (DNR) order to a patient's chart. They need not consult the family first if they do not think it is necessary—although often they do so.

    Write an argumentative essay in which you present your opinion on the right thing to do about DNRs and try to persuade the reader that you are correct.

2. Animal rights groups are opposed to using animals for scientific purposes in laboratories. Their opponents believe we need to use animals for testing so that human beings can benefit from the scientific breakthroughs.

    Write an argumentative essay in which you present your view in a persuasive manner.

3. Many people are concerned about violence in sports, which can sometimes cause serious injury and end an athlete's career. There are many ethical questions concerning violence in sport, such as the following: What do you think should be the limit in measuring appropriate contact in sports? How should violence in sports be controlled? Do violent strategies learned in sport carry over to other aspects of life?

   Write an argumentative essay in which you present your view about violence in sport.

4. Choose another ethical issue or controversy that interests you. With your classmates, brainstorm and discuss a range of issues. Then write an argumentative essay on one of the issues, arguing for or against the specific issue.

| Writing Plan

1. After you have selected a topic, you will need to gather information and ideas before you write. Take a position and write down all the ideas you can. It is good to list both sides, pro and con. Since each controversy has two sides, you should be aware of both.

2. Make a list of the major points in your argument. Emphasize the side of the argument that has your opinion. It will be longer because that is what you want to support.

3. Write out your thesis statement, basing it on your information so far.

4. Organize your arguments in order of importance. To have the strongest impact, consider arranging your argument from least important to most important.

5. To present an argument that will persuade the reader, you will need to use either logic or emotion, or both. Look back at the readings "Ethics and Integrity: Personal and Professional" and "Medical Ethics: A Ghastly Way to Practice" and determine where logic was used and where emotion was used.

6. Gather information that supports each of your points. Use facts, examples, personal observation and experiences, quotations, imagery, and data, and be sure to cite authorities.

7. Select methods of development, such as definition, comparison, process, and cause-effect, that will help to present your opinion in the strongest possible way.

8. Present your counter-argument so that your essay is not one-sided. Use a transition to introduce the counter-argument. You may use the following expressions:

   Some may argue that. . .
   Critics of this position point out that. . .
   At this point, contrary opinions must be considered. . .

9. It is then necessary to argue against the counter-argument, showing that the point may be valid but that it is not strong or important. You must show that it is untrue or incorrect. You need to do this because your reader may believe it rather than accept your opinion or main argument.

Overall Plan of the Essay

To review the structure of an argumentative piece of writing on a controversial topic, look back at Reading 3, "Medical Ethics: A Ghastly Way to Practice," and Reading 1, "Ethics and Integrity: Personal and Professional." How are the arguments presented? Is it like Plan A or Plan B below, or does it have a different structure?

Plan A

Paragraph 1: introduction plus thesis statement
Paragraph 2: pro argument 1 (weakest argument that supports your opinion)
Paragraph 3: pro argument (stronger)
Paragraph 4: pro argument (strongest)
Paragraph 5: con argument and your refutation
Paragraph 6: conclusion and recommendation

Plan B

Paragraph 1: introduction and thesis statement
Paragraph 2: con argument plus your refutation
Paragraph 3: pro (weakest)
Paragraph 4: pro (stronger)
Paragraph 5: pro (strongest)
Paragraph 6: conclusion

These two plans, which are samples of possible approaches in organization, may have more than one paragraph devoted to pro or con points. Each essay is different and dependent on the writer's audience, purpose, thesis, and techniques of support.

Checklist

After you have written a draft of the essay, ask yourself the following questions as you revise.

1. Is it clear who my audience is?

2. Is the purpose of the essay clearly stated and explained?

3. Is there a clear thesis statement?

4. Have I supported the thesis statement with facts, examples, personal information, description, or research?

5. Have I argued pro and con?

6. Do my pro arguments provide strong evidence?

7. Have I refuted the con argument?

8. Have I concluded logically?

9. Have my paragraphs been connected with appropriate connectors?

CHAPTER 8

Varieties of Intelligence

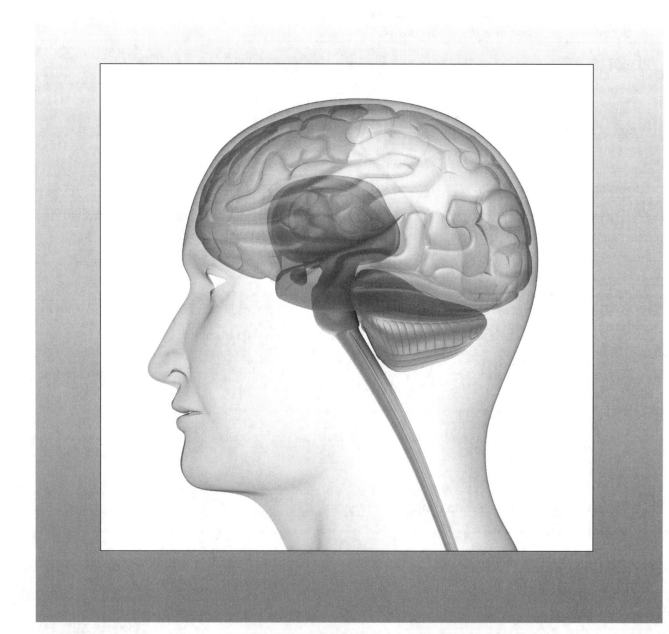

Introduction to the Chapter

What is intelligence? Who are the people who we believe are especially intelligent? What special knowledge or skills do these people possess?

Intelligence can be defined and explained in different ways. Reading 1, "A Description of the Eight Intelligences," discusses intelligence as it has been defined in education. Reading 2, "Do Grades Really Matter?" examines a particular form of intelligence called emotional intelligence.

As you work through this chapter, you will practise a variety of techniques that will help you remember the information and ideas in the texts you read. It is important to remember the main ideas and important details in the articles because, at the end of the chapter, you will be asked a series of questions based on the readings.

Reading 1—*A Description of the Eight Intelligences*

EXERCISE 1. PRE-READING—WRITING BEFORE YOU READ

Writing before you read is a strategy that can help clarify your thoughts and prepare you for reading. It can also make you more aware of your own biases; this may increase your understanding of the similarities and differences between your own ideas and the author's.

Answer the following questions before you read.

1. Name a historical figure or someone you know whom you consider especially intelligent. What is it that makes this person intelligent?

   _____

2. What is intelligence? Write your own definition.

   _____

3. Have you ever taken an IQ test? What is your opinion of IQ testing?

   _____

A Description of the Eight Intelligences

[1]   In his 1983 book, *Frames of Mind*, Howard Gardner presented his Theory of Multiple Intelligences that reinforces his cross-cultural perspective of human cognition. The intelligences are languages that all people speak and are influenced, in part, by the cultures in which we are born. They are tools for learning, problem-solving, and creating throughout life. A brief description of Gardner's eight intelligences follows.

[2]   **Linguistic intelligence** consists of the ability to think in words and to use language to express and appreciate complex meanings. Authors, poets, journalists, speakers, and newscasters exhibit high degrees of linguistic intelligence.

hand in!

[3] **Logical-mathematical intelligence** makes it possible to calculate, quantify, consider propositions and hypotheses, and carry out complex mathematical operations. Scientists, accountants, engineers, and computer programmers all demonstrate this intelligence.

[4] **Spatial intelligence** instills the capacity to think in three-dimensional ways as do sailors, pilots, sculptors, painters, and architects. It enables one to perceive external and internal imagery, to recreate, transform, or modify images, to navigate oneself and objects through space, and to produce or decode graphic information.

[5] **Bodily-kinesthetic intelligence** enables one to manipulate objects and fine-tune physical skills. It is evident in athletes, dancers, surgeons, and crafts-people. In Western societies, physical skills are not as highly valued as cognitive ones, and yet elsewhere the ability to use one's body is a necessity for survival and an important feature of many prestigious roles.

[6] **Musical intelligence** is evident in individuals who possess a sensitivity to pitch, melody, rhythm, and tone. Those demonstrating this intelligence include composers, conductors, musicians, critics, and instrument makers, as well as sensitive listeners.

[7] **Interpersonal intelligence** is the capacity to understand and interact effectively with others. It is evident in successful teachers, social workers, actors, or politicians. Just as Western culture has recently begun to recognize the connection between mind and body, so too has it come to value the importance of proficiency in interpersonal behaviour.

[8] **Intrapersonal intelligence** refers to the ability to construct an accurate perception of oneself and to use such knowledge in planning and directing one's life. Some individuals with strong intrapersonal intelligence specialize as theologians, psychologists, and philosophers.

[9] **Naturalist intelligence** consists of observing patterns in nature, identifying and classifying objects, and understanding natural and human-made systems. Skilled naturalists include farmers, botanists, hunters, ecologists, and landscapers.

[10] Gardner is careful to explain that intelligence should not be limited to the ones he has identified. He believes that the eight, however, provide a far more accurate picture of human capacities than do previous unitary theories. Contrary to the small range of abilities that many standard IQ tests measure, Gardner's theory offers an expanded image of what it means to be human. He also notes that each intelligence contains several sub-intelligences. For example, there are sub-intelligences within the domain of music that include playing music, singing, writing musical scores, conducting, critiquing, and appreciating music. Each of the seven other intelligences also encompasses numerous components.

[11] Another aspect of the Multiple Intelligences is that they may be conceptualized in three broad categories. Four of the eight, spatial, logical-mathematical, bodily-kinesthetic, and naturalist, may be viewed as "object-related" forms of intelligence. These capacities are controlled and shaped by the objects that individuals encounter in their environments. On the other hand, the "object-free" intelligences, consisting of verbal-linguistic and musical, are not shaped by the physical world but are dependent on language and musical systems. The third category consists of the "person-related" intelligences with inter- and intrapersonal intelligences reflecting a powerful set of counterbalances.

[12] Each intelligence appears to have its own developmental sequence, emerging, and blossoming at different times in life. Musical intelligence is the earliest form of human giftedness to emerge; it is a mystery why this is so. Gardner suggests that excelling at music as a child may be conditioned by the fact that this intelligence is not contingent upon accruing life experience. On the other hand, the personal intelligences require extensive interaction with and feedback from others before becoming well developed.

[13] Gardner believes that since each intelligence can be used for good or ill purposes, all eight are inherently value-free. Goebbels and Gandhi both had strong interpersonal intelligence, but applied it in dramatically different ways. How individuals go about using their intelligences within society is a moral question of crucial importance.

[14] It is evident that creativity can be expressed through all the intelligences. Gardner notes, however, that most people are creative within a specific domain. For example, although Einstein was gifted mathematically and scientifically, he did not exhibit equal genius linguistically, kinesthetically, or interpersonally. Most people appear to excel within one or two intelligences.

Source: Adapted from L. Campbell, B. Campbell, and D. Dickinson. *Teaching and Learning through Multiple Intelligences,* 3rd ed. (Boston: Pearson, 2004), xx–xxii.

Exercise 2. Comprehension Check

Using your understanding of the reading, answer true or false to the following statements. Then, on a separate sheet of paper, modify all the false statements to make them true.

1. The intelligences that I exhibit are not influenced by my culture. _____

2. Communications experts have a high degree of linguistic intelligence. _____

3. Pilots demonstrate spatial intelligence by working well under pressure. _____

4. Craftspeople demonstrate bodily-kinesthetic intelligence through their many innovative ideas. _____

5. Intrapersonal intelligence refers to our understanding of ourselves. _____

6. Gardner's theory would support the use of standard IQ tests. _____

7. The naturalist intelligence is considered an "object-related" intelligence. This is because naturalist intelligence refers to knowledge of the external environment. _____

8. "Person-related" intelligences are among the earliest intelligences to develop in children. _____

9. Most people excel in more than two of the intelligences. _____

Exercise 3. Vocabulary in Context

Find a word in Reading 1 to match each of the definitions given below.

Example: A word meaning *more than one* (paragraph 1) multiple

1. *knowing* or *thinking* (paragraph 1) _____

   (Can you find the adjectival form of this word in paragraph 5? _____)

2. *pertaining to language* (paragraph 2) _____

3. *to show evidence of* (paragraphs 2 and 14) _____

4. *to show clearly* (paragraph 3) _____

5. *ability* (paragraphs 4, 7, 10, and 11) _____

6. *to be aware of* (paragraph 4) _____

   (Can you find the noun form of this word in paragraph 8? _____)

7. *clearly seen* (paragraphs 5 and 6) _____

8. *to meet* (paragraph 11) _____

9. *order* (paragraph 12) _____

10. *a large amount of* (paragraph 12) _____

11. *to do something very well* (paragraph 14) _____

   (Can you find the gerund form in paragraph 12? _____)

Exercise 4. Applying What You Have Read

Find someone who can do each of the activities listed below and ask him or her to sign your page. A person can sign your page only once.

_____ 1. likes to write articles and have them published.

_____ 2. can tell if someone is singing off-key.

_____ 3. can calculate numbers easily in his or her head.

_____ 4. likes to read books with many pictures.

_____ 5. likes to dance.

_____ 6. likes doing puzzles and mazes.

_____ 7. regularly spends time meditating.

_____ 8. can list three things that help him or her to learn.

_____ 9. can draw a picture of his or her favourite food.

_____ 10. has a good joke to tell.

_____ 11. will sing part of a favourite song.

_____ 12. sings in the shower.

_____ 13. can easily identify at least 10 different kinds of flowers.

_____ 14. finds it hard to sit for long periods.

_____ 15. is often involved in social activities at night.

_____ 16. loves to teach people new skills.

Exercise 5. Critical Analysis

Discuss the following questions with your classmates.

1. Which of Gardner's intelligences is represented in each of the statements in Exercise 4?

2. For each of the intelligences, name at least one or two people in your class who demonstrate that form of intelligence.

3. In addition to the ways suggested in Exercise 4, in what ways do you demonstrate each of the eight intelligences in your daily life?

4. According to the article, "Gardner is careful to explain that intelligence should not be limited to the ones he has identified." (paragraph 10) Can you think of other forms of intelligence not identified by Gardner?

5. Do you agree with Gardner's concept of intelligence? In your opinion, does it take away from or add to the traditional view of intelligence represented in IQ testing?

The Study Summary

Writing a summary is one of several aids to remembering information. Writing can help you clarify your thoughts about what you have read. To write a study summary, follow these steps.

1. Read the text carefully, thinking about the author's main purpose for writing.

2. Understand the major points in the author's explanation or argument.

    a) Identify the structure of the argument. Ask yourself how the writer has organized his or her text (e.g., comparison or contrast, extended definition, cause and effect, or a combination of those forms).

    b) Identify topic sentences and summary statements.

3. Look for the important details within each point. Note definitions that you may need to know. Also note any significant examples that will help you remember the information.

Note: Look for facts and examples that are connected to your own experience or knowledge. This will make the information easier to remember. (In this case, you might associate one member of your class with each of the intelligences.)

EXERCISE 6. WRITING A SUMMARY

Write a summary of the original text, using your own words. When you use the words of the original author, put quotation marks around them so that later you will know which words are your own and which come from someone else.

Your study summary should include the following:

1. the title, author, and page numbers of the material that you are summarizing;

2. the main ideas of the original text; and

3. any important details (e.g., definitions or examples) that you need to remember.

Also, in your summary you may note

1. any connections that you have made between the content of the reading and your own life; and

2. questions that you still have about the reading.

When you have completed a draft, compare your summary to those of at least two of your classmates. Note especially the information that each of you has included. Then rewrite your summary to clarify the ideas and to strengthen any sections in which information is lacking.

Reading 2—*Do Grades Really Matter?*

EXERCISE 7. PRE-READING DISCUSSION

Many people in the North American workplace believe that "emotional intelligence" is important for success.

1. What do you think is meant by emotional intelligence?

2. How might emotional intelligence be different from cognitive intelligence?

3. What characteristics would a person with emotional intelligence possess?

EXERCISE 8. PRE-READING—SKIMMING AND SCANNING

The reading below is an excerpt from a longer article that was published in *Maclean's* magazine called "Do Grades Really Matter?" Discuss the following questions before you read.

1. Scan the reading below for a definition of emotional intelligence. How similar was your idea of emotional intelligence to the definition given in this text?

2. Read the title, subtitle, and first and last paragraphs of this excerpt. What is the main topic and point?

3. For what specific audience do you think this article was originally published?

Do Grades Really Matter?

A growing body of evidence suggests grades don't predict success—
C+ students are the ones who end up running the world.

[1] A generation ago, David McClelland, the Harvard psychologist, was asked to find out why so many of the best students from Ivy League schools floundered in the US foreign service. It turned out that top performers on the job took the time to learn all about their potential audience before making a move. They considered how other people were feeling and thinking and adjusted their message accordingly. The Ivy League kids who were flailing did not do this.

[2] Roger Martin, dean of the University of Toronto's Joseph L. Rotman School of Management, may have found a reason why. In a previous job at the consulting firm Monitor, Martin used to hire the top scholars from Harvard, but he noticed they didn't perform any better than other people. Why? "They're told over and over again that they're right. Then they go out to the world and try to be right, and they're flabbergasted when people don't follow."

[3] A lack of insight into people can be dangerous in the corner office. "When a CEO gets let go, or is derailed, it's almost never because he's poor at math or couldn't express himself verbally," says Gary Latham, a professor of organizational behaviour at Rotman. "It's a lack of emotional intelligence, the ability to read yourself and others. A lot of CEOs get in trouble because they can't read their own board. They see heads nodding, but that doesn't necessarily mean agreement."

[4]   In 1973, McLelland proposed a radical new way to hire people. Instead of just relying on marks and IQ, employers should identify the behaviours that distinguish the people who succeed in that position, and hire people who behave like that. Drawing on this research, the Hay Group identifies the behaviours needed for any given job, which can vary depending on the job. Many of the competencies are emotional, such as the ability to listen, self-control, flexibility, and the ability to work in a team.

[5]   These kinds of attributes, of course, don't get a grade in high school, so it would be easy to overlook a future star in business. Take Paul Clinton. He wasn't interested in school, much to the distress of his father, a senior high school administrator in Vancouver. But after dropping out of college, he turned on when he took a sales job at a major packaged goods company. By his early 40s, Clinton was promoted to be North American head of the global beverage company Diageo. Knowing how to sell was critical. So was the ability to cut through the clutter, identify what was critical for success, and deliver it. And he wouldn't have hit the big time if he didn't know how to manage people—especially in a company that has to sell the products.

[6]   Some schools are getting it. In Toronto, for instance, Greenwood College School was launched in 2002 with a $10-million donation from Richard Wernham, a former lawyer and money manager. Wernham, the son of educators, says he started the private school because he noticed, in his professional and business career, that the top performers were not necessarily A students in high school. They were often people who had struggled. Success, Wernham thought, was driven by personal qualities like resilience, determination, initiative, the ability to work in a team. Greenwood sets the tone from the start when Grade 7 and 8 students head out for a two-week camping trip. Canoeing teaches perseverance, resilience, interdependence and integrity, says David Thompson, the principal. "It's an incredible leveller. It doesn't matter if an A student is in the bow, and a C+ student is in the stern. Marks are irrelevant. It's how you are."

[7]   Meanwhile, Ontario's Education Ministry is trying to instill "character development initiative" in all provincial schools. Teachers will be encouraged to show kids how to read other people's feelings from non-verbal clues, says Avis Glaze, Ontario's chief student achievement officer. Kids might not get a grade for empathy, but it will help them in later life, she says. "In my career as a teacher, I always said, 'Do not write kids off because their marks are not high. They will be stars in the workplace. Why? Because they have the qualities that will assist them.'"

[8]   Angus Reid used to sit in the classroom watching the clock to see how long he could hold his breath before getting out of there. Reid was dyslexic and had to complete Grade 12 English in night school. Then, he says, "I began to read stuff I wanted to read," and he ended up with a doctorate. "To be successful, everyone needs the same thing—a sense of self-esteem," Reid says. "The most important ingredient, whether the academics are good, bad or ugly, is that your self-esteem is intact at the end of the day, so you don't leave high school thinking you're a loser, that you'll never get anywhere in life. I think that's the single most important ingredient, and the one that parents, unwittingly steal from their kids."

Source: Excerpted from Sarah Scott. "Do Grades Really Matter?" *Maclean's* (30 August 2007), http://oncampus.macleans.ca/education/2007/08/30/do-grades-really-matter/, retrieved 14 October 2011.

Exercise 9. Comprehension Check

1. What, according to David McClelland, is important for success?

   _____

2. Do David McClelland and Roger Martin have the same ideas about what leads to success? Be prepared to explain your response.

   _____

3. Gary Latham is quoted as saying, "It's a lack of emotional intelligence, the ability to read yourself and others. A lot of CEOs get in trouble because they can't read their own board. They see heads nodding, but that doesn't necessarily mean agreement." (paragraph 3) What is the meaning of "CEOs" and "their own boards"? What is the main point that the author is making here?

   _____

4. The article discusses the experiences of Paul Clinton. Why does the author discuss Clinton's experience?

   _____

5. The article also discusses the experiences of Angus Reid. Why does the author discuss Reid's experience?

   _____

6. According to the article, does success in high school guarantee success later in life? Be prepared to explain your response.

   _____

7. Based on your reading of the excerpt, what personal qualities contribute to emotional intelligence?

   _____

Exercise 10. Vocabulary in Context

Find the listed words in the text. Then, in groups of three, think of a synonym, a definition, or the general sense of each of the words. Also, note any clues provided by the context that helped you to discover the meaning of the words.

Note: Do *not* use a dictionary for this exercise.

> **Example:** *floundered* (paragraph 1)
>
> Meaning: struggled; had difficulties
>
> Clues: The main idea of the paragraph leads us to this meaning. McClelland is a psychologist who is asked to help understand something that must be a problem. What is the problem? Students from good schools *are struggling* in the US foreign service.
>
> "David McClelland . . . was asked to find out why so many of the best students from Ivy League schools struggled in the US foreign service." The word *struggled* makes sense in this context.

1. *flailing* (paragraph 1)

     Meaning: _____

     Clues: _____

2. *flabbergasted* (paragraph 2)

     Meaning: _____

     Clues: _____

3. *gets let go* (paragraph 3)

     Meaning: _____

     Clues: _____

4. *radical* (paragraph 4)

     Meaning: _____

     Clues: _____

5. *vary* (paragraph 4)

     Meaning: _____

     Clues: _____

6. *competencies* (paragraph 4)

     Meaning: _____

     Clues: _____

7. *attributes* (paragraph 5)

     Meaning: _____

     Clues: _____

8. *turned on* (paragraph 5)

     Meaning: _____

     Clues: _____

9. *resilience* (paragraph 6)

     Meaning: _____

     Clues: _____

10. *initiative* (paragraph 6)

     Meaning: _____

     Clues: _____

Share your predictions and the clues provided by the context with the other members of your class.

Remember: When you encounter a new word in your reading, you must decide how important that word is for your comprehension of the text. If the word does not seem crucial to your overall understanding of the text, it may be enough to have a general sense of the meaning of the word. However, if the word is important for your comprehension of the text, you should try to understand it. Use the context to help you understand the word and, if you are not sure that you have understood the meaning correctly, look in a dictionary.

Writing

Underlining and Annotating

Underlining and annotating are two techniques that may help you remember what you have read. Underlining can be used to highlight important ideas so that when you review the text later, you can easily concentrate on what is most important. Annotating, or using marginal notes, can be used along with underlining to help you remember important ideas, examples, and definitions. The following hints may help you underline and annotate effectively:

- Read part of the text first and then go back and underline. After you have read a portion, you will know which ideas are most important.
- Underline only the most important words. If you underline too much, the purpose of underlining is lost.
- When you annotate, you may use either symbols or a brief paraphrase. Some symbols that you might use are

  ex. — example   *def.* — definition   * — important idea

It is a good idea to devise your own symbols. Think of symbols that you could use for

- a paragraph that summarizes the main idea of a text
- an important point that may be the focus of a test question.

Now, study the following examples from "Do Grades Really Matter?" in which a reader has used a system of underlining and annotating.

Example 1

A lack of insight into people can be dangerous in the corner office. "When a CEO gets let go, or is derailed, it's almost never because he's poor at math or couldn't express himself verbally," says Gary Latham, a professor of organizational behavior at Rotman. "It's a lack of emotional intelligence,   *def.* the ability to read yourself and others. A lot of CEOs get in trouble because they can't read their own board. They see heads nodding, but that doesn't   *ex.* necessarily mean agreement."

Example 2

In 1973, McLelland proposed <u>a radical new way to hire people</u>. Instead of   *
just relying on marks and IQ , employers should identify the behaviours that
distinguish the people who succeed in that position, and hire people who
behave like that. Drawing on this research, the Hay Group identifies the
behaviours needed for any given job, which can vary depending on the job.
<u>Many of the competencies are emotional</u>, such as <u>the ability to listen</u>,   *ex.*
<u>self-control, flexibility, and the ability to work in a team</u>.

Creating Maps

Drawing a map or diagram is another way to help remember the main ideas of a text. A map should show
the main and supporting ideas of a text and the relationships between the ideas.

To create a map, write the main topic at the top or centre of a page. Then write down each of the
important supporting ideas; draw lines to show how these ideas are related to one another.

"A Description of the Eight Intelligences" is an excerpt from a textbook called *Teaching and Learning
through Multiple Intelligences*. It is quite straightforward to map the ideas in this excerpt because the
organization is clear and logical.

A sample map of "A Description of the Eight Intelligences" is shown.

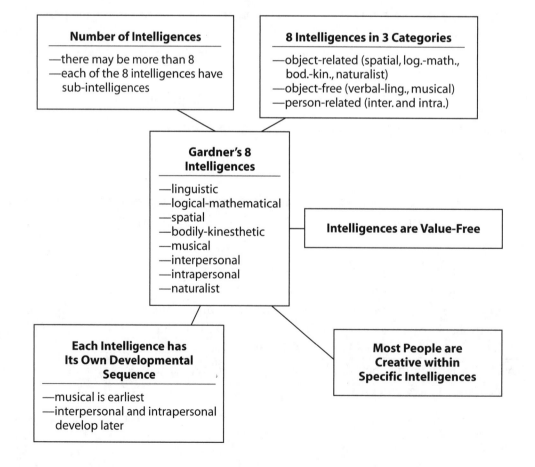

EXERCISE 11. UNDERLINE OR MAP

Decide which system (underlining and annotating or mapping) would be best for helping you remember the ideas in "Do Grades Really Matter?". Then underline or map the main ideas in the excerpt.

EXERCISE 12. CRITICAL ANALYSIS

Discuss the following Questions with your Classmates.

1. Examine the image below. What is the creator of the image saying about the relationship between IQ and EQ? Do you agree with the creator of the image? How important do *you* think EQ is for success in the workplace?

2. How might measuring EQ be helpful? How might it hurt people?

3. What might some of the difficulties be in evaluating a person's EQ?

4. Overall, do you think EQ testing is a good idea? Why or why not?

Short-Answer Questions

When you begin your academic studies, it is very likely that you will have to write formal tests that evaluate your knowledge of course content. One kind of question you will probably encounter is the short-answer question, which requires the student to write one or more paragraphs in response.

Answers to short answer questions should be

- Concise. Provide as much content as you can that relates to the question; do not add extraneous or irrelevant information.
- Well-organized. Introduce your ideas with topic sentences that pertain directly to the question. Avoid long introductions; writing them wastes precious time.
- Grammatically well written. Even though you may be pressed for time, your grammar must be as correct as possible.

| Vocabulary in Short-Answer Questions |—————————

To respond to short-answer questions precisely, it is important to understand the instructions. Some of the most common words used in short-answer questions are listed below.

Words that ask for retelling of information in readings or lectures

define	Give the meaning.
describe	Create a picture of an event, a process, or an object by using words.
list or enumerate	Give a series of related items.
summarize	Give a concise account of a body of information.

Words that ask you to make sense of information or ideas

analyze	Discuss the meaning of information that you have read about or discussed in class.
compare	Show similarities and differences.
contrast	Present a topic in detail (perhaps including your own analysis).
discuss	Show differences.
exemplify	Support a point by using examples.
explain	Make clear (e.g., show the causes or effects of something, discuss reasons).

Words that ask for your own opinion

evaluate	Give your opinion of a body of information or ideas.
rank, rate, order	Put in order of importance or strength.

EXERCISE 13. WRITING SHORT-ANSWER QUESTIONS

Write five short-answer test questions based on the readings in this chapter. Use some of the instruction words listed above, but do not use any instruction word more than once.

Exercise 14. Studying for the Short-Answer Test

Do the following to prepare for the short-answer test at the end of this chapter:

1. Review your notes for each reading.

2. Reread any texts in which the content is still unclear to you.

3. Prepare answers for the five short-answer questions you wrote.

4. Answer the short-answer questions of your classmates.

Exercise 15. Short-Answer Test

1. List the eight intelligences identified by Gardner. Suggest one way in which each is exhibited.

2. Define *emotional intelligence*. Give three examples that show how emotional intelligence is manifested.

3. Which of the eight intelligences are highlighted in EQ theory? Explain.

4. Discuss the strengths and weaknesses of EQ testing.

5. In this chapter, you practised using several methods designed to help you remember information (i.e., writing study summaries, underlining and annotating, and mapping). Evaluate the effectiveness of each of these methods.

CHAPTER 9

Canadian Demographics

Introduction to the Chapter

In Canada, much has been said and written about demographics, a field that describes the characteristics of segments of the population. Studying demographics can help to explain trends (e.g., consumer patterns) and can help to predict future needs within the population (e.g., in health care and social services). Through studying Canadian demographics, we can learn a great deal about life in Canada.

In this chapter you will read several articles that analyze Canadian demographics. You will read about the baby boomers and the millennials. You will also learn about writing a formal critique, and at the end you will write your own critique of an article called "The Four Biggest Reasons for Generational Conflict in Teams."

Note: To complete Exercise 12 in this chapter, you will need a yellow highlighter and a pink highlighter.

Reading 1—*By Definition: Boom, Bust, X and Why*

EXERCISE 1. PRE-READING DISCUSSION

Discuss the following questions before you read.

1. Examine the graph from Statistics Canada. What observations can you make about the population of Canada?

Age Pyramid of the Canadian Population in 2006

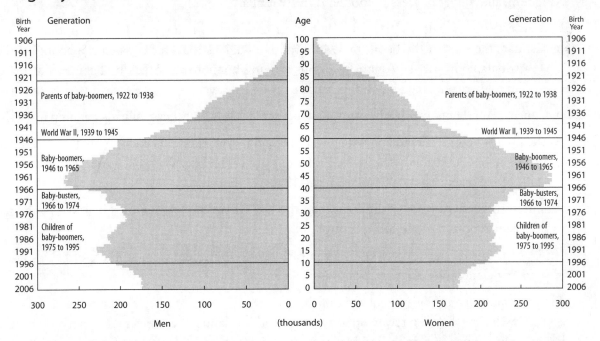

Source: Statistics Canada. "Census Snapshot of Canada—Population (Age and Sex)." *Canadian Social Trends* (December 2007): 38. http://www.statcan.gc.ca/pub/11-008-x/2007006/article/10379-eng.pdf, retrieved 15 October 2011.

2. Canadians born between the mid-1940s and the mid-1960s are often referred to as baby boomers. What does the word *boom* mean to you? Why would Canadians born between the mid-1940s and the mid-1960s be called *baby boomers*?

3. What does the word *bust* mean to you? Why would Canadians born between 1966 and 1974 be called *baby busters*?

4. Think about a country other than Canada. How have particular generations within that country been labelled? Why have they been labelled in this way?

Read the article below from Canadian newspaper the *Globe and Mail* to learn more about the Canadian baby boomers.

By Definition: Boom, Bust, X and Why

[1] Who exactly is a baby boomer? For today's special section, *The Globe* is using the definition of University of Toronto demographer and economist David Foot: A Canadian boomer is anyone living here (including immigrants) born from 1947 to 1966.

[2] Prof. Foot made his case in his 1996 bestseller, *Boom, Bust & Echo*, counting in the boom every age group that numbered more than 400,000 at the time. "You can't use that now," he says, "since the front end of the baby boomers, in their late 50s, is beginning to pass away."

[3] According to Statistics Canada, boomers make up a bit more than 30 percent of the population. In his book, Prof. Foot dubbed Canada's boom the "loudest . . . in the industrialized world." The population spike was shorter in the United States, much shorter in Europe and the United Kingdom, and longer but less pronounced in Australia.

[4] However, the bookends of 1947 and 1966 don't conform to many people's assumptions. They may situate the start of the boom in 1946. Prof. Foot agrees that this is when the boom hit the US—attributable in part to American troops arriving home to start making babies—but many Canadian soldiers remained behind in Europe for an extra year.

[5] In Canada, Prof. Foot says, "births were going up in the 1940s, but they really took a jump in 1947."

[6] At the boom's height, Canadian women were averaging four offspring each, a rate that peaked in 1959, when 479,000 babies were born. Prof. Foot places the boom's end at 1966, "halfway down the hill" of the declining fertility rates of the 1960s.

[7] Again, in this case, Canada is different than the US, where the boom ended in 1964, likely due to the faster adoption of the birth-control pill.

[8] "In Canada, births started declining in the early 1960s, but there were still lots of babies born. They're my Generation X," Prof. Foot says.

[9] Many people born in this final quarter of the boom aren't happy to be called boomers. They see Gen X as having had far fewer opportunities, and so define themselves in opposition to the boom. "Their experience at the tail end of the baby boom is totally different from that of an older brother or sister born in the first half," Prof. Foot admits.

[10] Culturally speaking, they have more in common with what Prof. Foot calls the "baby bust," born 1967 to 1979—which in common parlance is often also referred to as Gen X.

[11] "There's a shadow effect culturally. Someone born in 1968 will have a lot in common with someone born in 1964 or 1965. It's not nearly as clear-cut at the back end as at the front. They were a pretty disadvantaged group. Their lives are back on track now."

[12] However, they were still a relatively large cohort compared with those who followed—and that, by Prof. Foot's calculation, makes them boomers.

[13] "Numbers. It's just numbers," he says. "We don't control when we're born, but it can have a major implication on our life and life experiences."

Source: Tralee Pearce. "By Definition: Boom, Bust, X and Why." *Globe and Mail* 24 June 2006. http://www.theglobeandmail.com/archives/article831408.ece, retrieved 15 October 2011.

EXERCISE 2. PRONOUN USAGE

The quotes below are taken from Reading 1, "By Definition: Boom, Bust, X and Why." In each quote, a pronoun (or pronouns) has been underlined. Determine the meaning of each pronoun by examining the context within the passage.

1. "'You can't use that now. . .'" (paragraph 2)

    _____

2. "They see Gen X as having had far fewer opportunities, and so define themselves in opposition to the boom. 'Their experience at the tail end of the baby boom is totally different from that of an older brother or sister born in the first half,' Prof. Foot admits." (paragraph 9)

    They: _____

    themselves: _____

    Their: _____

3. "It's not nearly as clear-cut at the back end as at the front." (paragraph 11)

    It's: _____

4. "They were a pretty disadvantaged group. Their lives are back on track now." (paragraph 11)

    They: _____

    Their: _____

5. "However, they were still a relatively large cohort compared with those who followed—and that, by Prof. Foot's calculation, makes them boomers." (paragraph 12)

    they: _____

    those: _____

Exercise 3. Comprehension Check

1. "By Definition: Boom, Bust, X and Why" discusses the baby boom and the baby bust. On a separate sheet of paper, create a timeline that shows the years of the baby boom and the baby bust in Canada, according to Foot.

2. Draw a timeline for the baby boom in the United States using information from Foot. How is the timeline different from the one you drew for Canada? What are Foot's explanations for the differences?

3. Why does Foot place the end date of the baby boom at 1966 in Canada?

   _____

4. Compare the start and end dates of the baby boom and the baby bust proposed by Foot with the start and end dates proposed by Statistics Canada in the graph "Age Pyramid of the Canadian Population in 2006." What are possible reasons for the differences in the information?

   _____

5. What does Foot mean when he says that Canada's baby boom was the "loudest . . . in the industrialized world"? (paragraph 3)

   _____

6. According to Foot, how do some people who were born near the end of the baby boom feel about being called baby boomers? What is the reason that he gives for this feeling?

   _____

7. What is the difference between the baby bust and Gen X?

   _____

Exercise 4. Vocabulary in Context

Using the context provided by Reading 1, choose the best meaning for each of the terms listed below. (*Hint:* When using the context to guess a meaning, you may have to read the sentences before and after the sentence in which the word is used.)

1. *to pass away* (paragraph 2)
   a) to decrease
   b) to get older
   c) to die
   d) to develop

2. *don't conform to* (paragraph 4)
   a) don't result in
   b) don't fit with
   c) don't create
   d) don't belong with

3. *assumptions* (paragraph 4)

   a) beliefs without evidence
   b) beliefs based on evidence
   c) educated opinions
   d) knowledge

4. *attributable … to* (paragraph 4)

   a) at the same time as
   b) after
   c) resulting in
   d) caused by

5. *offspring* (paragraph 6)

   a) baby boys
   b) grandchildren
   c) infants
   d) children

6. *declining* (paragraphs 6 and 8)

   a) stable
   b) increasing
   c) decreasing
   d) unpredictable

7. *major* (paragraph 13)

   a) important
   b) not important
   c) most important
   d) small

8. *implication* (paragraph 13)

   a) role
   b) responsibility
   c) possible effect
   d) source

EXERCISE 5. WRITING

1. On a separate sheet of paper, paraphrase the following excerpts from Reading 1, "By Definition: Boom, Bust, X and Why."

   a) "Prof. Foot made his case in his 1996 bestseller, *Boom, Bust & Echo*, counting in the boom every age group that numbered more than 400,000 at the time. 'You can't use that now,' he says, 'since the front end of the baby boomers, in their late 50s, is beginning to pass away.'" (paragraph 2)

b) "Prof. Foot dubbed Canada's boom the 'loudest . . . in the industrialized world.' The population spike was shorter in the United States, much shorter in Europe and the United Kingdom, and longer but less pronounced in Australia." (paragraph 3)

c) "'Numbers. It's just numbers,' he says. 'We don't control when we're born, but it can have a major implication on our life and life experiences.'" (paragraph 13)

2. Drawing on the information in Reading 1, "By Definition: Boom, Bust, X and Why" and your own knowledge, write an extended definition of the term *baby boomers*.

⊣ **Reading 2**—*Canada's Emerging Millennials* ⊢

EXERCISE 6. PRE-READING DISCUSSION

Gen X. Baby Busters. A variety of "labels," or names, can be given to the same generation of Canadians. An often-used name given to children born in the early 1980s and later is "Millennials." Examine the cartoons below by R.J. Matson, from the book *Millennials Rising* by Neil Howe and William Strauss (2000).

Source: N. Howe, W. Strauss (auths.), and R.J. Matson (illust.). *Millennials Rising*. (New York: Vintage Books, 2000). pp. 17, 99, 170, 313.

1. What comment does each cartoon make about millennial children?

2. What comment does each cartoon make about the environment in which millennial children grew up?

Reading 2 is an excerpt from an article called "Canada's Emerging Millennials" by Reginald W. Bibby. Do the following before reading the excerpt:

- Read the short biography at the end of the passage to learn more about the author.
- Read the introduction (i.e., the first four paragraphs) and the subheadings.
- Examine the table and figure in the text.

What do you think this author will say about Canadian millennials?

Canada's Emerging Millennials

[1] Over the years, I have collected a lot of data through my national surveys of teenagers and adults. When I present the findings, I constantly remind people that I am not interested in numbers; I am interested in ideas. The numbers, after all, are not just cold, human-less statistics. On the contrary, behind each number is an individual Canadian who has offered a response to a question I have asked.

[2] And so it is that people should recognize themselves and their worlds in the numbers I collect. I have enjoyed "trying out the numbers" on the people around me, starting with family and friends. One person who invariably offered blunt, honest, real-life responses was my mother.

[3] Her "take" on the youth survey findings for 1984, 1992, and 2000 was pretty much consistent: "I wouldn't want to be trying to raise a teenager today." If she were alive today, I suspect her response would be the same—and, if anything, more emphatic. In light of the technological explosion that seemingly has transformed life—a wireless world headlined by the Internet, Facebook, Twitter, YouTube, cell phones, text messaging, digital television, endless communicating and unlimited and uninhibited expression of thought—she, like so many grandparents and other adults, would find parenthood to be bewildering and troubling.

[4] But you know what? Mom and I would find ourselves with a disagreement on our hands. My latest, 2008 national survey of more than 5,500 teenagers has unveiled some important and surprising positive findings about young people. The evidence points to the fact that things are looking better, not worse, for teenagers and their parents, and, consequently, for the rest of us, as well.

Almost Everyone Worries about Teenagers

[5] Historians tell us that anxiety about teenagers is something that goes back as far as, well, probably the first teenager. To put things in historical perspective, we only need to recall the famous lament of Socrates, no less: "Children today are tyrants. They contradict their parents, gobble their food, and terrorize their teachers." In late 2000, a prominent Canadian pollster told the Canadian Conference of Catholic Bishops, "I tremble to see what kind of society today's young people are going to produce in twenty to twenty-five years." As of 2005, 54% of Canadians maintained that their communities should have curfews for children under the age of 16. Think that is high? In 1995, the figure was 62%; in 1965, on the heels of the "happy days" era, it was 76%.

[6]   My Project Canada surveys of adults, carried out every five years from 1975 to 2005, along with the national teen readings in 1984, 1992, 2000, and 2008, provide us with a lot of information on how things have changed and not changed in Canada since the 1960s. Added to the information available from other sources, the surveys point to an extremely important conclusion: for all the consternation, today's teens are looking very good. In fact, they are looking better than any of our teen cohorts dating back to the early 1980s.

Their Values

[7]   When adults think of teenagers, many assume that young people are not inclined to place much importance today on characteristics like honesty, compassion, and politeness. Our survey findings do not support such impressions.

[8]   More than 8 in 10 teens say that traits such as *trust* and *honesty* are "very important" to them, while close to the same proportion say the same thing about *humour*. More than 6 in 10 maintain that they place very high levels of importance on *concern for others* and *politeness*. A majority also view *forgiveness* and *hard work* as extremely important. Speaking of civility, even *cleanliness* is widely valued.

Table 1. Valued Interpersonal Characteristics of Teenagers
% Viewing as "Very Important"

	Nationally	**Males**	**Females**
Trust	84	76	90
Honesty	81	74	87
Concern for others	65	56	73
Politeness	64	57	70
Forgiveness	60	53	66
Cleanliness	59	56	62
Working hard	55	52	58

Source: Reginald Bibby, The Emerging Millennials, 2009:10.

[9]   What's more, a number of things that teens are seen as doing that irritate adults also receive the disapproval of fellow teenagers. These transgressions include—with their disapproval levels in brackets:

* parking in a handicapped [space] when a person isn't handicapped (82%);
* not saying "sorry" when accidentally bumping into someone (77%);
* walking on a red light and making traffic wait (63%); and
* talking on a cell phone when driving a vehicle (56%).

Also contrary to rumour, some 80% of young males and females say that they "try to stay out of trouble," with even a slightly higher percentage in each instance reporting that they "have never got into trouble with the police."

[10]   When it comes to basic values, today's teenagers are looking good.

The Importance They Give to Relationships

[11]   As in previous surveys, we again have found that there is nothing more important to today's young people than relationships. Friends are their number one source of enjoyment, with 95% of males and females saying they receive "a great deal" or "quite a bit" of enjoyment from such ties. The Internet and sites like Facebook have expanded the possibilities for friendship. From 1984 through 2000, about 50% of teens said they had four or more close friends. Today, that level has jumped to almost 75%. Internet social networking now represents the no. 1 group activity for females and the no. 2 group activity—behind sports—for males.

[12]   Beyond friends, close to 80% say they are receiving high levels of enjoyment as well from their mothers, while around 75% say the same thing about their fathers. More generally, 87% of females and 65% of males indicate that "being loved" is very important to them. Stereotypes to the effect that teenagers are socially and emotionally detached are simply out of touch with reality. Teens, like the rest of us, supremely value relationships.

[13]   It also needs to be emphasized that teens today have greatly expanded social networks, compared to what their grandparents and parents knew. The Project Canada adult surveys have revealed that a mere 13% of Pre-Boomers (people born before 1946) felt that interracial dating was common when they were teenagers, with the figure rising to only 21% for Boomers (born between 1946 and 1965). Today such issues are virtually irrelevant for teenagers. No less than 51% of caucasian teens say they have at least one close friend who is not white—with the figure reaching 91% in Vancouver and 79% in Toronto; similarly, 68% of non-caucasians have at least one close friend who is white.

Their Enhanced Ties with Their Parents

[14]   What is striking about teens' enjoyment levels of parents is that they are significantly higher than the levels reported in earlier surveys. The near-80% figure in the case of enjoyment from mothers is up from around 70% in 1992 and 2000, and similar to what teens reported in the early 1980s. In the case of dads, the current enjoyment level of close to 75% represents a jump of about ten percentage points over the same period.

Figure 1. Enjoyment of Parents: 1984–2008

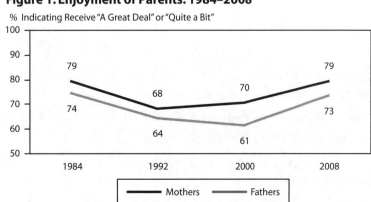

Source: Reginald W. Bibby. Project Canada Survey Series.

[15]   The enjoyment of parents is correlated with a number of important characteristics, including the influence of moms and dads, as well as the extent to which teens feel they can turn to parents when they are facing serious problems. Some 89% maintain that their moms have a high level of influence on their lives, while 82% say the same thing about their dads—both findings up about ten points since the 1980s. The level for friends is 86%.

[16]   What's more, the evidence points to an improved level of understanding between young people and their parents. In 1992, 58% of teens said they were troubled about not being understood by their parents; today the figure has fallen to 39%. Even the weekly-plus arguments are down—from 52% a decade ago to 42% now.

[17]   Why are parents and teenagers getting along better? One basic reason seems to stand out: moms and dads are doing a much better job of finding a balance between careers and family life. Despite the well-documented stresses and strains of this juggling act, parents seem to be benefiting from improvements in levels of enjoyment, influence, and reduced conflict with their children.

[18]   Between 1960 and 2000, the percentage of mothers employed outside the home jumped from about 30% to 60%. It was a major social change that put new and unanticipated pressures on Boomer parents and teens alike. The good news is that, as they shared in this transformation, those same teenagers learned a lot about what they wanted—and didn't want—from their own careers and family lives.

[19]   So it is that, today, as younger Boomer and post-Boomer moms and dads, they seem determined to do a better job than their parents did of balancing the attention they are giving to their careers and the attention they are giving to their kids. Ties between Canadian teens and their parents today are far from perfect. But it's clear that, for all the hand-wringing and publicity given to problems, things are actually moving forward in homes across the country.

Author's biography: Reginald Bibby holds the Board of Governors Research Chair in Sociology at the University of Lethbridge. For almost four decades, he has been monitoring social trends through a series of adult and youth surveys, and has shared the results with Canadians through twelve best-selling books. The latest is *The Emerging Millennials: How Canada's Newest Generation Is Responding to Change and Choice* (Lethbridge: Project Canada Books, 2009).

Source: R.W. Bibby. "Canada's Emerging Millennials." *Transition* 39, 3(Fall 2009): 2–6. http://www.vifamily.ca/pub_page/9, retrieved 17 October 2011.

EXERCISE 7. COMPREHENSION CHECK

Answer the following questions on a separate sheet of paper.

1. What is the main point that Bibby makes in this article? Find his thesis statement and underline it in the text. Then rewrite Bibby's main point using your own words.

2. What points does Bibby use to support his position? Under your paraphrase of Bibby's thesis statement, create an outline of these main points.

3. What evidence does Bibby use to support his main points? Fill in your outline with the evidence that he uses, in your own words.

4. Now look back at the introduction. What information and ideas does Bibby include in the introduction to lead the reader to his thesis statement? Why do you think he introduces his main point in this way?

Understanding Mixed Patterns

In previous chapters of this book, you have read and analyzed a variety of organizational patterns in written texts. One advantage of recognizing these patterns while reading is that it helps you remember information and ideas. Once you have identified an organizational pattern, you can use that pattern to organize information in your memory.

In previous chapters we have discussed patterns for describing objects and processes, comparing and contrasting, showing causes and effects, defining, and persuading. Often, you will find these patterns combined in one text.

EXERCISE 8. IDENTIFYING ORGANIZATIONAL PATTERNS

Name the organizational pattern demonstrated in each of the excerpts below. Then, in the space provided or on a separate sheet, either outline or draw a map of each excerpt.

1. Paragraphs 3 and 4

   "[My mother's] 'take' on the youth survey findings for 1984, 1992, and 2000 was pretty much consistent: 'I wouldn't want to be trying to raise a teenager today.' If she were alive today, I suspect her response would be the same—and, if anything, more emphatic. In light of the technological explosion that seemingly has transformed life—a wireless world headlined by the Internet, Facebook, Twitter, YouTube, cell phones, text messaging, digital television, endless communicating and unlimited and uninhibited expression of thought—she, like so many grandparents and other adults, would find parenthood to be bewildering and troubling.

   But you know what? Mom and I would find ourselves with a disagreement on our hands. My latest, 2008 national survey of more than 5,500 teenagers has unveiled some important and surprising positive findings about young people. The evidence points to the fact that things are looking better, not worse, for teenagers and their parents, and, consequently, for the rest of us, as well."

   Organizational pattern:

   _____

   Outline or map:

2. Paragraph 5

   "Historians tell us that anxiety about teenagers is something that goes back as far as, well, probably the first teenager. To put things in historical perspective, we only need to recall the famous lament of Socrates, no less: 'Children today are tyrants. They contradict their parents, gobble their food, and terrorize their teachers.' In late 2000, a prominent Canadian pollster told the Canadian Conference of Catholic Bishops, 'I tremble to see what kind of society today's young people are going to produce in twenty to twenty-five years.' As of 2005, 54% of Canadians maintained that their communities should have curfews for children under the age of 16. Think that is high? In 1995, the figure was 62%; in 1965, on the heels of the 'happy days' era, it was 76%."

Organizational pattern:

_____

Outline or map:

3. Paragraphs 7 and 8

"When adults think of teenagers, many assume that young people are not inclined to place much importance today on characteristics like honesty, compassion, and politeness. Our survey findings do not support such impressions.

"More than 8 in 10 teens say that traits such as *trust* and *honesty* are 'very important' to them, while close to the same proportion say the same thing about *humour*. More than 6 in 10 maintain that they place very high levels of importance on *concern for others* and *politeness*. A majority also view *forgiveness* and *hard work* as extremely important. Speaking of civility, even *cleanliness* is widely valued."

Organizational pattern:

_____

Outline or map:

EXERCISE 9. VOCABULARY IN CONTEXT

In Reading 2, "Canada's Emerging Millennials," the author uses a number of figurative or idiomatic expressions. Some of these are listed here. Using the context of the article, guess the meanings of the expressions from the context. Under each guess, note the clues that you used. After guessing your meanings, discuss your guesses and the clues with your classmates.

1. *to try out* (paragraph 2)

Meaning:_____

Clues:_____

2. *a "take" on* (paragraph 3)

   Meaning: _____

   Clues: _____

3. *on our hands* (paragraph 4)

   Meaning: _____

   Clues: _____

4. *on the heels of* (paragraph 5)

   Meaning: _____

   Clues: _____

5. *out of touch with* (paragraph 12)

   Meaning: _____

   Clues: _____

6. *to be striking about* (paragraph 14)

   Meaning: _____

   Clues: _____

7. *to turn to* (paragraph 15)

   Meaning: _____

   Clues: _____

8. *to stand out* (paragraph 17)

   Meaning: _____

   Clues: _____

EXERCISE 10. CRITICAL ANALYSIS

Discuss the following questions with your classmates.

1. According to the cartoons in the pre-reading discussion, how would you characterize millennial children's relationships with their parents? Do the cartoons express a similar point of view as is expressed by Bibby regarding millennial children's relationships with their parents? Be prepared to explain your response.

2. Do you agree with the way millennials are portrayed in the cartoons? Be prepared to explain your response.

3. Do you agree with the way millennials are described by Bibby? Be prepared to explain your response.

4. As demonstrated in the first two readings in this chapter, several generations in Canada have been labelled and described in very specific ways. In your opinion, is this just another form of stereotyping or is there value in analyzing generational differences and perspectives? Justify your opinion.

Writing

The Formal, Academic Summary

One type of common academic assignment is the summary. A formal, academic summary should

- express the ideas of the original author accurately;
- maintain the balance of the original text, emphasizing the ideas that were most important to the original author; and
- be written in such a way that a reader who has not read the original article or book could understand the basic ideas discussed in the original text.

A formal, academic summary should *not* include your own opinion.

How to Write a Formal Summary

In many ways, writing a formal summary to be submitted to your professor for evaluation is similar to the writing of a study summary (see Chapter 8). However, because the final written product is more formal, there are a few differences.

A. Reading

The following suggestions for reading may help you with your analysis.

1. For journal or magazine articles, read the title, subheadings, introduction, and conclusion first; note any charts or graphs. For books, read the title page, the table of contents, and the preface, and skim the bibliography. As you read, think about the author's main purpose for writing, the intended audience, and especially the author's main point.

2. Read the entire text. As you read, do the following:

   a) Confirm or modify your earlier understanding of the writer's purpose and main point.
   b) Highlight the important points the author uses to support his or her thesis. It will be crucial to include these points in your summary.
   c) Make annotations in the margins so that important examples and definitions stand out.

   Overall, when you read, focus on what the author *is doing* in the text. Does the author *describe, compare, argue*? What type of evidence does the author use to support his or her main points?

B. Writing

The following suggestions may help you draft your formal summary.

1. Create an outline or a map that shows the main ideas of the original article or book.
2. Look for any gaps in your outline or map.

   If some of the ideas in your outline do not have a clear connection, it may be because you have missed an important point in the original text. On the other hand, this may be because there is a weakness in the ideas or the argument of the original author. It is important to go back to the original text to fill in the gaps or determine why there are gaps in your outline.

3. Write an introduction to the text. Your introduction should prepare the reader for the main ideas of the text. Include
   - the title of the article or book;
   - the name of the author; and
   - the main point or purpose of the text.

4. In the body paragraphs, summarize the author's supporting points. Include important definitions or examples that will clarify the ideas for your reader.

   Use your own words to express the ideas of the original author. Though you may use some direct quotations, your summary should not be a stringing together of the original author's words. Remember, through your summary, you are showing your instructor how thoroughly you have understood the text.

   Where you *do* use the original author's words, be sure to put quotation marks around them. If you do not, it is considered plagiarism.

   Refer to the author as you summarize his or her ideas, focusing on what the author *is doing* in his or her text.

   Examples: Shaw argues that . . .

   Shaw concludes that . . .

   Shaw provides examples that . . .

5. Write a brief conclusion that again summarizes the main point and purpose of the text.

6. Revise your draft. Look for weak connections between ideas and strengthen them. Look for points that may be unclear to the reader. Clarify these by adding a brief explanation or an example.

   Check the length of your summary. Your summary must fall within the limits set by your instructor.

   Check your paragraphing. The general rules for paragraphing also apply to summaries.

7. Add a bibliographical entry for your book or article at the top of the first page.

EXERCISE 11. WRITING ASSIGNMENTS

1. Complete the following sentences.
   a) Bibby argues that _____.
   b) Bibby uses _____ to support his argument.

2. Write a brief, formal summary of the excerpt from "Canada's Emerging Millennials." (Approximate number of words: 180–200.)

Critiques and Reviews

A critique, which is sometimes called a review, is similar to a summary in that it is also based on the main ideas of a given text. In a critique, however, you must take things one step further: in addition to a summary, you must include your own response to the writer's ideas.

Key Questions for the Critique

A critique should answer the following three questions:

1. What is the author's main point or purpose for writing?

2. How does the author support that point or achieve that purpose?

3. To what extent is the author successful in doing what he or she intended to do?

Read the review of "Canada's Emerging Millennials" below. Then complete Exercise 12.

Article Review

Bibby, R.W. (2009). Canada's Emerging Millenials. *Transition* Fall 2009:
The Vanier Institute of the Family. 2–6.

[1]   Public opinion and the media often portray the current generation of youths, including Canadian teenagers, as far worse than their parents with regard to societal values and behaviour (Ng, Schweitzer, & Lyons, 2010). However, Canadian sociologist and researcher Reginald W. Bibby maintained a more positive view in his article "Canada's Emerging Millennials" (2009). Drawing on more than 35 years of national survey data he has gathered on Canadian adults and teens, he examined the change in attitudes and values of today's millennials born between 1980 and 2000 (Eubanks, 2006; Howe & Strauss, 2003; Sutherland & Thompson, 2001). His surveys revealed some "positive findings about young people" (p. 2), and he claimed that things are "looking better not worse, for teenagers . . . than any of [the] teen cohorts" (p. 2) since his surveys began in 1975. Though his evidence unwittingly pointed to some major flaws in categorizing generations, including the millennials, Bibby's analysis of six themes concluded somewhat successfully that about today's teens "overall, the message is one of considerable optimism and progress" (p. 6).

[2]   In developing the article, Bibby's approach was not to compare his findings with other literature in the field, such as Tucker (2006) or Oblinger (2003), but rather to rely on internal comparisons from his surveys, particularly of 1984, 1992, 2000, and 2008. This method allowed him to focus on long-term analyses of a reliable and similar Canadian sample. He illustrated his themes with seven helpful comparative tables and graphs that enhanced his message. One drawback, though, is that Bibby made only brief, unreferenced mention of the Project Canada surveys on which his findings were based. Still, an Internet search revealed his studies are accessible and part of the

International Social Survey Programme (ISSP). After gathering opinions from 1500 adults and 3500 teens in 200 Canadian schools, he evaluated responses with regard to values, social relationships, social behaviours, life outlook, and views of their futures.

[3]   The author's theme on basic values showed evidence that contrary to what some might think—recent riots in Toronto and Vancouver notwithstanding—"honesty, compassion, and politeness" (p. 2) are important to millennial teens and, as with adults, things that annoy them are similar, such as people who jaywalk and misuse of parking spaces for people with disabilities. Social relationships, now enhanced because of the Internet, bring high satisfaction to these teens. The author showed too an upswing, from the 1992 or 2000 results, of teen "enjoyment" (p. 3) of parents. He posited the reason for this increased family harmony as boomer parents (born 1946 to 1965) getting better at balancing "careers and family life" (p. 4). The problem with the boomer label is that many parents of this cohort are not boomers but Gen Xers (born 1966 to 1980) who have perhaps learned from difficulties their own boomer parents had. He failed to address this fundamental problem in labelling a group belonging to a 20-year span. While some millennials may have had boomer parents, the majority today have Gen-Xer parents, who have a completely different approach to life learned from boomer mistakes and successes.

[4]   Bibby offered percentages from Toronto and Vancouver to show a considerable increase in interracial friendships and dating within the millennials from the boomer and pre-boomer (born before 1946) cohorts. But what about other cosmopolitan cities, such as Edmonton, Montreal, or Winnipeg? Another theme Bibby explored on smoking, drinking, and illegal substance use showed a 25 percent reduction, as did reported victimization, such as school bullying, suicide attempts, or abuse at home. A final theme the article covered was self-concept and view of their futures. Bibby supplied the questions asked and the results in a comparative table that showed responses by gender across three cohorts. From the evidence he concluded that the millennials view themselves as good, well liked, and highly competent, and optimistically see their futures as bright.

[5]   Bibby devoted the final page to summarizing the major findings from Project Teen Canada (2008), insisting boomers left a legacy that allowed Canadian society to improve peoples' lives and that video gaming and social networking leave little time for teenage vices. Certainly, he has made a significant contribution to understanding society with these studies. Yet this article's brevity prevented him from providing details, or giving references, and left the reader searching to find out more. Though agreeing with Howe and Strauss (2003) in their predictions of positive outcomes for this generation, he did not attempt to reconcile the opposite findings of Twenge (2006) and others who argued millennials are self-absorbed, demand immediate success, care less about others or their opinions, and "are more likely to flaunt society's conventions" (Eubanks, 2006, p. 2).

[6]   Clearly, Bibby's studies have engendered praise from academics, the media, educators, and parents. This one-of-a-kind series of social opinion has been called a Canadian "national treasure" (Project Canada Survey Series, 2010) and will no doubt encourage other countries to imitate it and do comparative analyses.

[7]   Bibby's optimism is highly infectious, but the reader should use caution and question whether these are analyses from a certain demographic of Canadian teen society. Were the responses only from urban schools? Finally, the reader needs to ask, Does this analysis really represent the millennials or only some of them?

References:

Bibby, R.W. (2009). Canada's emerging millennials. *Transition, 39*(3), 2–6.

Eubanks, S. (2006, April 24). Millennials – Themes in current literature. Retrieved from http://eubie.com/themes.pdf

Howe, N., & Strauss, W. (2003). *Millennials go to college.* American Association of Collegiate Registrars and Admissions Offices and Life Course Associates.

Ng, E.S.W., Schweitzer, L., & Lyons, S.T. (2010) New generation, great expectations: A field study of the millennial generation. *Journal of Business and Psychology, 25*(2), 281–292.

Oblinger, D. (2003). Boomers, gen-xers & millennials: Understanding the new students. *EDUCAUSE Review, 38*(4), 37–47.

Project Canada Survey Series. (2010). Project Canada Codebooks & Data. Tracking & Translating Trends. Retrieved from http://www.reginaldbiddy.com/codebooksdata.html. Accessed 15 August 2011.

Sutherland, A., & Thompson, B. (2001). *Kidfluence: Why kids today mean business.* Whitby, ON: McGraw Hill Ryerson Limited.

Tucker, P. (2006). Teaching the millennial generation. *The Futurist, 40*(3), 7.

Twenge, J. (2006). *Generation me: Why today's young Americans are more confident, assertive, entitled – and more miserable than ever before.* New York: Free Press (Simon and Schuster).

Author biography: Chris Butterill, Ph.D., has worked for many years with students at undergraduate and graduate levels, teaching courses that enhance students' skills in critical thinking, reading, and academic writing. Besides lecturing in history, she recently completed a 12-year term as dean of studies at St. Paul's College and a term as acting director of University One at the University of Manitoba.

EXERCISE 12. ANALYZING THE MODEL

Introduction

1. Where does the name of the article first appear in the critique?

   _____

2. Where is the purpose of Bibby's article discussed in the introduction?

   _____

3. Where is Chris Butterill's overall opinion of Bibby's article expressed? This is the thesis statement of Butterill's critique.

   _____

Body Paragraphs

1. In paragraph 2 of the critique, Butterill discusses Bibby's approach and the source of Bibby's information. In pink, highlight strengths Butterill sees in Bibby's approach. In yellow, highlight weaknesses pointed out by Butterill.

2. In paragraphs 3 to 5 Butterill summarizes Bibby's main points. Annotate these three paragraphs, writing "Sum" in the margins where Butterill is summarizing and "Crit" in the margins where Butterill is giving her opinion.

3. In paragraphs 3 to 5 for each section where you wrote "Crit," indicate whether Butterill's opinion of Bibby's analysis is positive (+) or negative (−).

4. To what extent does the writer of the review use direct quotations from the original text?

5. Highlight in yellow each place in the critique where Bibby's name is mentioned. Also, be sure to highlight in yellow the pronoun "he" when it is used to refer to Bibby. Then, highlight in pink any verbs following the mention of Bibby's name that describe what he was doing in his article.

   Example:

   Reginald W. Bibby in sentence 2 of paragraph 1 should be highlighted in yellow.

   The verb *maintained* should be highlighted in pink.

   Notice the wide range of verbs used by Butterill to describe what Bibby is doing in his article.

6. Are there any points in the critique that are unclear? How might the writer of the review clarify these points?

Conclusion

1. How does the writer conclude her review? What is her overall view of Bibby's article?

2. As the reader of the critique, are you satisfied with the conclusion? Why or why not?

The Structure of a Critique

The review of "Canada's Emerging Millennials" illustrates one way of organizing a critique. The model is presented in the first diagram below. Another way of organizing a critique is shown on the next page.

1. What are the advantages and disadvantages of each of these models?

2. When might one model be more suitable than the other?

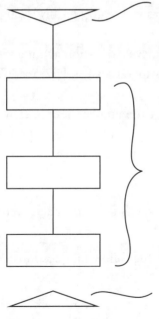

Introduction
• name of author, title of article
• major points to be analyzed (short summary)
• your thesis: opinion about the main points of article

Body
Each body paragraph should contain
• major point to be analyzed in that paragraph
• direct quotes from the article, demonstrating the point being made (opinion)
• your topic sentence which states agreement or disagreement with the main point
• your proof of the effectiveness or ineffectiveness of that major point: facts, examples, physical description, personal experience
• perhaps a suggestion for the improvement of the author's major point

Conclusion
• perhaps only one sentence
• probably an opinion which you have proved within your essay

Source: Reid, J. *The Process of Composition*. 2nd ed. (Englewood Cliffs, N.J.: Prentice Hall, 1988), 114.

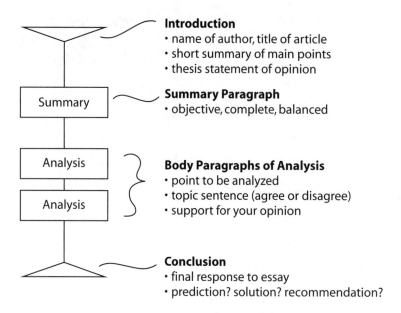

Introduction
• name of author, title of article
• short summary of main points
• thesis statement of opinion

Summary Paragraph
• objective, complete, balanced

Body Paragraphs of Analysis
• point to be analyzed
• topic sentence (agree or disagree)
• support for your opinion

Conclusion
• final response to essay
• prediction? solution? recommendation?

Source: Reid, J. *The Process of Composition*. 2nd ed. (Englewood Cliffs, N.J.: Prentice Hall, 1988), 123.

How to Write a Critique

Reading the Original Text

Follow the steps outlined in "How to Write a Formal Summary—A. Reading" on page 202. Remember, your purpose in reading is to discover the author's main purpose or point and to draw out the important supporting points.

For a critique, you should also make note of your responses to the text as you read (i.e., any strengths or weaknesses that you discover in the text).

Your responses to the text may not be well developed. You may simply have a question about an idea discussed in the text. You may see connections or contradictions with other materials you have read. You may see contradictions within the text itself.

It is important that you record all these impressions since you may not remember them later when you are writing your critique. You may either record them briefly in the margins of the text or you may take notes. (If you take notes, be sure to include the page number for the idea to which you are referring.)

Writing

1. Think about the significance of the author's main idea. Think about how well the author achieved his or her purpose.

   Depending on the text that you are reviewing, you might also consider the following questions:

   • What did the author use as sources? Are these sources current?
   • To which school of thought do the ideas in the text belong? What are the strengths within this perspective? Does the author successfully overcome any of the limitations of this school of thought?
   • Does the text make an important contribution to its field? When it was published, did it introduce new ideas or was it a restatement of older ideas?

2. Write a preliminary thesis statement that expresses your view of the text.

3. Find support for your thesis statement. Depending on the formality of the assignment, this could come from your own experience or from source texts. What support can you find for your position? To a great extent, the effectiveness of your critique will depend on the quality of the support that you find for your position.

4. List the points you will use to support *your* thesis statement. Be sure that you are critiquing significant points from the article or book.

5. Plan your critique. Which model will you use? Will you summarize the original text first and then critique the ideas, or will you integrate the summary and the critique?

6. Draft your critique.
   - Keep the focus of your writing on the author and what he or she is doing in the text.
   - It is sometimes a good idea to include direct quotations from the original source that illustrate the author's points especially well. In most instances, however, you should use your own words to paraphrase and summarize.

7. Revise your critique.
   - Have you named the text and authors and briefly stated the main idea of the original text in your introduction?
   - Does your thesis statement clearly state your overall view of the text you are critiquing?
   - Have you summarized the original text sufficiently in the body of your critique?
   - Is the position in your thesis statement consistently supported in the body of your critique?
   - Have you supplied convincing reasons for your own analysis of the text?
   - Have you used a balance of direct quotations, paraphrases, and summary statements?

You will practise this process as you write a critique of a blog post called "The Four Biggest Reasons for Generational Conflict in Teams."

Reading 3—*The Four Biggest Reasons for Generational Conflict in Teams*

EXERCISE 13. PRE-READING DISCUSSION

Discuss the following questions before you read.

1. Have you ever had a close friendship with someone from an older generation? Describe this friendship. What do you think made it successful?

2. Have you ever had a close friendship with someone from a younger generation? Describe this friendship. What do you think made it successful?

3. Have you ever worked closely with a member of a different generation? Was this workplace relationship affected by the difference in ages?

Exercise 14. Pre-reading

Read the title of and the introduction (i.e., the first two paragraphs) to the following blog post from HBR Blog Network. What is the author's main purpose?

_____

Read the entire blog post. As you read, note your responses to the ideas in the text. You may record your responses in the margin or you may take notes.

The Four Biggest Reasons for Generational Conflict in Teams

[1]   Today most of us work closely with colleagues that span at least three, if not four, generations. The possibility that we'll misunderstand another team member's behavior is high. It's easy to form a hasty and incorrect impression of someone from another generation.

[2]   While inter-generational mis- understandings can occur in a variety of situations, for teams, I find generational conflict unusually centers around four essential team activities:

- Choosing where and when to work
- Communicating among team members
- Getting together
- Finding information or learn- ing new things

[3]   **Choosing where and when to work.** Listen to the language: many older colleagues speak of "going to work." Members of older generations often view work as a place—a location you go to at a specified time, say from 8:30 am to 5 pm. This synchronicity stems from a time when the nature of most work required that workers to be present together, for example, to run a manufacturing assembly line. Over time, of course, the nature of work in most sectors of the economy has changed; today most tasks do not require synchronous activities, yet many in older generations—including many senior executives—continue to expect syn- chronous behavior.

[4]   Younger workers, in contrast, tend to view work as something you do—anywhere, any time. They have grown up in an asynchronous world—filled, for example, with digital TV recorders that allowed them to watch any show at any time. Many Gen Y's consider the rigidity of set work hours an anachronism from another era.

[5] It's easy for team members to misinterpret each other's behaviors around time and place. Is someone who arrives at 9:30 necessarily working less hard than other team members who are there at 8:30? Is it okay for some members to work from alternate locations? Is adherence to time and place norms important for the team to accomplish its task? Is it viewed by some as an important sign of team commitment?

[6] **Communicating among team members.** No surprise that many Gen Y's and X'ers are comfortable using electronic communication. They text (or Yammer or Twitter) or post to various social networking sites much more frequently than most older colleagues do.

[7] The crux of most technology-based team misunderstandings is not the technology *per se*—it is how team members interpret each others' intentions based on communication approaches. Younger members are accustomed to rapid responses from peers; they are likely to feel frustrated and, at time, rejected if they don't hear from older colleagues for a day or so. Team members from older generations may not only be uncomfortable with digital communication, they may even feel offended by a lack of face-to-face or at least voice-to-voice interaction, or left out of the loop.

[8] **Getting together.** Boomers and X'ers are planners and schedulers; Gen Y's are coordinators. When faced with a need to meet, Gen Y's are likely to ascertain each other's immediate coordinates, and then home in on each other. Older colleagues would almost certainly prefer to rely on pre-planned schedules—and may be very annoyed by younger team members' seemingly seat-of-the-pants approach. To Y's, the extent of scheduling that goes on in most workplaces today seems stultifying and inefficient.

[9] **Finding information or learning new things.** Boomers and Traditionalists are linear learners—most are inclined to attend training classes, read manuals, and absorb the requisite information before beginning the task at hand. Gen Y's are largely "on demand" learners—they figure things out as they go, reaching out to personal contacts with relevant expertise for information or referrals, as needed. Y's are likely to be bored and turned off by a project that begins with a lengthy training phase. X'ers and Boomers may be annoyed by Y's' frequent questions and requests for input.

[10] As you work with colleagues from other generations, your first priority should be to avoid forming quick negative conclusions. Bring the team members' diverse perspectives out in the open—help everyone on the team understand the multiple points of view—and legitimize each person's view in the eyes of the team.

[11] Decide together which norms will work best for your team—for example, how flexible you are about time and place, how you'll communicate different types of information, how scheduled you need to be, and so on—based on collective preferences and the work you need to accomplish.

[12] And, so we all can learn more, I hope you'll share your multigenerational team experiences. What issues do you face in working together well? How have you addressed them?

Author's biography: Tammy J. Erickson has authored the books *Retire Retirement, Plugged In* and *What's Next, Gen X?* She is the co-author of four *Harvard Business Review* articles and the book *Workforce Crisis*.

Source: T.J. Erickson. (16 February 2009). "The Four Biggest Reasons for Generational Conflict in Teams" *HBR Blog* Network (blog), *Harvard Business Review*, 16 February 2009, http://blogs.hbr.org/erickson/2009/02/the_four_biggest_reasons_for_i.html, retrieved 17 October 2011.

Exercise 15. Highlighting

Read "The Four Biggest Reasons for Generational Conflict in Teams" again. Highlight the important points that the author uses to support her main point. Note any important examples.

Exercise 16. Comprehension Check

1. In Reading 3, the author refers to "Gen Ys." Who does she mean? Confirm your guess by checking online.

    _____

2. What is the writer's main point in the post?

    _____

3. In her four supporting points, how does Erickson characterize members of the baby-boom generation and members of Gen Y?

    _____

4. How many suggestions are given for improving intergenerational communication and relationships in the workplace? Paraphrase these points.

    _____

    _____

Exercise 17. Vocabulary in Context

As a class, choose eight words from "The Four Biggest Reasons for Generational Conflict in Teams" that are unfamiliar to you and that are important to understanding the main ideas.
List these words below.

1. Word: _____ Meaning: _____
    Clues: _____
2. Word: _____ Meaning: _____
    Clues: _____
3. Word: _____ Meaning: _____
    Clues: _____
4. Word: _____ Meaning: _____
    Clues: _____
5. Word: _____ Meaning: _____
    Clues: _____
6. Word: _____ Meaning: _____
    Clues: _____

7. Word: _____ Meaning: _____

   Clues: _____

8. Word: _____ Meaning: _____

   Clues: _____

On your own, guess the meanings of the words from their contexts and write them beside the words. Under each guess, note the clues that you used. After guessing your meanings, discuss your guesses and the clues with your classmates.

EXERCISE 18. CRITICAL ANALYSIS

Discuss the following questions with your classmates.

1. According to Erickson, "It's easy to form a hasty and incorrect impression of someone from another generation." (paragraph 1) Do you believe that intergenerational conflict is important and widespread? Why or why not?

2. Do you agree with the way Erickson characterizes baby boomers and GenYs in her blog post? Be prepared to explain your response.

3. If you agree with Erickson that it is easy to form the wrong impression of someone based on generational differences, do you also agree with Erickson that the conflicts centre on the four activities that she discusses?

4. In your opinion, how useful are the suggestions made by Erickson for improving communication in the workplace? Justify your answer.

EXERCISE 19. WRITING ASSIGNMENT

Write a 250-word critique of the blog post "The Four Biggest Reasons for Generational Conflict in Teams."

Refer to "How to Write a Critique" on pages 208–9. Remember that the process suggested in this textbook is general; that is, it may not suit you and this particular writing situation exactly, so you may need to modify it to suit your own needs.

| Revising Your Critique |

1. Have you named the text and authors and briefly stated the main idea of the original text in your introduction?

2. Does your thesis statement clearly express your overall view of the blog post?

3. Have you sufficiently summarized the original text in the body of your critique?

4. Is the position in your thesis statement consistently supported in the body of your critique?

5. Have you supplied convincing reasons for your own analysis of the text?

6. Have you used a balance of direct quotations, paraphrases, and summary statements?

CHAPTER 10

Global Citizenship

We don't have to wait for things to break apart
if you weren't involved before it's never too late to start
you probably think that it's too far to even have to care
well take a look at where you live what if it happened there?

—Lyrics by Drake, from the song "Wavin' Flag" by K'Naan

Introduction to the Chapter

This chapter focuses on the theme of global citizenship. *Global citizenship* is a phrase that is frequently used in the Canadian media and in education. But what does global citizenship mean? According to Keeping and Shapiro, "The term 'global citizenship' is increasingly heard, especially in Canada, but rarely defined. This leads to confusion because it is often not clear what a particular writer or speaker means by the term."

In this chapter, you will explore the meaning of global citizenship. You will read about people who could be considered global citizens and analyze theoretical discussions of global citizenship. As you read the articles, you will practise paraphrasing, note-taking, comparing perspectives, and evaluating ideas. In the end, you will write a research paper that provides your definition and evaluation of the term *global citizenship*.

Source: J. Keeping and D. Shapiro. "Global Citizenship: What Is It, and What Are Our Ethical Obligations as Global Citizens?" *LawNow* (July/August 2008). http://findarticles.com/p/articles/mi_m0OJX/is_6_32/ai_n30979385, retrieved 19 October 2011.

Here is the topic for the final research paper:

> *Global citizenship* is a term that is frequently used in the Canadian media. In a 550- to 650-word paper, discuss two to three aspects of global citizenship that are emphasized in current definitions. Use information and examples from at least three of the readings in this chapter to help you explain these aspects. In your concluding paragraph, respond to this question: Does the term *global citizenship* provide new meanings, or is it a new term for an old concept?
>
> Be sure to reference all sources using one of the styles discussed in this chapter.

Reading 1—*Christopher Opio*

EXERCISE 1. PRE-READING DISCUSSION

Discuss the following questions before you read.

1. What does it mean to be a "citizen"? As a class, brainstorm the various aspects of citizenship.

2. After you have completed your brainstorming as a group, pick out the aspects of citizenship that you think are the most important. The aspects that you select may be different from those selected by your classmates.

3. As a class, discuss possible meanings of the phrase *global citizenship*.

4. In your first or primary language, is there a similar phrase? What is the phrase? Does the phrase in your first or primary language have exactly the same meaning for you as the phrase *global citizenship* in English, or does it have additional or different meanings?

Readings 1 and 2 will introduce you to two exceptional Canadians. Reading about these Canadians and discussing the questions that follow in the critical analysis exercise may help you expand and refine your thinking about global citizenship.

Christopher Opio

Where there's a well there's a way.
A Canadian helps Africans tap into better health.

[1] Vivid memories of the dirty, unsafe water his family drank to survive, and the preventable deaths of so many from water-borne illnesses, inspired Dr. Christopher Opio, professor of forestry at the University of Northern British Columbia, to find a way to help the people of his native Uganda gain access to clean and safe water.

[2] In 2007, Opio and fellow UNBC colleague Tony Donovan founded the Northern Uganda Development Foundation. Dedicated to improving the standard of living for Ugandans, the foundation is focused on promoting locally sustainable sources of safe drinking water, as well as improving farming practices, health education, and small business enterprises in partnership with the local people.

[3] Opio immigrated to Canada in 1982, but was haunted by powerful memories of the struggle and hardships his family endured. "I was born and raised in northern Uganda in a war-torn, poverty-stricken area. We walked barefoot, had to drink dirty water that was shared with animals, and suffered from parasites and many other water-borne diseases. We spent a considerable amount of time travelling long distances to collect unsafe drinking water."

[4] It was against this tragic backdrop that Opio decided to put his academic and scientific training to work to help the people of northern Uganda. To date, the Northern Uganda Development Foundation has opened 29 wells, providing more than 42,000 people access to clean water.

[5] The NUDF coordinates the efforts of Canadian volunteers with local Ugandans to supervise the digging and construction of the wells. Once the wells are completed, a small local committee is appointed to oversee care and maintenance. Founding the Northern Uganda Development Foundation—and the ability to help save lives—has both inspired and changed Opio. "I've learned how important it is to give back to the community. It gives me great joy and satisfaction to see how NUDF is positively affecting the children, women and men in rural northern Uganda. People are healthier, children can go to schools, and many locals are engaged in income-generating projects like goat production, beekeeping, and tree planting."

[6] In a land where clean water can literally mean the difference between life and death, Opio has met many people along the way who have deeply affected him. One such person was northern Ugandan Engola Dicken, who told NUDF: "I thought I would die without ever drinking clean water."

More about Volunteer's Cause

[7]   Dirty water is the most common cause of developing-world illness: diarrhea, killing 1.4 million children every year—more than AIDS, malaria and measles combined, says the World Health Organization (WHO). In fact, it's estimated 2.2 million people die every year from diarrhea caused by contaminated water. Children are especially vulnerable.

[8]   Pathogens like bacteria, viruses and parasites can contaminate reservoirs—lakes, rivers, ponds, streams, creeks or water wells—that are being used as water supplies.

[9]   Best solution? One that addresses access to water and sanitary facilities, and promotes hygiene and hand washing. This integrated approach, says the WHO, can reduce deaths by diarrhea by 65 percent. Next best? Install a proper water supply—well, borehole or piped-in system—close to where a community lives. According to The Water Project, when a village in Africa has access to safe water, the local infant mortality rate can be cut in half. As of 2010, UNICEF says about 60 percent of sub-Saharan Africa has access to clean water. Progress, yes, but this region still [has] one of the lowest rates in the world.

Source: Leah Macpherson. "Canada's Champions of Change: Finalist Christopher Opio," CBC.ca, http://www.cbc.ca/change/christopheropio.html, retrieved 20 October 2011.

EXERCISE 2. COMPREHENSION CHECK

Fill in the second column of the chart below, titled "Dr. Christopher Opio." When making your notes in the chart, be sure to use your own words. If you copy any phrases from the reading, note the phrases within quotation marks so that you remember later that these phrases are not yours and come from the original text.

	Dr. Christopher Opio	Lindsay Willms	Dr. David Suzuki
Description of the individual			
Description of the individual's unique contribution			
Explanation of the importance of the individual's work			

Exercise 3. Vocabulary in Context

Skim the article for the verbs listed in the left column below and underline them. These verbs are used by the writer to describe different aspects of how Opio and his organization, the Northern Uganda Development Organization, support the people of Uganda. Then, using the context provided by the article and a dictionary, match each word in column A with its meaning in column B.

A	B
1. *to found*	a) to make better
2. *to promote*	b) to manage
3. *to improve*	c) to create
4. *to put . . . to work*	d) to give
5. *to provide*	e) to apply
6. *to coordinate*	f) to increase knowledge of something
7. *to supervise*	g) to manage
8. *to oversee*	h) to organize

Exercise 4. Vocabulary in Context

Take a moment to look at the title of the text box, "More about Volunteer's Cause." The word *cause* is used in a special way in this title.

1. What does *cause* mean in this context?

_____

2. What does the expression *to have a cause* mean?

_____

—| Reading 2—*Lindsay Willms* |—

Exercise 5. Reading for Specific Information

Read the following article about Lindsay Willms to learn about another Canadian who uses her time to support others. As you read, fill in the third column of the chart on page 217, titled "Lindsay Willms", again using your own words.

Lindsay Willms

A special-ed high school teacher heads to the hills to offer
challenged children a rare taste of freedom.

[1] Lindsay Willms truly is a volunteer for all seasons: in summer, she gives her time to kids with cancer at Camp Goodtimes, in Maple Ridge, BC, and in winter she spends every weekend on the slopes helping children with disabilities enjoy snow sports at the Whistler Adaptive Sports Program (WASP).

[2] For Willms, it's a labour of love: she considers her many volunteer hours fun, not work. Her hope is that her volunteer work has an impact: to show people the positive power of giving back to the community. Camp Goodtimes gives children battling cancer a much-needed break from the rigours of treatment and the stress of living life with a devastating disease (it offers them a taste of "normal" childhood).

[3] Willms first volunteered at the camp in 2002. She has returned every year since. Cost-free, Camp Goodtimes offers a medically supervised program for children between the ages of 6 and 15 and their parents and siblings are invited along, too. Like their healthy peers, the camp allows kids with cancer to enjoy activities like hiking, fishing, campfires, and crafts in an environment that encourages them to escape from their health worries and enjoy the moment.

[4] When the snow flies, Willms travels up the Sea to Sky Highway from Vancouver to Whistler to help kids (and adults) with disabilities learn to ski and snowboard. The program makes accommodations for a wide range of medical challenges. "I've worked with all kinds of people," she says, "from blind and hearing-impaired adults to kids with autism and partial paralysis. WASP is a wonderful program and has helped so many people enjoy winter sports."

[5] Lindsay also joined the 2009 Ascent for Alzheimer's teams, climbing 19,340 feet on Mt. Kilimanjaro to raise over $250,000 for the Alzheimer Society of BC, each step of their journey honouring the over 70,000 British Columbians whose lives have been impacted by Alzheimer's disease or dementia.

[6] Devoting her time and energy to all these causes has changed Willms' life—and the course of her career. She had planned to go to law school, but her volunteer experiences have inspired her to instead become a special-education teacher.

[7] Currently, Willms is working toward a master's degree in education at the University of British Columbia at night—but she won't stop volunteering. "I recall watching a parent's face as she watched her child—who sits in a wheelchair all day—on the mountain, slicing through powder, screaming with joy and excitement, well, it was beyond words. I've seen parents—who spend

nights at the hospital, eating horrible hospital food and watching their child lying in a bed—come to camp and see their child swimming, laughing and having the time of their life in a safe environment. The smiles I have seen, the tears I have seen, they have changed me."

[8]   All kids need to play—even sick and disabled ones, says Dr. Pat Longmuir, a researcher at the Hospital for Sick Children (Sick Kids) in Toronto. Why? Because until about age 10, children don't sit and talk to bond with peers—they mostly do it through play and physical activity. If that opportunity is off the table, says Longmuir, especially due to an illness or disability, kids don't reach their potential targets of physical and emotional growth.

[9]   We develop motor skills in childhood, and need to be physically active to do so. The window of development starts closing, says Longmuir, as we grow older—so even sick kids have to learn skills like running, jumping and throwing when young.

[10] Sports and play help keep sick kids physically on track with their peers, so they're not left behind—or simply behind, once well.

[11] It also wards off social marginalization. The more physically active kids are the more they're included in group activities like playground sports or field trips, despite an illness or disability. Exercise releases chemicals in the brain that elevate mood—and this applies to sick and well kids alike.

Source: Leah Macpherson. "Canada's Champions of Change: Finalist Lindsay Willms," CBC.ca, http://www.cbc.ca/change/lindsaywillms.html, retrieved 20 October 2011.

Exercise 6. Comprehension Check

In groups of three, compare your notes in the chart on page 217. Is there any important information that you missed? Talking with your classmates will help you identify relevant information. Be sure to add any information you missed to your chart.

Exercise 7. Vocabulary in Context

This article discusses how Willms helps individuals with various health-related challenges stay active. Examine the list of words below. Some of these words have to do with health challenges (i.e., illness or disease) and some of these words express ways of keeping active (in the words of the author, "enjoying the moment"). In small groups, discuss the meaning of these words. As you discuss the words, sort them into the graphic provided; place the words that describe health challenges in the smaller circle and the words that describe ways of keeping active in the larger circle.

cancer (paragraph 1)   *fishing* (paragraph 3)   *running* (paragraph 9)

hiking (paragraph 3)   *laughing* (paragraph 7)   *jumping* (paragraph 9) *campfires* (paragraph 3)   *partial paralysis* (paragraph 4)   *throwing* (paragraph 9)

crafts (paragraph 3)   *Alzheimer's disease* (paragraph 5)   *playground sports* (paragraph 11)

skiing (paragraph 4)   *dementia* (paragraph 5)   *field trips* (paragraph 11)

snowboarding (paragraph 4)   *swimming* (paragraph 7)

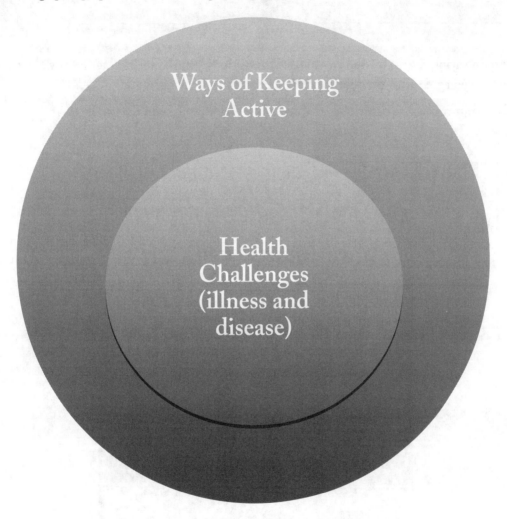

Exercise 8. Skimming for Information

In Chapter 2, you read an article about a well-known Canadian scientist, David Suzuki. Skim through the article in Chapter 2 and fill in as many boxes as you can in the fourth column of the chart with information about David Suzuki.

Exercise 9. Critical Analysis

You have read about three exceptional individuals. Discuss the following questions with your classmates.

1. How does each individual exemplify global citizenship? (To help you respond to this question, you might refer to the ideas you discussed in Exercise 1.) Be prepared to explain your response.

THINK

ACT

glObally → locally

2. A common saying that is related to global citizenship is "think globally, act locally." What does this mean? Do you agree with the sentiment expressed in this saying?

3. Based on your reading so far in this chapter, what do you think are the qualities of a global citizen?

Reading 3—*Concept and Definitions on Global Citizenship and Social Justice Education*

The three readings that follow present ideas about global citizenship on a more abstract, theoretical level. Read the following passage from an article in a Centennial College publication called *Global Citizen Digest*. (Please note that this is not the complete article. Only the first section of the article is reprinted here.) As you read, focus on information that describes the characteristics of a global citizen, according to the author of this text.

Concept and Definitions on Global Citizenship and Social Justice Education

Global Citizenship

[1] Global Citizenship as a concept is not new, but has taken on new meaning as a result of globalization and the understanding that what happens at local and national levels does have an impact globally. "Lynn Davies (2006) suggests global citizenship education has grown out of the practice of global education which had its focus in international awareness through participatory learning and engaging in holistic learning activities (p. 6). She argues that adding citizenship into the concept reflects the shift towards a focus on human rights and responsibilities, implying a more active role that moves beyond an awareness of the issues." (Shultz and Jorgenson)[1]

What does it mean to be a global citizen?[2]

[2] We are living in an increasingly global world. Travel by air, sea, and land make it possible to move across great distances and cross boundaries and borders, as tourists, immigrants, volunteer workers, and business travelers. Advances in communication technology enable us to communicate with others around the world, even in remote places.

[3] As citizens around the globe and as part of the whole world, we need to recognize and value the diversity and differences of others. We may also see that there can be differences in economic and environmental resources, political and social systems, human rights, and access to technology that may give advantages to some people and disadvantages to others. We recognize that inequities exist.

[4] The global citizen becomes aware of the world and their place in it as citizens. A citizen participates in their community, whether it is local or global and takes responsibility for their own actions.

[5] To be a citizen in the global sense means recognizing that we must all be aware of our use of the world's resources and find ways to live on the earth in a sustainable way. When we see others are treated without justice, we know that we are responsible for trying to ensure that people are treated justly and must have equitable opportunities as fellow citizens of this world. We must think critically about what we see, hear, and say, and make sure that our actions bring about positive changes.

---

[1] Shultz, L. and Jorgenson, S. Global Citizenship Education in Post-Secondary Institutions: A Review of Literature.

[2] Centennial College, http://www.centennialcollege.ca/AboutUs/SignatureLearningExperience/global

Source: "Concept and Definitions on Global Citizenship and Social Justice Education." *Global Citizen Digest* (Fall 2009): 10–14. http://www.centennialcollege.ca/Default.aspx?DN=d05db1dd-09d6-4cdf-81f1-fdc6089ba45e, retrieved 20 October 2011.

EXERCISE 10. COMPREHENSION CHECK

1. According to the author of this article, is *global citizenship* a new concept? Be prepared to explain your response.

   _____

2. The author discusses *awareness* as an important aspect of global citizenship throughout the text, using such phrases as "we need to recognize . . ." and "we may also see that. . . ." In what ways is awareness important to the author? In the graphic below, list these ways in the box called Awareness.

3. The author also discusses *participation* and *action* in the article. In what ways are participation and action important to the author? In the graphic below, list these ways in the box called Participation/Action.

4. Does the author of Reading 3 give more importance to local or global action? How do you know?

   _____

EXERCISE 11. VOCABULARY IN CONTEXT

Skim Reading 3 for the words listed below. As you find each word, think about possible meanings for it. Additional examples that use each word have been provided to help you determine the meaning of each word. Write your own definition of the words in the space provided and then create one of your own sentences for each word.

concept	*access to*
globalization	*inequities*
human rights	*sustainable*
recognize	*justice*
diversity	

1. The *concept* of generational differences is important in the study of demographics.

   Meaning: _____

   Original sentence: _____

2. When the Canadian factory moved to a country outside of Canada, it was another sign of *globalization*.

   Meaning: _____

   Original sentence: _____

3. Freedom of speech is an example of a basic *human right*.

   Meaning: _____

   Original sentence: _____

4. The university provides free tutoring in writing for all students, and in this way, *recognizes* that it must support students' development.

   Meaning: _____

   Original sentence: _____

5. *Diversity* and multiculturalism are important themes in Canada especially since many Canadians were born in countries outside of Canada.

   Meaning: _____

   Original sentence: _____

6. The government must make sure that all citizens have *access to* clean drinking water.

   Meaning: _____

   Original sentence: _____

7. Many women have worked hard to address the *inequities* that have existed for many years between men and women.

   Meaning: _____

   Original sentence: _____

8. They had a strong interest in living a *sustainable* lifestyle and one of the ways they demonstrated this was to ride their bicycles to work each day.

   Meaning: _____

   Original sentence: _____

9. With her strong interest in *justice*, she left her teaching job in the suburbs and taught in a neighbour-hood where the children had very little money and few opportunities.

   Meaning: _____

   Original sentence: _____

EXERCISE 12. NOTE-TAKING

Look back to the instructions provided at the beginning of this chapter for the research paper that you will be writing. Using your own words and Reading 3, add information or ideas that will help you write your paper to the box below.

Global citizenship as a new/old idea

Important elements of global citizenship

Reading 4—*Key Elements for Global Citizenship*

Oxfam is an organization that works on projects in many parts of the world, especially projects that seek to meet basic human needs. The graphic below is an expression of how Oxfam staff view global citizenship. It lists the elements that are especially important to them.

Study the graphic below.

Key Elements for Global Citizenship

Knowledge and understanding

- Social justice and equity
- Diversity
- Globalization and interdependence
- Sustainable development
- Peace and conflict

Skills

- Critical thinking
- Ability to argue effectively
- Ability to challenge injustice and inequalities
- Respect for people and things
- Co-operation and conflict resolution

Values and attitudes

- Sense of identity and self-esteem
- Empathy
- Commitment to social justice and equity
- Value and respect for diversity
- Concern for the environment and commitment to sustainable development
- Belief that people can make a difference

Source: Oxfam Development Education Programme. *Education for Global Citizenship: A Guide for Schools* (Oxford: Oxfam GB, 2006). http://www.oxfam.org.uk/education/gc/files/education_for_global_citizenship_a_guide_for_schools.pdf, retrieved 21 October 2011.

EXERCISE 13. READING FOR CONNECTIONS

1. Put a check mark beside any of the points in the graphic where there is clear agreement between the authors of this graphic and the author of Reading 3 about the key elements of global citizenship.

2. Focus on the elements of global citizenship presented in the graphic that are different from those discussed by the authors of Reading 3. How do these elements add to your understanding of global citizenship?

EXERCISE 14. CRITICAL ANALYSIS

So far, you have examined two explanations of global citizenship. In Reading 3, you saw that awareness and participation were important to the author's understanding. In the graphic on page 226, you saw that knowledge and understanding, skills, and values and attitudes are important to the authors. Which of these two perspectives fits best with your way of thinking about global citizenship? Be prepared to explain your response.

Reading 5—*Educational Travel and Global Citizenship*

EXERCISE 15. PRE-READING DISCUSSION

The author of Reading 3 discusses various ways in which individuals can think and act as global citizens. In your opinion, is action in any particular area (e.g., promoting human rights, protecting the environment, promoting democracy) important to your definition of global citizenship?

Reading 5 is a short excerpt from an article called "Educational Travel and Global Citizenship." As you read the article, think about how the authors define global citizenship.

Educational Travel and Global Citizenship

[1] The notion of citizenship is typically associated with the rights and duties of a particular nation-state; however, global citizenship cannot be extended in this way since there is no global government (Noddings, 2005). While contemporary definitions of global citizenship remained focused on notions of obligations and justice, they also incorporated a concern for environmental protection and many argued that global citizenship was firmly rooted in an environmental context (Attfield, 2002; Bryant, 2006; Dobson, 2003; Dower & Williams, 2002; Shallcross & Robinson, 2006; Winn 2006). Attfield (2002), for example, suggested "environmental responsibilities form the most obvious focus of concern for global citizens, as well as the territory where global obligations most clearly arise" (p. 191). Similarly, the environment provided the basis of Dobson's (2003) post-cosmopolitan view of citizenship, as an obligation to reduce our ecological footprint to sustainable levels; i.e., to act as an "Earth Citizen."

[2] According to Dobson (2003), the concept of justice is used to distinguish between a community of citizens and that of humans; A "Good Citizen" is one who accepts a political obligation to act

in a just and fair manner, in contrast to a "Good Samaritan" who may act out of a duty. The distinction between justice and duty is illustrated using the example of climate change, "if global warming is principally caused by wealthy nations, and if global warming is at least a part cause of strange weather, then monies should be transferred as a matter of compensatory justice rather than as aid or charity ... globalization then changes the source and nature of obligation" (Dobson, 2003, p. 31). The global nature of many environmental issues such as climate change, ozone depletion, the supply and distribution of renewable and non-renewable resources, and biodiversity and species loss transcend national boundaries with effects distributed across the planet. It follows therefore, that the civic concern expressed by citizens most appropriately concerns the sustainable use and conservation of earth's resources. As such, global citizens are not simply international by reason of their world travel but as a result of their ecological footprint—the quantity of nature (specifically, the amount of natural resources) required and consumed to sustain their lifestyle choices and behaviors. Moreover, global citizenship in this sense is not just a matter of being a good community member, rather in recognizing an ethical imperative or willingness to reduce one's ecological impact and support a sustainable footprint that may have no immediate, personal value but ultimately benefit others around the world.

[3]   Westheimer and Kahne (2004) have proposed three types of citizens: (a) *personally responsible citizens* (someone who acts responsibly in his/her community, obeys laws, recycles, gives blood, and/or volunteers in times of crisis); (b) *participatory citizens* (someone who is an active member of civic and community organizations, organizes community efforts such as environmental clean-ups, etc.); and (c) *justice-oriented citizens* (someone who critically assesses social, political, and economic structures to see beyond surfaces and challenges injustice, knows about social movements, and explores the root causes of problems). The distinction among these three citizen-types is described as follows, "if participatory citizens are organizing the food drive and personally responsible citizens are donating food, justice-oriented citizens are asking why people are hungry and acting on what they discover" (p. 3). Westheimer and Kahne, as well as others (e.g., Brown, 2006; Bryant, 2006; Dolby, 2007), further maintained that academia, and educational systems generally, have failed to foster civic obligations and responsibilities, especially at the justice-oriented level, resulting in a student body apathetic to the politics of democracy and global citizenship. While students may gain the practical skills (and concerns) of personally responsible citizenship (recycling, park and river clean-ups, donating blood) and of participatory citizenship (participating in civic and community groups and organizations), the programs rarely empowered students to address social problems through a critical assessment, with the goal of affecting profound social change and justice.

[4]   By definition, these three types of citizens (plus a fourth group, not explicitly addressed by Westheimer and Kahne but included in our study, of non-citizens) are likely to differ with respect to their support for sustainable (pro-) environmentalism; however, there are no known published findings to this effect. Westheimer and Kahne acknowledged that, "a focus on justice guarantees neither the motivation nor the capacity to participate in democratic change. Many—ourselves included—would applaud programs that manage to emphasize justice-oriented citizenship inextricably linked to a desire and capacity for participation" (2004, p. 6).

References:

Attfield, R. (2002). Global citizenship and the global environment. In N. Dower & J. Williams (Eds.), *Global citizenship: A critical reader* (pp. 191–200). Edinburgh, UK: Edinburgh University Press.

Brown, N. (2006). Embedding engagement in higher education: Preparing global citizens through international service-learning. In B. Holland & J. Meeropol (Eds.), *A more perfect vision: The future of campus engagement.* Providence, RI: Campus Compact. Retrieved from http://www.compact.org/20th/papers

Bryant, D. (2006). The everyone, everywhere: Global dimensions of citizenship. In B. Holland & J. Meeropol (Eds.), *A more perfect vision: The future of campus engagement.* Providence, RI: Campus Compact. Retrieved from http://www.compact.org/20th/papers

Dobson, A. (2003). *Citizenship and the environment.* Oxford, UK: Oxford University Press.

Dolby, N. (2007). Reflections on nation: American undergraduates and education abroad. *Journal of Studies in International Education, 11*(2), 141–156.

Dower, N., & Williams, J. (2002). *Global citizenship: A critical reader.* Edinburgh, UK: Edinburgh University Press.

Noddings, N. (2005). Global citizenship: promises and problems. In N. Noddings (Ed.), *Educating citizens for global awareness* (pp. 1–21). New York, NY: Teachers College Press.

Shallcross, T., & Robinson, J. (2006). Education for sustainable development as applied global citizenship and environmental justice. In T. Shallcross and J. Robinson (Eds.), *Global citizenship and environmental justice* (pp. 175–194). New York, NY: Rodopi.

Westheimer, J., & Kahne, J. (2004). Educating the "good" citizen: Political choices and pedagogical goals. *PSOnline.* Retrieved from www.apsanet.org

Winn, J.G. (2006). Techno-information literacy and global citizenship. *International Journal of Technology, Knowledge, and Society, 2*(3), 123–127.

Source: Tarrant, M. A., Stoner, L., Borrie, W. T., Kyle, G., Moore, R. L., & Moore, A. (2011). Educational travel and global citizenship. *Journal of Leisure Research, 43*(3), 403–426. Retrieved from Academic Search Premier (Accession no. 65236936).

EXERCISE 16. COMPREHENSION CHECK

1. In sentence 2 of paragraph 1, the authors state, "many argued that global citizenship was firmly rooted in an environmental context." To whom does the word *many* refer?

_____

2. In paragraph 1, the authors quote a writer named Attfield.

   a) Using your own words, explain what Attfield believes about global citizenship.

   _____

   b) In the same paragraph, the authors also refer to the work of a writer named Dobson. Do Attfield and Dobson share the same point of view about citizenship? How do you know?

   _____

   c) Do the authors of Reading 5 agree with Attfield? How do you know? (Hint: You may have to look beyond paragraph 1 for the answer to this question.)

   _____

3. In paragraph 2, the authors contrast two approaches to justice.
   a) What are the two approaches that the authors contrast? Be sure to use your own words to express these ideas.

   _____

   _____

b) What example is given in paragraph 2 to illustrate the difference between the two approaches? Explain the example, using your own words.

_____

_____

4. Find and underline three sentences in paragraph 2 in which the authors clearly state their position on the meaning of global citizenship.

5. In paragraph 3, the authors describe three types of citizens.

a) Describe these three types of citizens in your own words.

_____

_____

b) Find and underline an example in paragraph 3 that illustrates the difference in these three types of citizens.

6. According to the authors in paragraph 3, in what way have education systems failed?

_____

7. In paragraph 4, the authors mention a fourth type of citizen. What type of citizen do they mention?

_____

8. What level of citizenship do the authors of Reading 5 favour? How do you know?

_____

9. Do the authors of Reading 5 agree with the author of Reading 3 that participation and action are important to global citizenship? How do you know?

_____

10. In your own words, how do the authors of Reading 5 define global citizenship?

_____

EXERCISE 17. PARAGRAPH ANNOTATIONS

To help you understand the ideas in Reading 5, annotate the reading by writing the main idea of each paragraph in the margin. Be sure to use your own words. After you have finished, compare your annotations with those of your classmates.

EXERCISE 18: VOCABULARY IN CONTEXT

For the following vocabulary study, your instructor will divide you into groups. Work with the members of your group to come up with definitions for the following words. Use your group members' knowledge and the context to help determine the meanings. Note the context clues that help you.

1. *notion* (paragraph 1)

   Meaning:_____

   Clues:_____

2. *duty/duties* (paragraphs 1 and 2)

   Meaning:_____

   Clues:_____

3. *contemporary* (paragraph 1)

   Meaning:_____

   Clues:_____

4. *obligation* (paragraphs 1, 2, and 3)

   Meaning:_____

   Clues:_____

5. *to be rooted in* (paragraph 1; note also the use of *root causes* in paragraph 3)

   Meaning:_____

   Clues:_____

6. *ecological footprint* (paragraphs 1 and 2)

   Meaning:_____

   Clues:_____

7. *to transcend* (paragraph 2)

   Meaning:_____

   Clues:_____

8. *civic* (paragraphs 2 and 3)

   Meaning:_____

   Clues:_____

9. *conservation* (paragraph 2)

   Meaning:_____

   Clues:_____

10. *apathetic* (paragraph 3)

    Meaning:_____

    Clues:_____

Exercise 19. Note-Taking

Look back to the instructions for the research paper that you will be writing, provided at the beginning of this chapter. Using your own words and Reading 5, add information or ideas that will help you write your paper to the box below.

Characteristics of global citizens

Examples of global citizenship

Exercise 20. Synthesizing Information

In academic writing, you will often have to work with a variety of perspectives on a topic. When you compare the ideas of different authors, you are synthesizing. This is an important academic thinking and writing skill. This exercise will help you practise synthesizing information.

Complete the following statements using the information in Readings 3 to 5.

1. Similar to the description of global citizenship provided by Reading 3, "Concept and Definitions on Global Citizenship and Social Justice Education," the framework provided by Oxfam in Reading 4, "Key Elements for Global Citizenship" includes _____ _____ .

2. Unlike the description of global citizenship provided by Reading 3, the framework provided by Oxfam in Reading 4 includes _____ _____ .

3. Similar to Reading 5, "Global Citizenship," the framework for global citizenship provided by Oxfam in Reading 4 includes _____ _____ .

4. Unlike the description of global citizenship provided in Reading 3, Reading 5 emphasizes _____ _____ .

5. In contrast to the framework for global citizenship provided in Reading 4, Reading 5 focuses on

_____

_____.

Source: Based on an exercise from C. Feak and B. Dobson. "Building on the Impromptu: A Source-Based Academic Writing Assessment." *College ESL* 6, 1(1996): 73–84.

EXERCISE 21. WRITING

On a separate sheet of paper, in approximately five sentences, describe your understanding of global citizenship. Are environmental awareness and action important parts of your definition?

Writing

Discussing Research

The writer of Readings 1 and 2 about Christopher Opio and Lindsay Willms uses information from expert sources to persuade the reader that both of these individuals are involved with important causes. The writers of Reading 5, "Educational Travel and Global Citizenship," use information and ideas from scholarly sources to persuade. The use of research from expert sources is a fundamental element of persuasion and of academic writing. References to research demonstrate that the writer has a strong basis for his or her point of view.

However, it is essential to give credit to the researchers whose work you use. First, a writer who does so is sure to avoid plagiarism. Plagiarism occurs when words or ideas are taken from another source but that source is not provided for the reader; plagiarism is seen as stealing words or ideas. By giving credit to the authors whose words and ideas you use, you will avoid plagiarism and demonstrate that you are honest and not trying to take credit for work or ideas that are not your own. Second, giving credit allows readers to find studies or related articles if they want to read them for themselves.

There are two basic techniques for naming the sources of information in writing: lead-in expressions and documenting information.

Lead-in Expressions

Academic writers frequently use lead-in expressions in the body of their texts to introduce the authors whose works they are including. Lead-in expressions include the names of the scholars whose work is being discussed and often a verb that indicates how those scholars presented their information.

Examine the following lead-ins from Reading 5, "Educational Travel and Global Citizenship," the article by Tarrant, Stoner, Borrie, Kyle, Moore, and Moore.

> *Lead-in:* X suggested
>
> **Example:** Attfield (2002), for example, suggested "environmental responsibilities form the most obvious focus of concern for global citizens, as well as the territory where global obligations most clearly arise" (p. 191).

> *Lead-in:* X proposed
>
> **Example:** Westheimer and Kahne (2004) have proposed three types of citizens. . . .

EXERCISE 22. SCANNING

Scan Reading 5 to find other examples of lead-in expressions.

More Lead-In Expressions

The following lead-in strategies can also be used to introduce authors with their ideas. The examples provided below are drawn from the article review in Chapter 9 by Dr. Chris Butterill.

1. For problems, questions, or issues

    X discusses + a problem, a question, or an issue

    X examines + a problem, a question, or an issue

    X addresses + a problem, a question, or an issue

    X explores + a problem, a question, or an issue

    Example: Drawing on more than 35 years of national survey data he has gathered on Canadian adults and teens, [Bibby] examined the change in attitudes and values of today's millennials born between 1980 and 2000 (Eubanks, 2006; Howe & Strauss, 2003; Sutherland & Thompson, 2001).

    Example: Another theme Bibby explored on smoking, drinking, and illegal substance use showed a 25 percent reduction, as did reported victimization, such as school bullying, suicide attempts, or abuse at home.

2. For suggestions

    X recommends + a suggestion

    X suggests + a suggestion

    X proposes + a suggestion

3. For opinions

    X believes + an opinion

    X contends + an opinion

    X posits + an opinion

    X claims + an opinion

    X argues + an opinion

    X maintains + an opinion

    Example: However, Canadian sociologist and researcher Reginald W. Bibby maintained a more positive view in his article "Canada's Emerging Millennials" (2009).

4. For original insights or ideas presented by the author

    X points out + an original insight or idea

    X reveals that + an original insight or idea

    Example: [Bibby's] surveys revealed some "positive findings about young people" (p. 2), and he claimed that things are "looking better not worse, for teenagers ... than any of [the] teen cohorts" (p. 2) since his surveys began in 1975.

Documenting Information and Avoiding Plagiarism

To avoid plagiarism and to give credit to the writers whose work they are using, academic writers also include bibliographic information. This helps the reader find the books and articles that were used to write the academic text. When writers include this bibliographic information, they are *documenting information*.

There are several different styles in which information can be documented. These include APA (American Psychological Association), MLA (Modern Language Association), Chicago, and CSE (Council of Science Editors). You should find out what documentation styles your professors require for their courses. The APA and the MLA styles are illustrated here.

APA

APA uses an author-date system. The name of the author and the date of publication are integrated into the body of the text. Page numbers are included when material is quoted or a specific detail is given from the original source. Readers can then look up the authors' names in a reference list where they will find the complete publication information.

MLA

MLA uses an author-page system. The name of the author and the page number of the information or idea within the original source are integrated into the body of the text. Readers can then look up the authors' names in a reference list where they will find the complete publication information.

Examples

Examples that mention the author in the lead-in

APA

According to Dobson (2003), the concept of justice is used to distinguish between a community of
        author   date
citizens and that of humans;

MLA

According to Tomkins, when he has created a model that is similar to what his clients had wished for,
        author
Gehry's own design process really begins. He experiments with the model, modifying forms and the relationships between the forms pushing his model further and further (41).
                                                                                                        page

Examples that do not mention the author in the lead-in

APA

The notion of citizenship is typically associated with the rights and duties of a particular nation-state; however, global citizenship cannot be extended in this way since there is no global government (Noddings, 2005).
_{date}   _{author}

MLA

Gehry's way of working is to begin by listening closely to his clients. He not only takes note of their explicit requests, but also of their body language and facial expressions to give him cues as to their desires and wishes (Tomkins 41).
_{author   page}

Examples of referencing direct quotations

APA

The distinction between justice and duty is illustrated using the example of climate change, "if global warming is principally caused by wealthy nations, and if global warming is at least a part cause of strange weather, then monies should be transferred as a matter of compensatory justice rather than as aid or charity . . . globalization then changes the source and nature of obligation" (Dobson, 2003, p. 31).

MLA

Teenagers today may be healthier than we think. "[T]oday's teens are looking very good. In fact, they are looking better than any of our teen cohorts dating back to the early 1980s" (Bibby 2).

Reference List

As mentioned, the writer must also provide a reference list so that readers can find the complete publication information. The reference list must follow the specific conventions of the documentation style chosen by the writer; for example, if the writer has referenced information in the body of the paper using APA, the reference list at the end of the paper must also follow the conventions of APA.

Samples of references for books and journal articles are shown below.

Book

APA

Dower, N., & Williams, J. (2002). *Global citizenship: A critical reader.* Edinburgh, UK: Edinburgh University Press.

MLA

Dower, Nigel, and John Williams. *Global Citizenship: A Critical Reader.* Edinburgh, UK: Edinburgh University Press, 2002. Print.

Online journal article

APA

Tarrant, M. A., Stoner, L., Borrie, W. T., Kyle, G., Moore, R. L., & Moore, A. (2011). Educational travel and global citizenship. *Journal of Leisure Travel, 43*(3), 403–426. Retrieved from Academic Search Premier (Accession no. 65236936).

MLA

Tarrant, Michael A., Lee Stoner, William T. Borrie, Gerrard Kyle, Roger L. Moore, and Annette Moore. "Educational Travel and Global Citizenship." *Journal of Leisure Research* 43.3 (2011): 403–426. Web. 18 Sept. 2011.

Websites

APA

Macpherson, L. (2011). "Canada's champions of change: Finalist Christopher Opio." Retrieved from http://www.cbc.ca/change/christopheropio.html

MLA

Macpherson, Leah. "Canada's Champions of Change: Finalist Christopher Opio." *Canadian Broadcasting Corporation*. 2011. Web. 18 Sept. 2011.

EXERCISE 23. DOCUMENTING

Revise the following bibliographic entries so that they are consistent with either the APA or MLA guidelines. Use the model references presented above, paying special attention to the punctuation that should be used in each entry.

Books

1. Millennials rising by Neil Howe & William Strauss. Vintage Books. New York. 2000.

2. Hannah Friesen and Kathy Block. Creating meaning: advanced reading and writing. 2000. Oxford University Press: Toronto.

Journal articles

1. Barb Toews. (1996, Summer). A Fable for our Time. *Conciliation Quarterly*, 15(3), 2–4. Accessed on Sept 18, 2011. Retrieved from http://us.mcc.org/programs/restorativejustice/resources/print/conciliationquarterly

2. Reginald W. Bibby. Canada's Emerging Millennials. *Transition*, 39(3). Retrieved from http://www.vifamily.ca/media/node/148/attachments/Canadas_Emerging_Millenials.pdf, Fall. Retrieved on Sept 18, 2011, pages 2–6.

⊣ **Reading 6**—*Walking by the Crooked Water* ⊢

EXERCISE 24. PRE-READING DISCUSSION

Discuss the following questions before you read.

1. You have now thought about, read about, and discussed the meaning of global citizenship. In what ways is global citizenship an old idea?

2. Reading 6 is written from a perspective that is somewhat different from the earlier readings in this chapter. Before reading the article, study the title and the brief biography of the author given at the end of the article.

⊣ Walking by the Crooked Water ⊢

In a land with no lines, how do you define the end of one territory and the beginning of another?

[1] My Ojibwa family name is Wagamese. By itself, it means nothing. That is because when the registrars came to sign up the Ojibwa for treaty, they wrote down only the parts of the names they could pronounce. Or they gave us English translations, such as Redsky and Otter Tail, or English surnames, such as Green, Kelly, and Smith. Wagamese is part of a longer phrase that translates to "man walking by the crooked water."

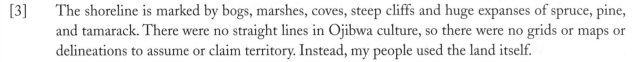

[2] The name refers to my great-grandfather. He is remembered in the northwestern part of Ontario north of Minaki for walking the 72-kilometre length of our traditional trapline along the Winnipeg River in both directions in three days. That river is the crooked water referred to in our name because of the way it snakes from Lake Winnipeg southeasterly to Lake of the Woods, close to the Canada-US boundary. It is the great landmark that allowed my family to declare the boundaries of our trapline.

[3] The shoreline is marked by bogs, marshes, coves, steep cliffs and huge expanses of spruce, pine, and tamarack. There were no straight lines in Ojibwa culture, so there were no grids or maps or delineations to assume or claim territory. Instead, my people used the land itself.

[4] Sometimes, the end of one family's or band's traditional territory and the start of another's was marked by a huge boulder or a cliff. Other times, a bend in the river itself referenced a boundary, even though there is no word for boundary in the Ojibwa language. There is no word for map either. There was only ever the land.

[5] For the Ojibwa and other native groups across North America, land could not be divided. It was whole, as defined by the Creator. It was sacred, because the idea of wholeness contained principles such as

sharing, harmony, and equality. When territory was decided upon, it was an honourable agreement based on those principles, and the agreement became sacred, too, because it involved the land.

[6]   The trapline my great-grandfather walked followed the twists of the river. There were beaver dams, muskrat lodges and plenty of foxes, wolves, mink and game, such as moose, deer, geese, ducks, and rabbits. It was rich and bountiful in everything our family needed. That was the other thing that defined territory; no band or family ever arranged for more than what it needed.

[7]   When I see the number of land claims negotiated these days and the reams of maps backing up those claims, I wonder how it all came to pass. The idea of the land as sacred remains a native principle. But nowadays, we have learned to see it in straight lines and value it in terms of the resources and money it could yield rather than the spiritual principles it gave our cultures.

[8]   There is a man walking by the crooked water. He stops to enjoy the feel of the land all around him. There are no boundaries between him and the world. There is only a critical joining: balance, harmony, belonging. No one ever needed a map for that.

Author biography: Richard Wagamese is an Ojibwa writer and storyteller from the Wabaseemoong First Nation in northwestern Ontario. He is the author of *One Native Life.*

Source: Wagamese, R. (2010). Walking by the Crooked Water, *Canadian Geographic, 130*(4), 52.

EXERCISE 25. VOCABULARY IN CONTEXT

In this reading, several words are used by the author that have very specific meanings related to Aboriginal history and culture in Canada. Skim the text and highlight the words that are listed below. Notice that some of these words are used more than once in the text. Be sure to highlight every instance in the text where the word is used.

Ojibwa	*treaty*	*territory*	*band*
the registrars	*traditional trapline*	*sacred*	*land claims*

If you are unfamiliar with the meaning of these words, ask your instructor for an explanation.

EXERCISE 26. COMPREHENSION CHECK

1. In paragraph 1, why does the author say his family name, Wagamese, "means nothing"?

    _____

2. What is the story behind the author's true family name? In other words, where did the name (which means "man walking by the crooked water") come from?

    _____

3. In paragraph 3, the author states, "my people used the land itself." What is the author referring to in this statement?

    _____

4. Examine paragraphs 5 to 7 carefully. What principles discussed by the author relate to sustainability? Who held these principles?

_____

_____

5. Examine paragraphs 5 to 7 once more. What principles discussed by the author relate to justice? Who held these principles?

_____

_____

EXERCISE 27. CRITICAL ANALYSIS

Discuss the following questions with your classmates.

1. After reading this article, in what ways do you see global citizenship as an old idea?

2. Are there ways in which global citizenship is a new idea? If yes, be prepared to explain your response.

EXERCISE 28. TAKING NOTES

Look back to the instructions for the research paper that you will be writing, provided at the beginning of this chapter. Using your own words and Reading 6, add information or ideas that will help you write your paper to the box below.

<table>
<tr><td>

Characteristics of global citizens

Examples of global citizenship

Ways in which global citizenship is an old idea

</td></tr>
</table>

Writing the Research Paper

You have now gathered a substantial body of information about the meaning of global citizenship. You have also thought about and discussed your own definition of global citizenship. Your perspective, along with the information that you have gathered, will be used to write a research paper. In its organization a research paper is similar to an essay: it contains a thesis statement that is supported in the body of the paper. However, when drafting a research paper, a writer uses research findings to support and develop his or her own analysis of the topic.

Research Paper Topic

Global citizenship is a term that is frequently used in the Canadian media. In a 550- to 650-word paper, discuss two to three aspects of global citizenship that are emphasized in current definitions. Use information and examples from at least three of the readings in this chapter to help you explain these aspects. In your concluding paragraph, respond to this question: Does the term *global citizenship* provide new meanings, or is it a new term for an old concept?

Be sure to reference all sources using one of the styles discussed in this chapter.

EXERCISE 29. FREE WRITING

In an academic paper, it is very important to include your own ideas; in fact, after reading your paper, your readers should come away with a clear understanding of *your* analysis of the topic. Therefore, it is important for you, as a writer, to clarify your own position.

To begin this research paper, think about your definition of global citizenship. What elements are important to a definition of this term *for you*? Write down your thoughts without worrying about organization or grammar.

_____

_____

_____

_____

EXERCISE 30. ORGANIZING AND DRAFTING YOUR PAPER

In the following outline, list the two to three aspects of global citizenship that you would like to discuss in your paper.

Next, go back to the notes that you have taken throughout this chapter. In point form, list the ideas from your notes that might help you develop these points. For example, fill in any details, direct quotations, or examples from the articles. Remember to name the source for the information, quotations, or examples as you add them to your outline.

Aspects of global citizenship emphasized in current definitions

Aspect #1: _____

Information from readings: _____

_____

_____

Examples from readings: _____

_____

_____

Aspect #2: _____

Information from readings: _____

_____

_____

Examples from readings: _____

_____

_____

Aspect #3: _____

Information from readings: _____

_____

_____

Examples from readings: _____

_____

_____

Does the term *global citizenship* provide new meanings, or is it a new term for an old concept?

_____

_____

_____

_____

Discard any points in your outline that seem unimportant.

Arrange the points in the order in which you will present them in your paper. This may be either from strongest to weakest or from weakest to strongest, depending on how you think the ideas best fit together.

Write a thesis statement that will express the main idea of your paper. Ask for feedback from your instructor or classmates to help you develop a clear thesis statement.

Thesis statement:

_____

_____

Consider what background information your reader might need in order to understand your thesis statement. Include this in your introduction.

Write your first draft. Do not revise until you have completed your first draft. However, you should document the information as you write.

EXERCISE 31. REVISING YOUR PAPER

Consider the following questions:

1. Is the main argument of your paper clearly presented in the thesis statement?

2. Is the thesis statement directly related to the topic of the paper?

3. Did you support the thesis statement with relevant ideas in the body of the paper?

4. Are your supporting ideas introduced to your readers in clear topic sentences?

5. Have you used information from the readings to develop your supporting ideas?

6. Where could you add information to strengthen your line of argument?

7. Have you overused direct quotations? Remember, your paper should not be a stringing together of ideas from other authors. It should express your own analysis of the topic.

8. Did you give credit to the authors whose words and ideas you have used by using lead-ins and documentation?

EXERCISE 32. OPTIONAL WRITING ASSIGNMENT

After you have finished the preceding assignment, write a letter to your instructor describing your writing process. What aspects of the assignment do you believe you did well? What aspects were difficult? Where do you need more help?

Appendix

SUFFIXES

Suffix	Meaning	Part of Speech of Resulting Word
-able, -ible	capable of	adjective
-ance, -ence	instance of an action	noun
-ation, -tion	the action or process of	noun
-er, -or	person connected with	noun
-ful	full of	adjective
-ic, -ical	having the form of	adjective
-ious, -ous	having the qualities of	adjective
-ish	relating to	adjective
-less	not having	adjective
-ly	in the manner of	adverb
-ness	the quality, state, or character of	noun

PREFIXES

Prefix	Meaning
ante-	before
anti-	against
bi-	two
circum-	around
con-, co-, col-, com-	with
counter-	against
de-	opposite of
dis-	opposite of
ex-, e-	out of, from
hyper-	above, excessively
hypo-	under, below
inter-	between
intra-	within
macro-	large
mal-	bad, badly

Prefix	Meaning
micro-	small
mis-	wrongly
mono-	one
multi-	many
non-	not
post-	after
pre-, prim-	first or before
pro-	for or before
re-	again
semi-	half
sub-, sup-	under
trans-	across or beyond
tri-	three
un-, im-, in-	no, not

Photo Credits

Literary Credits

138 Oxford Advanced Learner's Dictionary, 8th ed. Oxford University Press 2010.

141–42 David Suzuki with contributions from Jode Roberts. Courtesy: David Suzuki Foundation: www.davidsuzuki.org

144–45 Adapted from: Beverly Fehr, from Friendship Processes (Newbury Park, CA: Sage, 1996).

150–51 Courtesy: Dr. Sheryl Bermann Drewe, University of Manitoba.

155–58 Adapted from: CBC News, http://www.cbc.ca/news/canada/story/2009/02/09/f-assisted-suicide.html Retrieved August 17 2011; Adapted from: "The Fight to Die." The Tyee, 2011, published in http://thetyee.ca/News/2011/07/13/FightToDie/, retrieved 8 October 2011.

163–66 © Charlene Sadler

173–75 Campbell, Linda C.; Campbell, Bruce; Dickinson, Dee, Teaching and Learning Through Multiple Intelligences, 3rd edition, © 2004. Reprinted by permission of Pearson Education Inc, Upper Saddle River, NJ.

179–80 Macleans. http://oncampus.macleans.ca/education/2007/08/30/do-grades-really-matter/ Retrieved 14 October 2011. © Sarah Scott. Used with permission.

190–91 By definition: Boom, bust, X and why. Pearce, T. (2006, June 24). Globe and Mail. © The Globe and Mail Inc. All Rights Reserved.

195–98 Vanier Institute of the Family, Transition Vol. 39, No. 3, Fall 2009.

204–06 C. A. Butterill

210–11 Source: http://blogs.hbr.org/erickson/2009/02/the_four_biggest_reasons_for_i.html, retrieved 17 October 2011. © Harvard Business Review. Used with permission.

214 © 2010 Sony/ATV Music Publishing Canada, Bug Music, EMI Music Publishing, Publisher(s) Unknown. All rights on behalf of Sony/ATV Music Publishing Canada, administered by Sony/ATV Music Publishing LLC, 8 Music Square West, Nashville, TN 37203. Words and Music by Keinan Warsame, Philip Lawrence, Bruno Mars, Jean Duval, Edward Dunner, and Andrew Block. Copyright © 2009 Sony/ATV Music Publishing Canada, Roc Nation Music on behalf of itself and Music Famamanem, Mars Force Music, Northside Independant Music Publishing LLC, Bughouse, 67 Sounds and Coca-Cola Corp. All Rights on behalf of Sony/ATV Music Publishing Canada Administered by Sony/ATV Music Publishing LLC, 8 Music Square West, Nashville, TN 37203. All Rights on behalf of Roc Nation Music on behalf of itself and Music Famamanem Controlled and Administered by EMI April Music Inc. All Rights on behalf of Mars Force Music and Bughouse Administered by Bug Music. All Rights on behalf of 67 Sounds Controlled and Administered by Universal Tunes, A Division of Song of Universal Inc. International Copyright Secured. All Rights Reserved. Reprinted by Permission of Hal Leonard Corporation. Words by Harry Ruby, Music by Rube Bloom. Copyright © 2010 WB MUSIC CORP., NORTHSIDE INDEPENDENT MUSIC PUBLISHING, LLC, MARS FORCE MUSIC, MUSIC OF WINDSWEPT, MUSIC FAMAMANEM, DUSTY FOOT MUSIC, LITCHFIELD ENTERTAINMENT COMPANY, INC., and UNKNOWN PUBLISHER. All Rights Reserved. Used by Permission.

216–17 Retrieved from http://www.cbc.ca/change/christopheropio.html. © CBC. Used with permission.

219–20 Retrieved from http://www.cbc.ca/change/lindsaywillms.html. © CBC. Used with permission.

223 Global Citizen Digest. (Fall 2009): 10–14. http://www.centennialcollege.ca/Default.aspx?DN=d05db1dd-09d6-4cdf-81f1-fdc6089 ba45 retrieved 20 October 2011. Used with permission of Centennial College.

227–29 Journal of leisure research by WITT, PETER A.; NATIONAL RECREATION AND PARK ASSOCIATION Copyright 2011 Reproduced with permission of NATIONAL RECREATION AND PARK ASSOCIATION in the format Textbook via Copyright Clearance Center.

238–39 "Walking by the Crooked Water" Wagamese, R. (2010, July/August). Walking by the crooked water. Canadian Geographic, 130(4), 52.